A Century⁺ of Living:
The Autobiography
of
Cora Jones "Boot" McLeod

"Lord, Keep Me Day by Day"

Written by Dr. Beverly "Eagle" Rogers

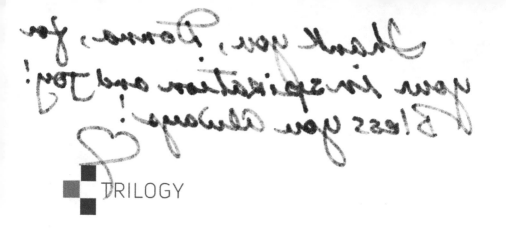

TRILOGY

A Century+ of Living: The Autobiography of Cora Jones "Boot" McLeod

Trilogy Christian Publishers A Wholly Owned Subsidiary of Trinity Broadcasting Network

2442 Michelle Drive Tustin, CA 92780

Rights Department, 2442 Michelle Drive, Tustin, CA 92780.

Trilogy Christian Publishing/TBN and colophon are trademarks of Trinity Broadcasting Network.

Cover design by: Natalee Groves

For information about special discounts for bulk purchases, please contact Trilogy Christian Publishing.

Manufactured in the United States of America

10 9 8 7 6 5 4 3 2 1

Library of Congress Cataloging-in-Publication Data is available.

ISBN: 978-1-68556-250-2
E-ISBN: 978-1-68556-251-9

DEDICATION

I dedicate my life story to my son, James F. McLeod, Jr., who believed in this fulfillment from the beginning of Beverly's vision. Thank you! Thanks, Barbara Jean McLeod, my other "daughter," for always giving encouragement and support.

To LaKishia, Karleshia, Krystal, Kassan, Khalil, Kaden, and Kayla, remember what Granny showed you through her walk of faith in God; let Him guide your lives by accepting and acknowledging Him first, and He will direct your paths. Pass it forward to future generations. Granny loves each of you!

To all my extended family and friends worldwide—I love you more. God bless!

Acknowledgments

With sincere acknowledgment to my Lord and Savior, Jesus Christ, for the grace, mercy, and longevity that he had blessed upon my life! All that I am and all that I hope to be, I owe it all to thee, Almighty God.

With great appreciation to the partners of the Investment Group and their seeds of love. May God bless you and your families—V. Davenport, P. Ferré, H. Lewis, W. Reese, A. Rogers, B. Rogers, C. Rogers and J. Veverka.

Special thanks to Gwendolyn McQueen Printing of Jennings, Florida for designing the center photo layouts. Your creativity and expertise is most eminent and esteemed!

Table of Contents

FOREWORD

Rarely in life do we encounter a person whose life has spanned a century. More rarely, still, do we get to hear that person's story in her own words, from her detailed and sharp memory. *A Century+ of Living: The Autobiography of Cora Jones "Boot" McLeod,* as written by her great-niece, Dr. Beverly "Eagle" Rogers, is such a story. It is the story of descendants of an African American family making progress, often against the odds. Most of all, it is a story of unshakable faith. Whether she is giving thanks or having to lean on her faith for strength, Mrs. McLeod continues to be a guidepost and a spark of light for her family and for all those who encounter her presence.

Mrs. McLeod's family story intersects at many points with larger American history. For example, her oldest brother Leroy "Yi" Jones was FDR's valet, and her youngest sister, Christine Jones Johnson, attended Hampton Institute before it became Hampton University. Mrs. McLeod and her siblings grew up during the segregation era in the rural part of Wake County, NC. She attended one of the 22 Rosenwald schools that African American communities in Wake County helped to construct. During the segregation era, African American Families paid their taxes, then raised funds, additionally, to obtain those schools for their children. This movement of building African American schools included North Carolina's 813 Rosenwald schools, built by the communities with the support of matching grants from philanthropist Julius Rosenwald.

After Mrs. McLeod's family moved to Durham, NC, during the Great Depression, she attended the historic W.G. Pearson Elementary School and historic Hillside High School, alma mater of civil rights activist, lawyer, Episcopal priest, and author Pauli Murray, as well as many other notable persons. While she married young, Mrs. McLeod later decided to go to school for cosmetology at the legendary DeShazor's Beauty College. This eventually led to her operating her own beauty business for decades. Upon entering beauty college, she notes that she also entered the world of enterprising African American women.

Throughout her long life as a daughter, wife, mother, businesswoman, and church leader, Mrs. McLeod has relied on her faith and integrity. She credits her father and mother, Rev. and Mrs. Junious and Olivia Jones, with instilling within her these values. Her teachers also played an important role in her development. Whether schools were Rosenwald-funded schools or whether they had other origins in the community, North Carolina's hundreds of historic African American schools set high expectations and standards. The motto of Winston-Salem State University, one of North Carolina's eleven HBCUs-along with NCCU, "Enter to learn, depart to serve," could well serve as their common motto. Ironically, that motto is also part of the mission statement of her beloved church, Mount Vernon Baptist, where she has attended for nearly eighty-eight years.

Mrs. McLeod's book paints an intimate portrait of her life. Through the stories, we see a life well-lived. Be prepared to chuckle, cry, hold your breath, feel joy—love—sorrow, laugh out loud, sing, smile, and whistle—all are possible in this genuine and moving chronicle of a special Centenarian's daring and delightful life. It is no wonder that Mrs. Cora Jones "Boot" McLeod is still a pillar and a rock of longevity for her church, community, and family. An amazing life!

—Claudia Stack's documentary films,
Under the Kudzu, Carrie Mae: An American Life,
and Sharecrop trace the history of Rosenwald schools
and sharecropping.

As a North Carolina native, I learned the power of Mrs. Cora Jones "Boot" McLeod's presence in the Durham community and the impact she made on many lives throughout the state. Like so many African American citizens, Mrs. McLeod's life is an encouraging story, complete with many entrepreneurial accomplishments and noted defeats. In this heartwarming autobiography, *A Century+ of Living*, Dr. Beverly "Eagle" Rogers steers her readers through the important lessons and challenges of a persistent, prayerful, and purposeful woman who built business and community while inspiring those around her; and who has lived 103 years to share her grateful journey. Mrs. McLeod's story is an American story that is long overdue. Well done!

—Congressman G. K. Butterfield

When one reads of the life and legacy of Mrs. Cora Jones "Boot" McLeod, it can appear that the poet, Ralph Waldo Emerson, had her in mind when he wrote, "What lies behind us and what lies before us are tiny matters compared to what lies within us."

Mrs. McLeod has presented to all who know her a life that is an ever-present example of self-determination and strength, steeped in godly faith, as epitomized in her book, *A Century+ of Living: The Autobiography of Cora Jones "Boot" McLeod.*

Born during the Spanish flu pandemic in 1918, Mrs. McLeod, at 103-years-old, maneuvers her way through this 21st century pandemic (COVID-19) with courage and faith that can only come from the Savior, Jesus, whom she has called Lord for over a century.

I am proud to be her pastor.

—The Rev. Jerome J. Washington, Ph.D.
Pastor of Mount Vernon Baptist Church, Durham, NC

INTRODUCTION

As I sat and listened to the oral history of the life of Mrs. Cora Jones "Boot" McLeod, every fiber of my body was awakened with excitement! I was sitting at the foot of wisdom. Sitting right in front of me was my great-aunt, Aunt Boot, a mountain of life, only a few months from her hundred years of living! She laughed a hearty belly laugh as she recalled family stories, life episodes, and historical moments since the early 1900s. How could she be so vibrant, so alert, and so detailed?

Certainly, she remembered walking two miles of country road to school with her baby sister, Christine; crying when her brother Otis died at the young age of twenty-one; driving the mule-pulled tobacco truck while standing on the handlebars; and getting all her long, nappy hair cut off and being called "Boy Boot."

In this real-time chronicle of her century-plus of living, God has blessed dear Aunt Cora beyond ordinary words. She gives Him all the honor, glory, and praise as she shares her life's journey with a newer generation of bloggers, Facebookers, Instagrammers, readers, and tweeters. May I introduce to millions of you, locally, nationally, and around the world:

A Century+ of Living: The Autobiography of Cora Jones "Boot" McLeod as shared by one of this world's nearly-new centenarians!

—Dr. Beverly Royster Edwards Rogers

Chapter 1
Happy 100th Birthday, Granny! August 2018

"Happy Birthday, Granny!" shouted Khalil, my middle great-grandson.

The other great-grandsons chimed in with Khalil shouting, "Granny, Happy Birthday!" My great-granddaughter, Kayla, shouted, "Happy Birthday, too, Granny!"

"Granny, it's your birthday. Guess how old you are?" asked baby girl Kayla.

"I don't have to guess. I know how old I am, Kayla. Granny is 100 years old today! God has blessed me to see a century of living. Thank you, Lord!" *I hardly know what to say.*

Tears began to roll down my face as the authenticity, the sheer reality of 100-years old, sank into my head. A landslide of thoughts flooded my mind. I thought of my mother, Mama Olivia. Papa was a close thought behind Mama. Vivid pictures of my sisters, Christine and Clelly and Mozelle popped up one after the other. I could visualize my brothers, Yi and Buddy and Budja running to the well to draw water. That old country road leading to our church appeared to be right in front of me as my mind traveled back down memory lane.

Visions of my late husband, Buster, smiling at me and of Lizzie shaking her head in disbelief flashed quickly through my mind. Lizzie was the oldest girl in the family and might have thought that she would beat me to the 100th birthday. "Sorry, Lizzie, now I am the oldest of the twelve Jones children." *I hardly know what to say.*

My heart began to beat faster. Excitement filled the air. A big 100th birthday celebration had been planned for me. Family, friends, church members, my Pastor, my former Pastor, neighbors, some of my old customers, and some of my customers' children were all coming to wish me a happy 100th birthday. I was sure there would be folks present that I remembered well and some that I had never met yet. People were coming from near and far to honor me, "lil ole" Cora Jones "Boot" McLeod. *I hardly know what to say!*

Who thinks about living a century? Many of us are living with hopes of making it through today's challenges, looking for a glimpse of light at the end of the week's tunnel, and if we can extend a little further, we may wonder why there is more "month" left after the end of the money?

Certainly, not everyone is facing life as a short fraction of time. Many of us have bright blueprints, great goals, and prepared plans for the future, such as athletic aspirations, businesses to birth, career opportunities, family dreams, graduations, marriage proposals, political plans, spiritual endeavors, travels to take—locally or worldwide, wild adventures—marathons to run, mountains to climb, movies to make; and perhaps, there comes a moment in the midst of our lives that we pause to acknowledge how swiftly time has flown by, and it is now, as for me, 100 years of living in the rearview mirror. *I hardly know what to say!*

Chapter 2
Take Me Back/"Boy Boot" Haircut

The first scripture that I ever learned was:

> The LORD is my shepherd; I shall not want. He maketh me to lie down in green pastures: he leadeth me beside the still waters. He restoreth my soul: he leadeth me in the paths of righteousness for his name's sake. Yea, though I walk through the valley of the shadow of death, I will fear no evil: for thou art with me; thy rod and thy staff they comfort me.
>
> Thou preparest a table before me in the presence of mine enemies: thou anointest my head with oil; my cup runneth over. Surely goodness and mercy shall follow me all the days of my life: and I will dwell in the house of the LORD forever.
>
> Psalm 23 (KJV)

These Bible verses laid a foundation for my life. They were a comfort, a consolation, and a covering to my young soul. I was five years old.

The 23rd Psalm takes me back to my youthful days in Wake County, NC. My Papa was a preacher man, Rev. Junious Jones. My Mama was a sweet lady. She was called Sister Olivia by the church family. Our church was Jones Chapel Baptist, named after Papa, and was built by some family members. There were lots of children in our church—mostly Joneses' children (smile). Papa and Mama Olivia led the way with twelve of their own. I was the knee-baby girl.

Sunday School was every Sunday at Jones Chapel at 10:00 a.m. In those days, church services rotated in the community. On the first Sunday, church was at Jones Chapel. On second Sunday, there was church at Malaby's Crossroad Baptist. Third Sunday church met at Riley Hill Baptist, and fourth Sunday service was at Macedonia Baptist Church. All the churches were within a few miles of each other. Papa grew up in Riley Hill, while Mama Olivia and her family were members of Macedonia. Families had a sense of unity and support. Our whole family accompanied Papa to all the church services throughout Wake County.

Jones Chapel didn't have a well for water, so my brothers, Yi and Buddy and Budja, had to go draw water for the church from down the road at Uncle Bud Watkins' house. He wasn't our real uncle, we just called him uncle, and we called his wife, Aunt Addie. I was grown before I really knew that we just called most of the elderly people, uncles, and aunts.

Uncle Bud hung gores around the well for folks to drink out of and provided a bucket for the church to draw out the water. That's the way we lived in the country. Everybody knew everybody and everyone helped their neighbors. Like the Perry

Family, who lived a coin toss from our church, they were one of our close neighbors and good friends. They were members of Jones Chapel, too, and Mr. and Mrs. Perry had three boys and three girls. The younger ones were our good playmates. I still hold fond memories of Bud, Do-Gal, and Sambo. Sis was their oldest sister, who mostly minded their home. Henry and the sister next to him had learned barbering for their trades. The Perrys were a great family!

My older brothers and sisters who were living at home were too busy working on the farm or courting the locals to play with us young 'uns. Mozelle, me, and Christine were the last of the Jones children, and we loved to play. Mozelle tried to keep up with me and Christine, but it was hard because of her limited eyesight. We would play horse and buggy, sail-a-way, knee bouncing, skipping across the road, and building frog houses. We had plenty of chores, and we had time to play with each other and our friends.

I remember one Sunday morning between Sunday School and church service that I left Jones Chapel and walked to the barber lady who cut hair right across the street from the church. At that time, Mozelle had medium-length hair—black and natural, Christine's hair was brownish and short, and I had a full head of thick, nappy, long, jet-black hair.

"Pet," that's what we called the Perry barber lady, knew I didn't have *no money*. But she was willing to cut my hair, anyway. Maybe she was getting practice cutting anybody's hair that sat in her chair. Her brother, Henry, cut all the guy's hair, and she cut all the lady's hair. She could cut rather good, too, like a professional barber. I would soon display how skilled she was with her shears.

All my life, as far as I can remember, I was called "Boot." Aunt Cora, Papa's sister, named me Cora. She had a daughter named Cora, and her husband's brother's child was named Cora Lee. I never heard a story, nor was told where the name "Boot" came from or how it got to stick on me. That Sunday, I sat in Pet's chair, and all my long, nappy, thick hair was spread out across the floor. My new hair style was shaped like a bob cut. Then, folks called me "Boy Boot."

I had not thought about what Mama Olivia would say about my haircut. But quickly, I thought about what Papa would say. He was used to us girls taking down our hair on Saturday night, combing it, and wrapping it up with strings. What would he say now that all my hair was gone and I looked more like one of his boys? To my surprise, Papa was not as upset as I expected. Mama Olivia looked at me and shook her head. "Take care of it yourself," she said. It was a brave and bold thing for a girl to do. What made me do it? Only the Lord knows, but yes, I did it!

How great our country living was! Simple, but great! Papa owned our farm. He bought the land from Mr. Hence Watkins. Mr. Watkins owned quite a lot of land in the community. He had lost his wife and was staying with his son, Henry. As the country preacher, my Papa was well-loved by the whole community. Mr. Watkins respected Papa. He sold him 100 acres. It was a huge farm.

I am not sure what year Papa purchased the land or why Mr. Watkins sold the land to a Negro man, but the farm was where I was born in the hot summer of 1918. I loved the farm.

We had plenty of room to play, with a big front yard and one huge hickory tree, big enough to throw shade over the entire yard. A small graveyard with a black iron fence was at the end corner of our house on the left side. Mr. Watkins gave us girls a dollar because we kept it cleaned and put flowers on it.

We had all types of other trees—butternut, hickory nut, pecan, and walnut trees. Plenty of fruits trees were scattered around our yard—peach, pear, and June-apple trees. We had blackberries and strawberries, but not blueberries. Mama kept our cupboard full of jams and preserves, and Papa supplied the meats and staples for the pantry.

Our home was a two-story house with a full porch across the front entrance. I recall that it was the color of the natural wood. I can't remember anybody painting their house in our community. They were all wood or log houses. We had two large rooms on the first level. Two front doors led into the house, one leading into each of the large rooms.

Everyone used the left side door because the right one went into the front room, which was also the teenagers' bedroom. Cete, one of my older sisters, had left home, married, and bore two beautiful daughters—Mary Ruby and Ramona. She then left her husband, John High, and came back home with their two babies. Cete's birth name was Annie Dora. She, the girls, and my teenage sister, Clelly, slept in that front room. When Papa had company to stay overnight, that, too, was the room where the guest slept.

The big room that we entered into the house was a combination living room, bedroom, and walk-thru to the back of the house. It had three wooden chairs—a rocking chair and two straw, straight backs. There was a huge dresser, a bowl in a washstand, and two beds. Papa and Mama Olivia slept on the one bed; me and Christine, and Mozelle, when she was home, slept on the other one. Yi, our oldest brother, had sent a Victoria record player with a horn-shaped needle from New York, along with a Rio oil lamp. They sat on a brown wooden table by the hearth of the red, brick fireplace, which blasted heat and warmth throughout the house.

The backside of our house had the kitchen on the left side and the pantry on the right. The walk-thru led to the back porch, which was in between the two. Later on, Papa closed the back porch in and made it into our dining room. He built a long dining table with two benches on both sides. The whole family could sit down and eat together. Papa included long viewing windows so we could watch the animals in the backyard.

Stairsteps led from the backside to the upper part of our house. Two more large rooms were upstairs that housed my five brothers, especially when they were all home. My three oldest brothers had left home by the time I was five: Yi, the byname for Leroy; Buddy, the byname for William; and Honey, the byname for Nathaniel.

Here's a quick glance at those elder siblings. Yi, who was born in 1896, had a story quite historic. World War 1 started the summer of 1914; Yi was on the draft list and went into the Army at eighteen. He served our country bravely. The war ended near the end of 1918, but he returned home early in September, just in time to meet me, his new baby sister, "Boot" (so the story was told). World War 1 ended on November 11, 1918, and it was called Armistice Day. I learned that in school!

Afterward, Yi secured a job as the personal valet to an upcoming politician, famously known as Franklin D. Roosevelt. Roosevelt was stricken with a crippling disease called polio. In an article about Roosevelt, it was written, "Leroy Jones, FDR's black valet, woke him each morning, bathed him, and dressed him." Yes, a historical story for a country boy from rural Wake County, NC, in the early 1900s.

Buddy took a different path than brother Yi. Although they were less than a year apart in age, Buddy decided to marry early to Lonie Lyons from the St. Matthew's community, another area not too far from us. In many talks that me and Lonie had thru the years, she would repeat that she was only thirteen years old when she and Buddy got hitched. A rumored country story detailed how Lonie's mother caught her and Buddy in the woods and put her out. The next thing that the family knew, Papa was marrying them.

Buddy learned how to cook and would get jobs almost anywhere. One day he was cooking at a nice hotel like the Washington Duke in Durham, NC; on another day, he had taken a job as the head cook for a restaurant; yet, another day, he was on a cruise ship as a head chef. It was a challenging life for him and Lonie. After having their two children, Jeff, byname for Johnny, and Lonie Mae, they had a split-up that lasted over thirty years.

Honey was more of the free-spirited one of the family. He was born around the turn of the century, 1900; maybe that played a part in his nature. Honey took off for Atlantic City when I was about four years old. That city was seen as a resort town with new hotels, fancy restaurants, and loads of taverns.

I heard Papa and Mama Olivia talk about the fast pace up in the North. Honey fitted right in!

That fast pace didn't stop my second, oldest sister, Chick, the byname for Aldonia, from heading to Atlantic City in 1924. She had turned eighteen and had married Otha Lucas, one of the Lucas twin boys from, again, St. Matthews. His family called him Buddy, and Otis was his double-take brother. Chick and Buddy had a fine-looking son, Irving Lee, who stayed with us in the country when they left. I helped take care of our two nieces and little nephew, and of course, me and Christine looked forward to new playmates.

We often wondered how Papa afforded to pay for our farm off of the preacher's minimal weekly donations. The story was told that Yi and Buddy and Budja would work, sometimes for more than a month, at Mr. Watkins' place to help pay for the farm. They traded their labor for debt payments. When the boys got grown, Papa gave each one an acre of land for their help in farming the land that we had been blessed to have.

The major source of survival for our family was, undoubtedly, the raising of animals and the growing of crops. We had a variety of chickens—a whole heap of chickens—hundreds of chickens. Yard chickens usually laid white, thin-shelled eggs. The Rhode Island bird produced light-browned, thick-shelled eggs, and Mama Olivia kept six or seven Guinea fowl that produced small brownish eggs—especially richer in color and taste and suitable for baking.

Papa, his brothers, and my brothers hunted rabbits and squirrels, and raised hogs in the daytime, and stalked possums and coons at nighttime. Plus, we had two cows! The cows belonged to me and Clelly. I milked my own cow, and Clelly milked her cow. We had to take our cows out to graze. We were fully responsible for those cows. While the cows ate, Clelly and I would play jack-rocks with our own smooth rocks. It was another one of our favorite games to play!

We grew all kinds of vegetables: beets, bush beans, butter beans, cabbage, carrots, collards, corn, cucumbers, peas, peppers, pole beans, string beans, sweet potatoes, white potatoes, and tomatoes. We grew cane and cotton, too. The raw cane was cut down and ran thru the refining machine that made our thick, dark-brown syrup-our own molasses.

Our biggest crop, by far, was the tobacco plant. We raised forty acres of tobacco each season. In early January, Papa began preparing the seedbeds for planting. That included burning the undergrowth, tilling, and fertilizing the soil, and using the ash as a good supplement for the tobacco seedlings. By February, it was time to plant the tobacco seedlings. This seedling process usually took six weeks for maturity.

During that waiting time, Papa had the field workers, usually my brothers, prepare the field for the seedlings, which had to be dug up and transplanted to the cultivated field that had been broken, plowed, fertilized, and the furrows had been created. As early as the beginning of April, weather permitting, the transplanting would start.

Transplanting required three different workers: the first worker made the hole in the furrow with a tobacco peg, the second worker placed the seedling in the hole, and the third worker added water mixed with fertilizer to the tobacco plant. Each plant was about two feet apart. Between transplanting and the harvesting time, the fields still had to be weeded, the pests controlled, and the plants topped off.

What did it mean, topped off? Well, when the tobacco plant started to flower, Papa had us help snap the buds from the top. That made other buds grow further down on the plant. The new buds were called "suckers," which had to be removed, as well. This process of "topping" and "suckering" made the plant stronger. It allowed nutrients to go down to the leaves and grow longer into the summertime.

The main pest enemy was the tobacco worm, also called hornworms. We had to explore every tobacco plant by hand and remove any worms found. This exploration included everyone, even Mama Olivia, who didn't get in the field as often. As children, it was an integrated function of our country lives.

Another job of mine was driving the tobacco truck. I was around eight years old when I learned how to handle it. The tobacco truck was a flatbed platform about six feet long and two feet tall with rafters on the sides. The long reins were attached to the bridle, which held the wooden or nickel bit in the mule's mouth. I felt proud to stand on the handlebars at the backend and drive the tobacco truck full of tobacco leaves from the field to the barn; then, drive the empty tobacco truck back to the field for the refill.

So, we grew the tobacco and gathered it from the field around late July or close to my August birthday. The tobacco leaves were tied onto sticks, cured in our barn, and let dry out; they turned yellow to the furnace heat. Everyone gathered at the big slab where the tobacco was graded by its level of quality. For example, the first grade was the top quality, second grade was good, and the third-grade level was trash. We weighed it, bundled it into "hands," pressed it down, and got it to the market. Uncle Dote, my Papa's brother, did all the hauling of the tobacco in his pick-up truck.

Like Uncle Dote, several families had a truck or car. We didn't. Papa never even drove. We walked everywhere—to church, school, stores and to visit our relatives. Surely, we got plenty of exercise and stayed healthy and strong. Isn't it amazing that Papa never drove, yet he pastored different churches in different cities? One day, to our surprise, he bought a Ford car for Budja, who was the oldest boy at home at that time. I will share more about Budja a little later.

I didn't mention that everyone had their own tobacco peg (used to set out the tobacco plant). Here's a funny story: One day, Clelly took my peg because she had lost hers. After we fussed and feuded about it, Papa told her to give me my peg. He knew it was mine because he had made all our pegs individually. I admired my Papa so much because he could make anything. In the country, when you didn't have the money to buy certain items, you invented them. Our Papa was a farmer, a preacher man, and an inventor!

Although life was stable for our family, there was an understanding of how life could be vastly different outside of our boundaries. We had a dirt path that led to our sheltered neighborhood; whereas, the Watkins and other white families lived on the highway, like Mr. Paul Robertson, owner of the country store. We were segregated in our own little world!

CHAPTER 3
Rosenwald School/
The Governor Morehead School

I was a smart learner, and being in school made me happy. Jones Chapel had school in the church for primer grade to sixth grade. It was a one-room classroom with one teacher who taught all the students for all the different grades. I fondly remember Mrs. Mayfield and Mrs. Thompson. They were both nice teachers during their teaching times. I can vividly recall the first book that I loved to read. It was The Child's World-Primer with stories about a little boy named Baby Ray.

Baby Ray has a dog.

The dog is little.

Baby Ray loves the little dog.

The little dog loves Baby Ray.

It was brought to my attention that The Child's World-Primer, written by Sarah Withers, was published by Johnson Publishing Company on January 1, 1917, and copies of this book are on sale today by online sellers. How amazing?

Although me and Christine, the baby child, were too young to start school, we went with Clelly to Jones Chapel and sat quietly with some of the other "too young" children. Clelly would get up early and cook breakfast while me and Christine washed up, made up the beds, and got dressed. Clelly prepared lunch for us all to eat at school.

We carried biscuits, fried sweet potatoes, and applejacks. Mama Olivia usually made enough applejacks for the whole week. She made them from dried apples—adding butter, milk, sugar, and nutmeg or vanilla flavoring to make the paste. Vanilla was her favorite flavor. She would roll out the crust with the rolling pin, pinch the sides of the crush, pour out the batter mix and bake our sweet treat for lunch.

On the way to school, we passed the second home on the farm where Lizzie and Burt lived and picked up little Mack, our nephew. He was toddler age and couldn't stay home by himself while Lizzie and Burt worked on the farm. He was part of our "too young" group.

We walked the country miles from home to Jones Chapel to get there by 8:30 a.m. The school day lasted until 3:30 p.m., with an hour lunch break at twelve noon. At lunch, we swapped our ham biscuits or sausage biscuits for our friend's peanut butter and crackers. That was the only time that I had eaten peanut butter, and it was the best swap to me! To this day, peanut butter is a favorite for me.

I learned a lot at Jones Chapel. I knew my alphabets, numbers, and site reading. However, when I was six years old, I started my first year at the Rosenwald School. For some reason, we were not really in the Jones Chapel school district, even though we lived closer. We were in the Rosenwald district, even though it was about five miles from our home. The school was closer to the Knightdale community than to ours. Our Uncle Jeff, Papa's brother, was on the board of education, and that was why we could go to Jones Chapel; but after he died, we were "put out" and had to go to our designated school district.

If you search the modern Internet, it is amazing to read the history of how the new Rosenwald School started. I lived as part of the story but never knew how the fire got in the potbelly stove, so to speak (lol).

The story began with a Jewish-American man, born in 1862, discussing the social situation in America after the Civil War with one of his business partners. The two men mulled for a while and came to an agreement that "the plight of African Americans was the most serious problem in the United States."

Shocked by the anti-Jewish violent riots in Russia, the Jewish-American fellow realized that the treatment of Negroes in the USA was no better; perhaps worse! Especially in the South, African Americans suffered disenfranchisement at the turn of the century, finding themselves treated as second-class in a segregated Jim Crow system. One main area of neglect occurred in education. Public schools for Negro children were "chronically and woefully underfunded." Our books were passed down from the White schools. Everything we had for schooling was used, and second or third-handed down.

The Jewish-American gentleman was named Julius Rosenwald, and he would change the course of the lives of Negro children in all eleven states that were in the original Confederacy, as well as other states from Maryland to Texas. Who was Mr. Rosenwald? And how did he actually impact the South and make so great of a difference during my early years?

Born to Jewish-German immigrants, Mr. Rosenwald learned from his relatives how to make clothing at an early age. He was quite fortunate to become a supplier for a growing business, later known as Sears, Roebuck, and Company. He became an investor in the company and eventually served as its president and chairman. He multiplied his investments and became an influential and wealthy man.

Paul Sachs, of a financial firm called Goldman and Sachs, was the business partner who often discussed America's social conditions with Mr. Rosenwald. It was Mr. Sachs who introduced him to Booker T. Washington. Mr. Washington was a famous educator during our time. He was the first principal and president of the "normal school," which he grew and developed into the well-known Tuskegee Institute in Alabama; presently, Tuskegee University.

National leaders and business owners, such as President Theodore Roosevelt, Andrew Carnegie, and Henry Huttleston Rogers (to mention a few), had tremendous respect for Booker T. Washington. It was Mr. Washington who encouraged Rosenwald "to address the poor state of African-American education in the U.S."

Mr. Rosenwald and his family had the financial resources. Mr. Washington had the knowledge, the contacts, the manpower, and the plan. Their collaboration was the beginning of a life-long partnership between the two men. The first step of Booker T. Washington's plan began by building six schools in the country areas of Alabama. Those schools were the models for more than five thousand, three hundred Rosenwald Schools built for the Negro children after 1913. The project included building more than two hundred boarding houses for teachers to live in while teaching at the schools, and hundreds of workshop buildings.

I was fascinated to discover how committed Mr. Rosenwald was to our Negro educational needs. The year before my birth, 1917, he used his wealth to create the Rosenwald Fund —"for the well-being of mankind"—and he created it in a smart manner.

He pledged to pay toward the building projects as a matching grant; so, the local white school boards and the local Negro communities had to commit and provide equal resources of money, land, and/or labor. It was reported that Negro communities raised 4.8 million dollars throughout the Southern regions to match his fund. What an accomplishment!

My first day at the Rosenwald School is etched in my memory for always. I enjoyed meeting my new classmates. All the students were excited about our new school. Meeting my teacher filled my heart with joy. Ms. Candace had a pleasant face and a bright, sunny smile. I was glad to be a part of history and didn't even know that I was. We were all ready to learn and grow and make our parents proud.

The five-mile walk to school took a toll on me. I was fighting as hard as I could not to fall asleep; nonetheless, I fell asleep on my first day at Rosenwald. When I woke up, I saw boys, mainly, and girls, too, pointing at a puddle of liquid under my chair. They were all snickering. I had peed on myself. That was quite embarrassing and not the way that I meant to start my school year.

Despite the mishap of my first day, excelling in school was what I did very well. Ms. Candace was my teacher from first to third grades. In third grade, we had to get up and recite our timetables. I knew my multiplications from Jones Chapel with Clelly and from Mama Olivia, having us recite them hundreds of times. I was one of the top students in arithmetic and spelling. Every Friday, we had a spelling match. I won the final spelling match, and our teacher took me to compete at other schools in our district. That was the first time that I had been to Wendell, NC, or outside of our area other than for church.

Another contest in school -that was fun—was pointing out the right sentences. The teacher wrote ten sentences on the board; then, she read out one of the sentences. The first student that picked out the correct sentence that was read got a ribbon. Yes, I won many blue ribbons and competed, again, in our district!

Ms. Forte was the teacher for the domestic room. That was the big room in the center of the school that we learned: cleaning, cooking, home budgeting, and sewing; even basic crocheting, embroidering, and quilting were introduced in the domestic room.

Mama Olivia enjoyed sewing. She sewed *all* our clothes: bloomers, breeches, coats, dresses, gloves, hats, nightgowns, shirts, and underclothing. She even made the sheets that went on the beds and could make a quilt in a night! She and Lizzie both had a talent for sewing, and both of them could cook delicious, mouth-watering meals.

Their love for sewing, cooking, and keeping house helped me do well in the domestic class, except I never finished the flowery dress that I started sewing. I slipped and took the dress home for Christine to finish it. She, too, like Mama Olivia and Lizzie, had the sewing talent. Without her help, I probably would never have gotten out of that sewing class. Now that I think about it, I was never a sewer, and I never quilted! (lol)

Dr. King was the principal of our Rosenwald school. On top of that, he was the teacher for the fourth to seventh grades. I picture him, still, as the strong, strict educator that held our school together. As a matter of fact, he was the main reason that our sister Mozelle got to go to the School for the Deaf and Blind in Raleigh, NC. Remember me mentioning that Mozelle had a problem seeing clearly? She didn't have more than six feet of vision.

The first eye doctor diagnosed her as having unrepairable congenital cataracts. He told Papa and Mama Olivia that she was born with them, and it wouldn't do any good to operate. Despite what was conveyed, Mama Olivia had Mozelle have three different operations on her eyes. They were failures, unsuccessful as pre-told.

Now, Dr. King lived in Raleigh and knew the Principal of the School for the Deaf and Blind, Rev. Williams. Both men were determined to help Mozelle attend there. It took a year, at least, before Papa and Mama Olivia agreed to send Mozelle to that school. Dr. King expressed that the three of us were being handicapped—Mozelle, me, and Christine.

The reason, he explained, was that me and Christine were like two little "bantam roosters" fighting kids who laughed or picked at Mozelle. If she stepped in a water puddle that she couldn't see, the kids laughed at her, we would fight. If she were in class and her eyes walled back in her head, the kids picked at her, and we would fight. It didn't take much for us to take up for our sister. We had her back. So, Dr. King let Papa and

Mama Olivia know that the fighting was handicapping me and Christine.

Principal Dr. King further explained that as smart as Mozelle was, she was being further handicapped because she was not learning and was not in an environment that supported her blindness; in addition, she was not being taught how to live an independent and productive life with her limited eye-sighted condition.

If allowed to attend, Mozelle would live on campus from September thru May and only be home June thru August. She wouldn't even come home for Christmas. Dr. King and Rev. Williams were convinced that this dedicated school would be the best avenue for Mozelle's success in life. Mozelle had never been away from home, and Mama Olivia had never been separated from her children; but, sure enough, it was truly her best path. Papa and Mama Olivia (after a year or so) made that right decision.

Here's a brief history of that school—It opened in May 1845 as the North Carolina Institution of the Deaf and Dumb and Blind. Governor John Motley Morehead received a letter from the Head of Virginia's School for the Deaf and Dumb and suggested that a similar school be established in North Carolina.

The Governor was known as an advocate for education and for the disabled. He swiftly jumped at the opportunity. He received the needed support, and the NC state legislature "approved an act to provide for the education of the poor and destitute deaf-mutes and blind persons in this state."

A building was secured near the Raleigh State Capital, and the school opened with four teachers and twenty-three deaf students. The growth of the school was steady, and after the Civil War, efforts were made to add a school for African Americans with disabilities.

An arrangement was made between the North Carolina Institution for the Education of the Deaf and Dumb and Blind and the United States War Department to acquire another facility. In the month of January 1869, this additional school opened with twenty-one deaf and seven blind students. Historically, this was the first institute in the United States for African American blind students.

Around 1905, the name of the school was changed to the State School for the Blind and Deaf. In 1912, seven years later, the school was recognized as the largest of its kind in the nation, with five hundred thirty-five students. Many changes have happened at the school through the years. The name was changed again in 1963 to the Governor Morehead School in honor of the governor who fulfilled the vision. By the 1970s, instead of a school for white blind students and a school for colored (black) blind students, there was a consolidation of both schools. It received reaccreditation by the Southern Association of Colleges and Schools.

Even now, nearly one-hundred-seventy-six years later, this school continues as North Carolina's premier institution educating and housing the blind from preschool through twenty-one years of age. The original motto remains, "By Faith, Not By Sight." How remarkable!

In the summer of August 1917, Hattie Mozelle joined the Jones Family as the tenth living child and the fifth daughter. Papa and Mama Olivia had no inkling that their daughter would attend this great school for the blind, that she would graduate with honors, become an educator and teach her entire career there! Yes, thanks to Dr. King and Rev. Williams, Mozelle became confident, self-reliant, and sharp.

Mozelle was so confident that, one time, she came home from school during her break, acting as if she had forgotten the house rules. One rule, in particular, was we did not go to the table till Mama Olivia said, "Dinner's Ready." Mozelle went and sat at the table as she asked, "What is it going to hurt if we sit at the table?" Before she could finish with the question, Mama Olivia had her by her coattail, grabbed a switch, and lit her up, all the way to the front porch. She usually did the switching, and Papa did the lectures and lengthy talks.

Budja and Big Baby picked at Mozelle from that day on. Every time she came home, they would tease her by asking, "What is it going to hurt? Oh, your behind (ha, ha, ha)." Me and Christine couldn't be the "bantam roosters" for Mozelle, then, because our brothers were much too big and it was a rather funny, family joke!

We did, however, play a bad trick on the brothers and the whole family. It really was a bad idea; but, one day, Mama Olivia sent Mozelle to the well. Mozelle, me, and Christine agreed to tell the family that Mozelle had fallen in the well. What made us do it? Maybe the devil made us do it? Anyway, me and Mozelle hid in the stable, and Christine ran to the house screaming, "Come quickly, Mozelle fell in the well!!"

We could hear the chairs turning over and hitting the floor as Papa, Budja, and Big Baby ran right by us toward the well.

They were scared to death. Mama Olivia stayed on the porch with her hand over her heart.

Around the well, rocks were built up about a couple of feet high. Papa shouted at Budja, "Go right down in there, Son." About the time Budja got ready to go in, Mozelle exclaimed, "No, I ain't in the well!!" Papa was so weak; he sat down by the well like he could've fainted. Budja turned apple red, and Big Baby just shook his head. Mama Olivia went back into the house. Papa finally said, "I'll deal with you three later." Needless to say, we never played another prank like that, ever! It was a very bad idea!

My last thoughts on the Rosenwald School experience end with a story of a tragedy. The older boys in the upper grades were responsible for making the fire in the potbelly stove each morning. Eli Smith and Allen Alexander would hustle to school to be the first arriving to start the fire. No one saw what happened; it was reported the boys got into a heated argument.

The next morning, Allen waited in hiding for Eli. When Eli came in to start the fire, Allen picked up a piece of wood and hit Eli over the head. The blow was deadly, and Eli was found lying in his blood puddle. The school was in a state of upheaval. Dr. King immediately canceled school, and all the students had to return back to their homes. The teachers were in disbelief. Our young minds could not understand such an evil act happening in our Rosenwald School.

My best friend in the sixth grade was Margaret Parker. We and other students were flower girls at the funeral service for little Eli. Allen turned himself in; he served his time for that Rosenwald school crime.

CHAPTER 4
My Brother Otis Died

Mama Olivia actually had fifteen children. She did not talk about the three that didn't survive. The losses might have been due to miscarriage or stillborn, but she nor Papa spoke about the details. As far as I knew, there were twelve healthy children comprising the Junious and Olivia Jones Family. I think about my incredible parents and siblings. I think about our happy, healthy clan. We were all that, until the day Big Baby died.

I've shared with you about Yi, my oldest brother, who worked for FDR and sent us fancy items from New York; about Buddy, the next oldest who had an array of career opportunities and married thirteen-year-old Lonie; and about Honey, the free-spirited, next brother, who became a pool shark in Atlantic City. This first trio of siblings were males.

The next trio of siblings were females. Lizzie was the oldest sister, wife of Burt Dunn, who Papa didn't want her to marry because he said Burt was our cousin; Chick came next as the fifth and feisty one, adored by all; and last of this trio was sister Cete who was most like Mama Olivia in nature—mild-mannered, practical, and strong.

Trio number three of the Joneses' offspring included Budja, Big Baby, and Clelly. Let me tell you about Budja and later more about Clelly. My brother Budja was one of a kind. He was cool as a cucumber and smooth as butter. He had this air about him that attracted others to him, naturally the ladies. Now, Budja worked hard and was diligent to do whatever was needed for the farm. He was Papa's right-hand son and Mama Olivia's pillar. If Mozelle, me, and Christine had to be watched, Budja would keep us. He was our big brother, and we looked up to him. He ranked seventh.

The eighth child was our brother, Otis, which I never heard anybody call him any other name other than Big Baby. He was Mama Olivia's baby boy. He was a gentle-natured fellow and didn't talk a lot. He was truthful and always did what he said he would do. We could have called him "Honest Otis."

One time, I was selling Baby Ruth candy (5 cents each) for Rosenwald School, and he asked me to loan him the dollar that I had raised so he could buy some gas. He was courting with a girl in Wake Forest, NC, and he promised that he would take me with him if I loaned him the money. I loaned him the dollar, which got him ten gallons of gas.

The next day I was coming down the staircase, and I jumped off the stairs onto a nail that went through my foot. "Oooooooouch," I screamed as my foot "swole up" as big as my head. When Big Baby came on Wednesday to take me with him, I couldn't go on account of my injured foot. He had kept his word to me; he always did!

One summer Sunday night, Big Baby went by Lizzie's house and ate some stewed corn that was sitting on the back of the stove. There were no refrigerators to store food. So, the leftover food normally went to feed the hogs. Perhaps the stewed corn was soured and upset his stomach. He felt nauseated.

The Baptist Association convention was starting on the upcoming Thursday. Big Baby was planning to attend. As he got ready to go to the convention, I was staring at him, combing his hair. The boys had a way of putting octagon soap on their hair to make it wavy. He looked in the mirror and said, "My eyes look weak," but he went on to the Baptist Association Convention.

It was said that at the convention on that Thursday night, Big Baby ate a piece of fresh cantaloupe, and it bent him over with a sharp pain. Yi was at the Baptist convention, and he brought Big Baby to Dr. R.R. Weathers, our family doctor—the only one in Knightdale, NC, that same night. The doctor told Yi that he wasn't sure what was wrong with Big Baby. There was the possibility of locked bowels or appendicitis. His stomach was swollen up big and hard. Dr. Weathers gave him an enema, hoping it helped.

Yi and Big Baby got home around midnight. Mama Olivia stayed up with him all night long and all the next day. When Mama Olivia got tired, she laid down and left me and Christine to watch Big Baby. He told us to bring him some water. I said, "Ain't no water in the bucket." He replied, "Go to the well and get some." We told him that we were scared, and he said to us, "Ain't nothing going to get y'all, it's bright as day out there."

Perhaps he had a fever because it was near nighttime and turning country-black outside. But me and Christine stumbled thru the darkness to get a bucket of water. When we brought it inside the house, I put some in a glass and gave it to him.

He must have been getting weak because he couldn't hold the glass of water, and it fell against his chest. "This water is cold," Big Baby murmured, so I helped him by holding the glass up to his mouth to drink. Not long afterward, we headed to bed.

My sister, Cete, was still home, and a few hours after we had gone to bed, she heard a noise. Big Baby had gotten up and walked to the water bucket to get more water. He headed back to lie down and fell forward onto the bed. Cete checked on Big Baby and hollered, "This boy is dying; his eyes are rolling back in his head!"

Mama Olivia had just gotten up and was holding Big Baby in her arms. "Go get the doctor, Budja," Mama said in a whispering voice. The last thing I heard Big Baby say was, "Bring some ice cream," and his head fell against Mama Olivia's breasts. That humid August day in 1931 brought pain in my heart that I had never before felt. Our brother was gone; my brother was gone. Big Baby just slipped away so fast; he left us in shock!

No one could believe it! No one thought it was serious; we thought it was a body ache or constipation, or bad food. He was only twenty-one. I recall that they didn't take his body from the house. The White undertaker came from Wendell, about ten miles away. He brought a grey casket with him, embalmed him in the house, and left him there until the funeral service.

I cried, and I cried, and I cried. I developed like a nervous spasm. I would shake and tremble and wince till Mama Olivia had to take me to Dr. Weathers. He told her that they would probably stop. But I continued to shake and tremble and wince for months, right till we got ready to leave the country and move to Durham City.

The homegoing service for Big Baby was held right on our farm. Folks from all around the many communities came to celebrate his life and say goodbye to a fine young man. Papa did the eulogy, and Mama Olivia shed silent tears. Most of the family attended this life-changing event.

Yi was home. He had moved back and married Luzelia Hartsfield from the Roseville community. Still separated, Buddy and Lonie and the children attended. Chick and her husband, Buddy, arrived from Atlantic City; she couldn't find Honey, who later came home to stay and help Papa on the farm.

Lizzie, Burt, and little Mack were close by Mama Olivia's side. Budja had married a young lady from Saint Matthews, Launa Thompson, and they were living in Virginia. He was not working yet and didn't make it home. Clelly, with her new husband, Robert Wall, was saddened and distraught; she was right next to Big Baby in birth. Cete, Mozelle, me, Christine, Mary Ruby, Ramona, and Irving Lee, all held hands. Our Jones circle had been forever broken!

Chapter 5
Moving to Durham in 1932

Who could have imagined the Joneses leaving their family and farm, home and land, there in Wake County, NC? How did Papa make such a crucial decision so soon after we lost Big Baby? Why Durham, the "Bull City"—as it was called? We studied that the Durham nickname came about in the late 1800s after the Blackwell Tobacco Company called its product "Bull" Durham Tobacco. Other tobacco companies would shortly find their way to the "Bull City."

I was thirteen when we departed from the Jones Chapel community, March 1932. I was still shaking, trembling, and wincing when we first arrived. I had graduated from Rosenwald as far as graduations go. We didn't get report cards or formal promotions; we just left one grade and went to the next one. I missed the teachers. I still thought about Eli, his senseless tragedy, and of his family. I thought about Allen and how his life would change from boyhood to manhood behind bars and of his family, too. I missed my best friend, Margaret, and I missed Big Baby. I had to adjust like the whole family had to make real-life adjustments.

One main reason Papa decided to leave the country was the lack of help to keep farming. Although Yi had returned home and he, Luzelia, and their baby girl, Katie, were living in the small house where Lizzie and Burt had lived, he was farming on his own.

Lizzie and Burt were living and sharecropping with the Ed Robertson family. Only Honey was left to help with the last harvest in the fall of 1931. Papa had a running tab at the Robertson grocery store where he would get supplies and staples on credit. Once the tobacco and crops were sold at the market, he paid out his balance, preparing to leave for the city.

Another important reason why Papa left the country and made his way to Durham was his pastorship of Northside Missionary Baptist Church on the second and fourth Sundays. Papa remained pastor at Jones Chapel on the first Sunday and pastor in High Point, NC, on the third Sunday. Sunday School was still taught at Jones Chapel by Mrs. Katherine Wright, wife of Rev. Wright, a long-time friend of Papa.

Papa had been doing this pastoring schedule for years. Remember, he didn't drive. It was easy for me to know how Papa managed to get to Durham each week because, on Friday afternoon, he would come to our Rosenwald School and catch a ride with Ms. Candace from the country to Downtown Raleigh. From there, he caught the Greyhound bus to Durham and was picked up by one of the Northside Deacons. One of the Deacons also transported Papa to High Point on the coordinating Sundays.

We lived on the south side of Durham at 215 and 217 Moline Street. However, from where we lived in Durham, Papa had to walk the ten-plus miles to the Walltown area, where the church was on the northside of Guess Road. I was Papa's partner and walked with him most Sundays. One of the treats of being with Papa was having Deacon James Holeman's daughter, Meneva, prepare dinner for us each week after the church service. We were friends, and she was also my classmate in school at Hillside High. Her mother, Mrs. Ada Holeman, was a gracious host and made us feel welcome each visit.

We were getting adjusted to city life. It was Papa, Mama Olivia, Honey, Cete and the girls, me and Christine, all settling in our new place. Mozelle was still at her school in Raleigh. It was a duplex on the upper hill of Moline Street with three rooms on each side and the bathroom on the outside porch. The community was delightful, with lots of Negro families who had lots of children and animals. We brought our chickens with us. Yes, the chickens had to come! Papa built the chicken coop behind the duplex.

Strangely enough, chickens got missing—one by one. Papa knew that Honey was stealing them and taking them down the street, selling them to a store merchant, or taking them to Millie to cook. Papa never accused him. He simply invented a fence with a wire strung from corner to corner. At the end of the wire was a tin can attached to the gate. When the gate was open, the can would rattle like an alarm bell, warning Papa of any intruder. Mysteriously, no more chickens went missing.

Honey did have it hard at that time, just like the majority of young men without work. By age thirty, he had not established a solid work ethic. Chick said that he had been living the bum life in Atlantic City—drinking, partying, and pool hopping.

Coming back to the country after Big Baby's passing helped change him for the better. But the state of our country affected him in our new setting.

Recalling history, The Great Depression had devastated our country in 1929. We didn't feel the blow as badly as others because Papa and the family faithfully worked the farm. But in the minds of many Americans, they blamed the new thirty-first President, Herbert Hoover. He had taken office as the economy deeply crashed. Seemingly, President Hoover failed to realize or understand how detrimental and severe this catastrophe affected American families. Although Hoover, from Iowa, had been successful as a mining engineer prior to his political run, he was "widely viewed as callous and insensitive toward the suffering of millions of desperate Americans."

That public opinion led to President Hoover being decisively defeated by New York Governor Franklin D. Roosevelt in the November 1932 presidential election, the very same FDR for whom our brother, Yi, provided valet services. One good remembrance of President Hoover that we learned in school was his signing the law that made Francis Scott Key's *The Star-Spangled Banner*, the American National anthem (March 1931).

Things got somewhat better for Honey and thousands of unemployed men after President Roosevelt took office. Throughout the nation, the unemployment rate jumped from three percent in 1929 to twenty-three percent the year we relocated to Durham. Millions of families lost homes, jobs, resources, savings and were driven to lengthy bread lines; many were forced to live in rundown areas known as "Hoovervilles."

President Roosevelt started economic relief programs and government reforms. He created The New Deal and the Second New Deal, plans to boost the economy. The WPA stands out clearly in my mind. Its initials are for the *Works Progress Administration*, part of a New Deal agency that helped men get jobs working on public works projects, usually in building construction or road development and maintenance.

The WPA furnished a well-stocked food bank. When Budja came to Durham, he worked so many hours for WPA and exchanged his hours for food. We had never eaten so much mackerel in all our lives! The Great Depression continued several years after we moved to Durham. The programs enacted by President Roosevelt helped to some degree; nevertheless, for many families, the repercussions were painful and permanent!

Flashback to the country—When I left Rosenwald in March, I was in the sixth grade, and we were learning to add and subtract fractions. I was looking forward to my new school and continuing in my progress. Well, at my new school, W.G. Pearson Elementary, which was near the famous Lincoln hospital, I was put back to the fifth grade. The sixth grade was further ahead in mathematics with multiplying and dividing compound fractions.

I didn't feel as bad for myself as I did for Christine. She, too, was put back a grade. Mama Olivia knew what to say to help us study hard and prepare for the next grade. Graduation was that June and both of us were able to finish all our schoolwork and get promoted to third and sixth grades, respectively.

Now in Durham, I could do something new that I had not done prior to leaving the country. I worked for money! Yes, I had a job. High School started in the seventh grade, and all my classes were in the morning. I was out of class by 12:30 p.m. So, I was able to keep a little boy after school till suppertime.

The little boy was named Jimmy. His dad had come across our street one afternoon looking for a lady to babysit Jimmy around noontime each day. As normal, I was sitting on the porch. He asked, "Do you want a job?" I ran inside and asked Mama Olivia if I could take on a job. She had me reassure her that my schoolwork would be first and that I would keep up my good grades. "Of course, I will," I told her, "Of course, I will." And she permitted me to keep little Jimmy.

His parents were Mr. and Mrs. White. I never knew their full names. Mrs. White played bridge in the afternoon and belonged to an upscale Bridge Club. Mr. White was a building contractor; he worked in our community. They lived behind a store on Chapel Hill Street, which was close to a five-mile walk from our home. That was no problem for me, remember I walked that distance at six years old to Rosenwald.

I hate to disclose that Mrs. White loved alcohol, not the rubbing kind (smile). She would beg Mr. White for liquor until he couldn't bear it any longer. She would drink until she passed out, and when she came around, she felt sorry for her behavior. Mrs. White needed her whiskey like a person in the desert needed water. She started sending me to the store with a gift box for the store manager to put a bottle in the box. One day the store manager looked at me and exclaimed, "Damn, she done started to hiring babies." I guess I was still a little youngster at that time.

Mr. White hired a big, White nurse lady to stay with Mrs. White for a week till the liquor got out of her system. Mrs. White would get off the whiskey for a few months, seeming refreshed and sharp. Then she and Mr. White would go to a party, and she'd start drinking all over again. Sure, she was an alcoholic, and Mr. White would get so mad at her that on occasions, he would give her a black eye. I liked Mrs. White. I felt sad for her and her life that was like a roller-coaster.

I loved little Jimmy. He had celebrated his fourth birthday when I started. He was a kid like no other kid I had known. When we were kids growing up, we had chores, discipline, house rules, plus we knew how to behave. Jimmy, on the other hand, did pretty much what he pleased. He was fun, playful, and vigorous! His vocabulary was quite colorful for a kid. If you asked Jimmy what he wanted to be when he grew up, he boastfully shouted, "I want to be a damn policeman." Most of his talking included a few "damns" scattered throughout his other words.

Mrs. White actually told me, "Don't let Jimmy curse, Cora." I asked myself, *how in the world can I stop Jimmy from cursing when he hears it from his parents?* I just looked at Mrs. White and smiled. I did find out that Mr. White's favorite dessert was a lemon meringue pie. I practiced making one. I kept trying to go by the book recipe. I finally made one that met Mr. White's tastebuds. He told Mrs. White, "Cora finally learned to cook a damn lemon meringue pie." The old saying that "the apple doesn't fall far from the tree" certainly applied to little Jimmy!

I had told Mama Olivia about me going to the store with the gift box to get Mrs. White the bottle of her choice. She expressed to Mr. White that she didn't feel comfortable with me running that errand. "What if the police stopped her?" the question was asked. Mr. White agreed. Mama Olivia had given me permission to work, and just like that, she had taken it away! I had enjoyed my four dollars a week job, learned a lot, and loved on little Jimmy till Mama Olivia nipped it in the bud.

Older people, especially your parents, told children nothing. What I mean is, they made decisions for the family, and that was that. In my day, nearly every child had a father in the home unless he had passed away. Fathers were the head of the homes; they made important and key decisions. The children had the responsibility of following and respecting whatever their father and mother told them to do.

Hence, when Papa started going to Mount Vernon Baptist Church, we—the family—did too. Prior to that, our neighbors behind us on Dunstan Avenue, The McKinneys, were going to Kyles Temple AME Church. It was a newer church built about three years earlier. Me and Christine would go to church with the McKinney family when I didn't go with Papa to Walltown. It was an easy walk right down from 202 Dunstan, where they lived, to 409 Dunstan, where the church was located and still is to the present date.

The McKinney Family were the first folks that we met when we arrived in Durham. They were the "rich people" on the block. Mr. Sam and his wife, Mrs. Lannie, had four boys and two girls. They had moved from the country, too, down past Rocky Mount, NC, to Durham for Mr. Sam to work at the tobacco factory. Their youngest son, John, stayed down there with his aunt and didn't move to the city.

The older McKinney sons were young men, each in their twenties. Charlie was the oldest, close to twenty-five, Walter ranked next at twenty-three, and Floyd, the next son, had turned twenty-one. He reminded me of Big Baby since he was close to the age that Big Baby was his last year. Sadie was the oldest daughter, almost grown, close to eighteen.

Christine's best friend was the baby girl, Elveater, who was the same age as Christine, eleven, when we became neighbors. My Durham best friend was Clara Mae Bagley, who lived right next door to us. Clara's brother Bill Bagley was perhaps my first boyfriend. I say "perhaps" because Mama Olivia was so strict that all we could do was make eyes at each other from a distance.

Anyway, we called Mrs. Lannie our second Mama because she treated me and Christine like we were part of her family. If we were not on the porch at our duplex, we were at the McKinney's place. One Sunday that we went to Kyles Temple with their family, we were surprised to hear a guest gospel group led by Mr. James "Big Jim" Caesar. He and his quartet group were well-known in the Durham communities and throughout the Carolinas.

He and his wife, Sister Caesar, had twelve children like Papa and Mama Olivia did. One of their daughters started singing with her father at ten years old, and she became a world-renowned gospel legend. She is known as the First Lady of Gospel Music and the Queen of Gospel Music, like Mahalia Jackson was named. This outstanding singer is also the pastor of Mt. Calvary Word of Faith Church in Raleigh, NC, not too far from where I was born. She inspired me as I grew up in Durham and still inspires me in my senior years. She loves the elderly and has always helped those in need. She is a faithful and true ambassador for Christ. She is Durham's one and only—Evangelist Shirley A. Caesar-Williams!

Once the Jones Family started going with Papa to Mount Vernon Baptist Church, we grew even more closer as a family. Rev. W. Williamson was the pastor at Mount Vernon, and he and Papa had become friends and brothers in the ministry. Papa had gotten sick a time or two, but he always bounced back and kept on pressing forward. One scary time that Papa got sick, he actually had a stroke while in the pulpit preaching at Northside Baptist. It was considered mild, and he slowed down a bit. Shortly afterward, Papa resigned as pastor of Northside. Slowly, his health improved. Praise God!

One particular Sunday, in summer 1934, Papa left early, heading to Mount Vernon, and said he would see us when we arrived a little later. When we got to church, Papa was already sitting in the pulpit. Pastor Williamson preached a soul-searching message. When he extended the invitation to join the church, Papa got up, Mama Olivia got up, too; and of course, the rest of the family got up and joined the church—which were Mozelle, me, Christine, and Cete's girls, Mary Ruby and Ramona. We were all surprised!

Pastor Williamson asked Papa to pray. What followed shook us to our foundations. Papa put up a prayer like I had never heard before, and I had heard Papa pray at least a million times. He cried out to the Lord, "God, I have no money to leave my wife and children, but I will leave them in the hands of your children at Mount Vernon. I know that they will need a shelter in the time of a storm." He prayed and he prayed. The whole church shouted for joy. We were officially new members of Mount Vernon Baptist Church!

Older folks would say that sometimes a person knows that he or she is coming to the end of his or her time. I wonder if Papa felt that sense of conclusion a few months earlier when he prayed at Mount Vernon like chariots were on the way to carry him home? Mama Olivia was enjoying her missionary group at church. Mozelle went back to school in Raleigh that September. I was back at Hillside High starting my eighth-grade year while Christine entered into the sixth grade back at Pearson School, along with Mary Ruby and Ramona.

Life was dancing right along when Papa had his last stroke. It was the last week in October. The weather was starting to get chilly and windy during this autumntime. Papa felt weak all day. His medical history recorded hypertension, coronary heart disease with congestive heart failure, and arteriosclerosis. That list of issues has plagued the Joneses for decades.

By that last Thursday evening in October, Papa's facial expression had turned grim, and his breathing was difficult. He was rushed to Duke Hospital, where he stayed ten days. Papa told Mama Olivia that he wanted to come home. The doctor told her that if she tried to move Papa and take him home, he most likely would die en route. Two days later, Papa was pronounced deceased. The strong tower of our Jones Family had taken his last lap around life's track. Another death date was etched into my memory, the third day of November 1934. Yes, I wept bitterly!

Everyone was home for the Homegoing Celebration for Papa: Yi, Luzelia, and Katie came from the country; Buddy and

Lonie came in together—yet, still separated, she had Jeff and Lonie Mae; Honey was close by, he had married Millie Moore in October the year before and had little Frances, they were living on Dunstan Avenue; Lizzie, Burt, and Mack arrived from Ed Robertson's farm; Chick, her new husband, Lumas Young, Jr., and Cete arrived from Atlantic City; Budja and Launa had returned home in 1933 when he began working with the WPA; and Clelly and her husband, Robert Wall, trailed in from Hopewell, VA. Mozelle, me, and Christine, along with Mary Ruby, Ramona, and Irving Lee, again, held hands at his service.

Papa had packed a lot of life into nearly sixty years. The actual years are debatable. A copy of his draft registration card verified that he gave 1875 as his birth year. His gravestone has 1874. Whichever date is right, he was so young and left us too soon. Big Baby and Papa are laid to rest together at Jones Chapel Graveyard.

Rev. Billy Graham, the famous Evangelist/Preacher from Charlotte, NC, who shared the same 1918 birth-year with me, had written words that helped me with Papa's departure. Rev. Graham wrote, "The physical death is but a transition from life on earth with Christ to the eternal life in heaven with Christ, if you know him." Rev. Junious Jones, our Papa, knew him—personally! Knowing that he had an intimate, personal relationship with the Lord helped. Even still, our Jones circle had once again been forever broken.

CHAPTER 6
"Jumping the Broom" & James, Jr.

Mama Olivia wore a cape of enduring strength. First, she said farewell to her baby son, Otis; then, a few, brief months later, she kissed her life partner of forty years goodbye. At the time, I couldn't envision living through such heartbreaking situations. Years later, I, too, had to face those same life challenges.

Wake County Courthouse records show that Papa and Mama Olivia were married on Monday, December 24, 1894. Her name was recorded as Livia. The "O" was left off for Olivia, and the "o" was left out of Junious. Supposedly, Papa was twenty, and Mama Olivia was eighteen. Truth, she was actually fourteen. Both ages were more than likely fudged.

So many records have conflicting dates because who truly recorded the information correctly and immediately? A midwife or an Auntie might have recalled a date from memory. The family Bible usually had a section in the front for birthdays, marriages, and deaths. Or, like me and Mozelle, we picked the birthdate we wanted (smile). Either way, know that historical data can be altered, subject to the documenter.

As you can imagine, Mama Olivia didn't let me and Christine take company. Papa was gone on with the Lord, and she tried to keep a hawk's eye on us. Just as mentioned, Budja and Launa, with their baby daughter, Pearline, had moved from Norfolk, VA, the year before Papa passed. Budja had been sick up there, and his doctor told him that he had six months to live. He told Papa and Mama Olivia that he was coming home to die. Budja lived over fifty-eight more years—surprisingly good for a dying man (smile).

Their second daughter, Catherline, arrived in April 1934. Papa enjoyed the few months that he had to tease her. He called her "Little Creole" because she was really light-skinned (like beige), and her hair was the same color as she was, which complimented her light brown eyes. Pearline welcomed her little sister as she was getting bigger and heading for her third birthday in the upcoming December.

With two little mouths to feed, Budja went for a job at Liggett & Myers Tobacco Company (L&M). When I first talked about the history of Durham and how it became "Bull" Durham, it was foretold that other tobacco companies were headed this way. Sure enough, it happened. Durham's famous Duke family started competing with the local tobacco company as early as the 1880s. They began focusing on tobacco cigarettes over the popular plug tobacco—a kind of chewing tobacco.

Duke and Sons rapidly became a major cigarette production company in Durham. With their prestige and wealth, the Dukes formed the American Tobacco Company (ATC) in 1890 by merging several leading tobacco companies and by buying smaller companies in their path from all over the country. Liggett & Myers was included in their purchases.

History buffs will know instantly the purpose of the Sherman Antitrust Act. The Dukes would find out its purpose when they were found guilty of violating it. Ironically, this Act was passed the same year as the American Tobacco Company (ATC) was formed to "prevent business monopolies." Because of the guilty verdict in the early 1900s, ATC had to split up their great, big company into four companies. I remember the top three were: the American Tobacco Company, R. J. Reynolds, and the Liggett & Myers Tobacco Company.

In spite of the split of the Duke Family's American Tobacco Company, the Dukes were exceptionally wealthy. For example, Mr. James B. Duke established the Duke Endowment that contributed part of his forty-million-dollar gift to transform what was Durham's Trinity College into the prominent Duke University. He bequeathed added millions to establish the Duke School of Medicine, Duke School of Nursing, and Duke Hospital, all for the goal of creating better health care in our city, state, and nation. That dream is being realized each day, as Duke Hospital ranks in the list of top hospitals in the USA. Plus, that's where our brown-eyed baby boy was born!

Now, Liggett & Myers had a sizeable factory in Downtown Durham occupying blocks of the city. Quite a significant population of Negros worked at L&M. Deacon Holeman and his wife, Mrs. Ada, worked there. Mr. Sam McKinney had been employed there for years. And the company was hiring folks from all races and genders, and it was paying a decent wage, about twenty dollars a week.

Budja got the job at Liggett & Myers and took on being the head of the house. Our Moline Street duplex still had three rooms on each side—it was now Mama Olivia's room, Budja, Launa, and the girl's room, Mary Ruby and Ramona's room, and me and Christine's room. We used one room as a parlor or living room.

Mama Olivia never worked outside of the home while Papa was alive. Her life's aim and contentment came with being there for Papa, preparing family meals, taking care of their children, and keeping the home clean and cozy. Not too long after Papa died, she started working for the Upchurch family, a prestigious White family in the Durham community. They owned property on Fayetteville Road with two brick houses on the lot.

Mama Olivia stayed in the big house. She was on the job from Sunday to Sunday, which meant she wasn't home like before when she had all eyes on me and Christine. Mr. Upchurch's son brought her home on Sunday morning in time for church and picked her up Sunday night before dark.

A fellow that stayed right behind us worked with Budja. He lived on Dunstan Avenue with his brother, George. Our back doors were facing each other. They were neighbors to the McKinneys. He would come to the house to see Budja, so he said. I think that was his alibi. Most days, me and Christine sat out on the porch after school. I don't know how this fellow stopped talking with Budja and started talking with me; because I repeat—I was not taking company, and no boys could come to see me!

Now, if we did go see a girlfriend or walk to the park, we knew we had to be home before dark. Somehow, someway, Buster, the neighborly fellow, convinced me to go with him to the Carolina Theater to see a flick. It was light outside when we went in and when we came out, the sun had gone down. We took off running the 1.09 miles to Moline Street. We had heard of Jessie Owens and his track records, but I had no idea that my life would depend on running like him!

Budja fussed us out! "You know that you had to be home before dark!" he shouted. I wanted to tell him, "This guy came to see you, not me," but I remained quiet. I did have a nice time. I liked Buster, and he liked me. We began to keep company with each other. We held hands, walked and talked, and laughed. We ate ice cream at the Ice Cream Parlor in Hayti. He took me to meet his family out in the country between Fayetteville and Lumberton, N.C.

Buster, the byname for James, came from a medium-sized family compared to other families during our time. There were seven children, with his mother raising them by herself. His father had passed. They did have a big farm like we did back home.

There were four girls—Mary, who was called "Sis," Julia, Rebecca, and Ann. The three boys were Buster, George, and Richard—the oldest brother who had left home, never to be seen again. This oldest brother, Richard, stopped through Durham at some point on his journey north; we had heard through the grapevine that he had a daughter in Durham on the West-End of town.

He had gone from Durham when me and Buster got together. Buster's mother shared that the last time she had heard from him, he sent a letter letting her know that he was admitted to a hospital in Baltimore, MD. She explained that if she would've had the money to go see him, she would have gone. But raising those children was a hard enough job, and the money was quite limited.

Did my future brother-in-law, that I would never meet, get well, live, and have his own family, or did he suffer and die all alone, right there in that Maryland hospital, with no proper homegoing service? It was a family mystery, and that question had no answer throughout the McLeod family.

Naturally, me and Buster fell in love. He made up in his mind that he was marrying me, and that was that! We had extra inspiration; I was in the motherly way. The laws of marriage in NC required that you had to be age eighteen. If you were underage, you would have to have your parent's consent. Buster came to our house to tell Mama Olivia that we desired to get married and ask for my hand in marriage. Little did I know that he had already gotten the marriage license and had put my age at twenty years old. I was only sweet seventeen.

We went to the Justice of the Peace uptown at the courthouse. George and his wife, Lucille, were our witnesses. It was a happy day to "jump the broom!" On Saturday morning, April 25, 1936, I became Mrs. James Frank McLeod. Afterward, we left uptown, came back to our community, and ate lunch at the Lincoln Café. We had what was called the *Blue Plate Special*. What a wonderful way to celebrate our special day!

I went back home to Mama Olivia, and Buster went back to George's house although he was renting a room elsewhere. Buster had a plan for us and our future family; I just didn't know all the details. I went back to school as normal. I was in class 9A at Hillside High. Somehow, I always was put in the highest class.

Two of my close classmates were Ruth Suitt (McCollum) and Minnie Moore (Hedgepeth). All three of us liked Mrs. Johnson, my accelerated teacher, but we found out that one of our classmate's dad sold liquor, and Mrs. Johnson was one of his best customers. She wasn't the only teacher that potentially had a drinking problem. A few other teachers fell prey to the same cycle of drinking. I remember praying for all the teachers and asking God to help relieve them from anxiety, pressure, and stress. I prayed that He would keep them strong.

From April to June of that year, Buster still rented a room from Mr. Get Buffalo and Mrs. Maggie. Then he found us a house. Mrs. Louise Morrison, one of the ladies he worked with at L&M, had a two-bedroom place available for rent on Gurley Street in North Durham. Her husband, Irving, worked at L&M, too, and he knew Buster. It was like the duplex that Papa had gotten for us, but a little different.

When you walked through the front door, there was a hallway where you turned either left or right. On the left side was the living room and a bedroom; on the other side was the kitchen and a bedroom. Yes, the bathroom was on the back porch with a tub and a commode. We didn't have any hot water; we just heated up the cold water. Julia, Buster's sister, came to stay with us, and we had a studio couch for her to sleep on. We were happy and waiting for our little bundle of joy.

Four months later, our blessing arrived. He sprang into our lives, all bright-eyed and plump, a solid nine pounds. He was strong and had an even temperament. Mama Olivia was excited about her new grandson, and Papa would have been proud that his knee baby girl had become a mother on the twenty-first of November, just two years after he transitioned.

Buster had come to the hospital early on that Saturday. Dr. Eleanor Easley was my doctor. She had made history by being the first woman to graduate from Duke's four-year medical school program. She also was the first female resident at the hospital. We crossed paths at the right time. She asked Buster to walk me around the hospital, and he did. He had me going up and down the stairs and back and forth down the hallway till I got tired. He had to leave and be to work by 4:00 p.m. Our bouncing, brown-eyed baby boy arrived at 7:00 p.m. We welcomed to our lives, James Frank McLeod, Jr.!

Before he had left the hospital, Buster stopped across the hall to see his first cousin, Vanilla. She had come to the hospital three days before I did. She had a pretty, newborn baby girl. Buster knew her husband, who worked with the rich man, Mr. Hill, along with Buster's uncles, Willie and George. Vanilla was Buster's Aunt's daughter, his Mama's sister's girl.

We didn't know that Vanilla was badly sick. She had gotten pneumonia. I heard her one night, barely getting the words out, "Nurse, Nurse." She passed away that night, nine days after her daughter was born.

I stayed in the hospital ten days. Nothing was wrong with me or James, Jr., that was the length of time that the hospital kept you—much different nowadays! Buster came to see me and the baby every day. He was proud to be daddy!

One day that he came, I knew that he had been to Vanilla's funeral. He didn't know that I knew that she had passed. He was quieter than usual, and I asked him if he went to her homegoing services. He told me, "Yes." He said that he was so grateful that I was healthy after having the baby, and he never knew that a woman could get sick and die after childbirth.

When he shared those thoughts with me, I, too, felt truly grateful. I thought back to Mama Olivia having fifteen pregnancies and three not making it, and she survived through all of them. I was thankful to Dr. Easley and how well she cared for me during my pregnancy. I had heard that having a baby is a close-to-death experience. Yes, I was thankful to God for His grace upon our family.

James, Jr. was born the Saturday before Thanksgiving, so my Thanksgiving dinner came from the hospital cafeteria. It was the first time that I had eaten pumpkin pie. It was rather good, along with the traditional holiday meal. Vanilla's mother-in-law came and took her granddaughter back with her. I often think of how she grew up without her mother, and I'm blessed to say that I've been a mother to my James, Jr. for eighty-five years. Only our God!

CHAPTER 7
I'm Gonna Do Hair

I had gained forty pounds carrying James, Jr. I lost most all of them taking care of him (smile). It was enjoyable being a new mother and a new wife. It took some getting used to the breast-feeding cycle, the sleeping routine, and Buster's work schedule.

We lived in a different community from on the Southside. Our new street, Gurley Street, was between Dowd Street and Gray Street. Mt. Gilead Baptist Church was right on the corner of Dowd and Gurly Streets. Occasionally, some of the missionary ladies from the church would come by to visit families in the community.

We didn't have a radio when we first got married. Seemed like everyone was excited about the big 1937 Championship fight with Joe Louis and Tommy Farr. Where we stayed on Gurley Street, there was a chain grocery store nearby. The guys gathered inside the store to listen to the fight. Farr fought hard, but Louis retained his title! Boxing was the sport for most of the fellows at L&M.

Even though Liggett & Myers hired a variety of people, they were segregated in their distribution of jobs and wages. They had white jobs and non-white jobs. The jobs for Whites were better jobs, like supervising jobs or running the big machines and repairing them. The non-white jobs included sweeping the floors and separating the wet part of the tobacco from the dry part, and cutting the wet part off. That was called the leaf department, "the dustiest and most labor-intensive part of the operation."

Negro men usually worked in what were called "bull gangs," which did the majority of heavy labor, such a carrying the weighty hogsheads of tobacco or working in the flavoring section. They worked in what was "the hottest and dirtiest part of the whole process." But it was the job that helped them take care of their families.

Papa would tell us all the time that the Lord works in mysterious ways. Somehow, a job position working on the machines came open, and Buster was considered for it. He said that he couldn't do it because he didn't have the education; plus, he needed to learn fractions to pass the test. The lead man told him, "That's all I have for you to do; if you can't do it, you have no job!"

For about a week or more, I helped Buster learn fractions. He brought home sample fraction recipes from work, like how much syrup was needed for the cigarettes. Buster really studied and understood. He passed the test! He then had four to five guys working for him. I was proud of my husband. He was proud of himself.

Without a doubt, there are things that you do not know about a person till you make vows for better or worse. Because Papa and Mama Olivia were Christian believers, I never heard a curse word in our home nor saw either one of them take a drink. Plenty of people in the country consumed moonshine and corn liquor that I knew. And I saw firsthand with Mrs. White's alcoholism how it affected her home and marriage.

Did I expect to see it in my own home? Absolutely not! Come to find out, Budja and Buster, and George drank on a regular basis. They drank so much that it ran their blood pressure up. That was something new that I had to process in our new marriage.

I chose to pray about the drinking situation and turn it over to the Lord. My focus was on the upcoming holiday. It was Christmastime! From a child, I had always loved the Christmas season—the joy, the love, the singing carols, the family and friends, the fun, the homemade cakes and pies, the exchanging of gifts, the decorations, the unity, and the reason for the season—baby Jesus, who was born in a manager.

Our first Christmas as a family was a great occasion. James, Jr. was just a month old. We started a few of our own traditions. The small Christmas tree was decorated with whatever ornaments that we could gather. Lizzie gave me colorful ribbons and trimmings. She was always trying to tell me what to do. Now, as a married woman, I listened more to what she said since she and Burt had been married for over ten years. It was the season to be jolly, and Buster, me, and James, Jr. had our first jolly Christmas.

After our second Christmas, we moved again, shortly after the new year in 1938. This time, it was on the West-End side of town. We lived on Milton Avenue, one street over from Carroll, the better-known street on the West-End. I had not made too many friends on Gurley, and even though we stayed on the West-End for a couple of years, I still had a minimum number of new friends. James, Jr. was growing like weeds and wildfire. He was walking and talking and learning what little boys learn as toddlers.

Yet, again, in 1940, we moved back to Dunstan Avenue. The North Carolina Mutual Life Insurance Company was investing in real estate and had built new houses on Dunstan Avenue. North Carolina Mutual is a success story in American History. It was the first Negro-owned insurance company in North Carolina. As well, it became the largest in the nation to be owned and operated by African Americans. When White institutions refused to lend in Negro neighborhoods, it was the newly developed Negro Financial institutions that made dreams a reality.

We had two options. The first stage of North Carolina Mutual's development project consisted of apartment complexes on the upper end of Dunstan Avenue. The new apartments had a living room, bedroom, and updated kitchen. The rent rate for these new apartments was one dollar a room, for three rooms—three dollars a week.

The second stage was single-family homes down on the lower end of Dunstan Avenue. To purchase a newly built home, it was only one hundred dollars down and thirty dollars a month for ten years.

Buster was bringing home nineteen dollars each week. His thinking told him that he might not be able to afford to buy a house. There was another World War that had started in the prior year, and it had him scared to take that leap. He was the husband, and I let him decide what was best for our family.

But I was about to make a decision to change my total dependency status to more independence! I had let Buster talk me out of finishing school and getting married, only months from graduation. I was proud of my baby sister. She didn't let anyone talk her out of completing school. Christine had graduated from Hillside High. We all celebrated her, and Mama Olivia beamed with joy.

Christine had a friend named Willie Lee Johnson, a sharp young man with a million dollar smile. He worked at Duke Hospital and at the Herald Sun. They had taken up company with one another and really grew close together. He asked Buster for permission to marry his sister-in-law. Buster told Mama Olivia. They both agreed. We accompanied them to the Justice of the Peace and were witnesses to their vows. On Monday, April 1, 1940, Christine became Mrs. Willie Lee Johnson. The baby girl was the last Jones offspring to "jump the broom."

After they married, they lived with us until Willie got hired by North Carolina Mutual to sell insurance. The "catch" was he had to relocate to Newport News, VA. Christine had always lived in North Carolina. She was a little nervous about the move. A couple of months later, they were residents of Virginia. Both she and Willie took classes at the nearby Hampton Institute. Willie took auto mechanics, and Christine took up cosmetology. It seemed like she was adjusting and enjoying her new life and being married.

We had heard about Hampton Agricultural and Industrial School as youngsters. There was talk in the country about how there was a school north of us that was established for freed Negros to go and get more educated. The school also helped Native Americas with educational programs.

The name changed to Hampton Institute and later to Hampton University. It is a historical black college (HBCU). One of the first students to attend Hampton was none other than Mr. Booker T. Washington, the same Washington that helped establish the Rosenwald Schools. It is a small world and amazing how the puzzle pieces connect one to another.

One day Buster came home and announced that we were going to VA to see Willie and Christine and stay for a week—a McLeod Road Trip? Buster invited Horace Hedgepeth, our next-door neighbor, to come along. His wife was my dear friend from High School, Minnie. Buster borrowed thirty dollars from the Credit Association in downtown Durham, right across from Lincoln Café. It was set up for us to repay three dollars a week for months. We didn't know anything about interest rates; we just took the money and headed North!

We had a great road trip. We all had a fun time. A few years had passed since the visit, and I was thinking that everything was good with Christine and Wille. Little did I know that Christine had gotten sick. She had a breakdown, a nervous attack. She was heading to Asheboro, NC, to stay with our sister, Clelly.

Clelly's first husband, Robert, had gotten sick and passed. Clelly left Hopewell, VA, and made her way to Atlantic City to stay with Chick. She met a gentleman, William Gailes, who was studying mortuary science in Philadelphia, PA. He was taken back by Clelly and proposed quickly after meeting her. Me and Buster were witnesses, once again, for our cherished sister. They were married and relocated to Asheboro, NC, to create Gailes Funeral Home, Inc., a historical landmark in that community.

Mama Olivia got the news about Christine, and she, too, headed to Asheboro. Clelly and Mama Olivia took Christine to different doctors, with the reports coming back the same. Something had triggered a bell in Christine's head, and she was coping by talking to herself and others she imagined. With time, she could be better and get back to being healthy-minded.

Mama Olivia and Christine came back to Durham, and Christine stayed with us until Willie relocated back to Durham. Me and Christine were always close. I loved her and hated to see her in a bad space. We talked and reminisced about life and growing up in the country.

Christine reminded me of the time that a girl from school named Daisy Watkins jumped on her, and I got a big tree limb and knocked her off. I screamed, "RUN, Christine!" and I took off running. Daisy almost caught me. She grabbed my head and pulled my hat off. I kept running. As soon as we crossed the branch, we were in her yard. We actually had to go through Daisy's yard to get to Rosenwald.

We shouldn't have called Daisy "Three-ears-Daisy," but we did because she had three ears, for real! I don't know if we even knew the meaning of this word, but she was also called a morphodite. I didn't think we were bad kids, but we weren't as nice to Daisy as we should have been. We remembered that her Daddy came to the house and spoke with Papa to instruct him to tell us not to mess with his daughter again! Along then, parents communicated with parents, not with their kids.

Having Christine at the house was good for both of us. She enjoyed her nephew, James, Jr., and he was crazy about her! He was six by then and had started first grade in the fall. She gave me lots of inspiration, especially when she talked about beauty school and all that she had learned. She was convinced that "cosmetology was a great field to be in for the future."

I discovered that "Madame" Jacqueline DeShazor had opened DeShazor's Beauty College on Fayetteville Street in the popular Hayti district. They were offering a six-month training from January-August 1943, complete with a beauty certification. This was my plan for more independence. I had decided! I was going back to school—beauty school! *I'm gonna do hair!*

CHAPTER 8
New Home in North Durham

Attending DeShazor's Beauty College changed my viewpoint on life. I had not been exposed to successful Negro women running their own businesses and making financial decisions. I've told you about Mama Olivia and her humble position in life. She loved being the wife and mother and being provided for by her husband.

I loved it, too, to a certain degree. However, I felt deep inside of me that there could be a more balanced side of life with a woman helping her husband and being responsible for other aspects of the family, home, and marriage. I respected Buster, and he knew that I wasn't the domineering, bossy kind of wife; but he also knew that I would stand up for herself and wouldn't take being abused, belittled, or mistreated, not from him or anybody else!

In a way, my sister, Chick, who remained in Atlantic City, NJ, for most of her life, was a good example for me. She had done well for herself. She found a good job working as a presser in a Pressing Shop. She made a sustainable living and enjoyed the growth of Atlantic City. Many articles and documentaries credit the Negro labor force, which included my sister, as the key component to the development of Atlantic City.

That was the reason so many of our family members and friends migrated there. Even Lizzie and Burt had gone to Atlantic City for a short stay. Burt was going to work at one of the hotels. They didn't like the city and came back to the country. That's when they chose to work for Ed Robertson. But many stayed and prospered.

One best-selling writer, Nelson Johnson, wrote, "If you take the black experience out of Atlantic City, this town never even happens… It was a shining example of just how black people overcame segregation and built a very successful city within a city" (2010).

The city of Durham had its own similar story of successfully creating a city within a city for the Negro residents. It was the combination of the famous Hayti District and Durham's "Black Wall Street."

Hayti was founded by freedmen as an independent Negro community not too long after the Civil War. It grew rapidly, accumulating more than two hundred black-owned and operated businesses that stretched along the border streets of Fayetteville, Pettigrew, and Pine—the Southern area of Durham.

The "Black Wall Street" portion of Durham was within walking distance to the Hayti District, located on Parrish Street. This area contained the newly established, black-owned Mechanics and Farmers Bank and the North Carolina Mutual Insurance Company (that built where we lived).

Once again, Mr. Booker T. Washington is directly involved in Negro communities by coming to this area in the early 1900s and hailing Durham's Negro business district as a model for American cities. He called it a "city of Negro Enterprises." The Hayti District, Durham's main Negro residential region, and the "Black Wall Street" together served as the central hub of life for the majority of our Black/Negro families in the "Bull City."

I graduated from DeShazor's Beauty College in August 1943 as planned, with great recognition as one of the top students. Mama Oliva was proud of me, like with Christine, for putting my mind to a goal and completing it. Buster was happier than I, and that felt wonderful! James, Jr. was heading to second grade, and I was heading to a career. I shared the Hayti history with you because, after graduation, I ended up in the heart of the Hayti District!

I started working at Berma Pretty's Beauty Salon, mid-center on Pettigrew Street. I fixed Mozelle's hair as my first demonstration for Berma to see my work. She was satisfied that I could do hair. In my very first week, I earned seventeen dollars. What! Me? Yes, almost as much as Buster! How truly amazing! Still, I had to learn the ends and outs of our business. I had to understand customer service, ordering supplies, tailoring to my customer's needs, and complimenting to get extra tips. If I didn't have customers, I didn't have any income.

Berma was an experienced business owner and exceptional hair stylist. She spoke well to me, like I had good sense to understand. Her teaching method worked well with me because I was excited to learn it all. Other ladies worked there prior to my coming. I met Dorothy "Dot" Steele, Elsie Keith, and Glady "Mo" Moore Best.

Dot was originally from Wake County, just like me, Elsie was from Durham, and her family lived out in the country area of Durham County, and Mo migrated from Clinton, NC, a city about ninety miles from Durham. All of us had attended DeShazor's Beauty College and found ourselves three blocks down the street at Bermas. We jellied together pretty good and enjoyed working with each other.

World War II was going full strength. It had been four years since its beginning in 1939. The government created an Army installation up the road from us in Butner, NC. It was called Camp Butner. I thought it was called Camp Butner after the city; I found out it was named after an Army General named Henry W. Butner, who was a North Carolina native.

This area was selected to be a major training area. They started ground-breaking construction at the beginning of 1942. We heard that by the summer, nearly two thousand buildings were constructed, and the facility could house over thirty-five thousand soldiers.

Well, the beauty business reaped a major benefit from those thirty-five thousand nearby soldiers! I mean, we reaped like a pot of gold at the end of a rainbow. Durham was rocking and rolling with military men. The women were dolling themselves up, dressing to impress Army admirers. The soldiers were footing the bills for many services—eyebrows, facials, hairdos, and nails. We could work on the weekends from seven in the morning till eleven at night! Sometimes we were so busy that we didn't eat lunch or dinner. I was loving every minute of it!

It was booming, the beauty shop business, that is. Berma opened up another beauty salon in Creedmoor, NC, and was dividing her time between her Hayti shop and the one in Creedmoor. I picked up quickly and acquired a steady and strong list of regular customers. Berma trusted to leave me in charge of running her salon while she was gone.

Work was going fine. However, changes were happening in our family. After Buster, me, and James, Jr. had moved back to Dunstan Avenue, we learned that my brother, Honey, had gotten sickly. It was later in his life that he asked Millie Moore to marry him; once he had flipped his life around, and decided to settle down.

He and Millie had been doing well, and Millie had given him the joy of his life, a precious bundle of baby joy, their darling daughter Frances! Honey's job was taking care of her, one job he loved beyond measure! One instance, little Frances had pneumonia, and I remember Honey sat up all night with her, with no fuss or complaints. She was born before Papa passed and brightened up our family tree.

Back in his high school days, Honey had a daughter by a high school girlfriend. She had been adopted and was unrevealed to the family. Mozelle found out about her when the daughter found out that Mozelle was her Auntie. Pearl, our newly discovered niece, was inserted into the family in time to meet me, Millie, and Frances and help her ailing father. She fit in well and hit it off with everyone.

At that time, I hadn't decided on going back to school, and I wasn't working, so I volunteered to help Millie with Honey. Millie secured her an upmarket job working for rich White folks who lived in the Forest Hill suburbs of Durham. She would leave early before light outside and return home late, way past dark time. I would go cook for Honey, help him with his medications and sponge him down. One afternoon, he wanted some fish for dinner. He sent little Frances, who was around eight years old, to Page's Store on Pine Street to get his favorite fish. I cleaned and cooked them for him. "Best meal ever, Boot," he raved, "Best meal, ever!"

Dr. Thompson was our new family doctor. On one of his visits with Honey, he needed my help in turning Honey over on his stomach. A smelly foam from his kidneys ran out of his mouth. It was a sign to me that time was running out. Honey had told Dr. Thompson that he didn't think that he was doing anything to help him. Dr. Thompson told Honey, "I don't think I or anyone else can help you unless the Lord comes down and gives you a new set of kidneys."

The free-spirited son of Junious and Olivia Jones caught the Friday afternoon, heaven-bound train on the first day of May 1942. I was thankful to have spent one-on-one time with Honey and gotten to know him better as an adult. I was so young when he left the country, and many of the tales about him growing up painted a different picture than the young man that I cared for that spring. He had matured to the age of forty-one—still a short lifetime to live!

With overwhelming grief, family members that could come home came to say goodbye to Nathaniel "Honey" Jones. It was a brief homegoing service at McLaurin Funeral Home on the corner of Umstead and Fayetteville Streets. They handled Papa's homegoing service, too, and transported Papa back home to Jones Chapel. Honey was laid to rest here in Durham.

Lizzie and Burt were among those attending Honey's home-going. Sadly to say, Burt passed away suddenly of pneumonia in October, only five months later. He had also lived a short lifetime. He was forty-two years young.

Changes were happening all around us. Another family adjustment occurred when Mack and Irving Lee, my nephews, both decided to join the Navy close to the same time. With Mack leaving and Burt gone, Lizzie couldn't handle the farming and sharecropping for the Robertson family alone. She asked if she could come live with Buster, me, and James, Jr. in Durham.

We didn't mind Lizzie coming; the situation was we only had three rooms. However, we made it work. She stayed in the living room, and James Jr. still had a twin bed in our bedroom.

Not long afterward, we found out that our friend, Floyd McKinney and his wife, Callie, had split up, and he'd moved back home with Mama Lannie. Floyd and his wife had built a splendid home on Dunstan Street, one that was appealing to me!

Me and Lizzie started talking about having a place with more space. She had gotten a job quickly, within a couple of weeks of moving here. She did pressing at a laundromat on Angier Avenue. She told Buster that she could help with the rent if we moved into Floyd's house. Lizzie still sewed and could always earn extra money by sewing for others.

By the first of the next month, we were packed and ready to move. The house had two bedrooms, a living room, dining room, and kitchen—five rooms and a bathroom on the inside! Me and Buster slept in the dining room, Lizzie had one of the bedrooms, and James Jr. shared his bedroom with Mack when he came home on leave. Still, there was no central heat, so we brought an oil heater, a smoking thing when it took a notion. Despite the finicky oil heater, we settled in, thankful to Floyd and God for our new place.

Things on the family front settled down a bit, and things at work continued to grow and progress. The War was coming to an end. Yet, our clients continued to delight in our services. One military gentleman would stop by often to see Elsie. We all noticed his frequent visits and the banana-like smile on Elsie's face. World War II ended in September 1945. Many military men remained in Butner and the surrounding areas.

Elsie's friend, who was from Polkton, NC, a small township southeast of Charlotte, was one of many who stayed in Durham. Me and Buster enjoyed spending time with Elsie and Brown. Brown received an honorable discharge from the Army in January of 1946. He asked Elsie to be his lawfully wedded wife, and on the 26th of February of that same year, the girls from Berma's beauty shop celebrated with Elsie Keith and her family as she became Mrs. John Brown Taylor.

Most of my friends had married. Elveater (Elvita) became the wife of Esther "Peewee" Monroe, who worked as a shoe shiner for the Sher's Shoe Shop on West Main Street. Meneva had married an Army guy, Ellison Wynn. Captain Wynn and their family were traveling the world. Dear Minnie married our local friend, Horace Hedgepeth, about three years after me and Buster married. And now Floyd was dating again and planning to remarry.

Floyd had chosen a nice young lady, Alease Jenkins, to be his new wife. A post-Christmas nuptial date was set. They married on the 28th of December 1947. We were happy for them, but the news that affected us was they wanted to move back into the house we occupied! While that was understandable, we had spent the last four years enjoying the comforts of a splendid home. We were not going backward. It was time to move forward.

Since the war was over, since I was doing well at Berma's, since Lizzie had been doing well for herself, and since there had been numerous promotions and raises at L&M, Buster had a different approach to us buying a home of our own. His fear was gone, and his desire was strong. He commented, "I used to have to buy you a new Easter dress every year, now you can buy your own Easter dress." I think that was his way of saying that I was carrying some responsibility and weight in our family. Even if that wasn't what he was saying, I liked the way it sounded!

Buster gave me and Lizzie the 'greenlight' to start looking for our new home. We had only lived in a few sections of Durham, where we were expected to live, and Durham had grown tremendously since 1932. New homes were built in various parts of the city. We soon found out that some areas we were welcome to look, and some areas were not ready for us yet.

We did get the help of a real estate guy. He was a minister, who enjoyed the real estate business because of the joy that it gave him to see families get their first home or upgrade to a better home. I believe his name was Rev. Bryant; that's the name that sticks out now. So, he took us to several areas of town—East Durham, North Durham, South Durham, and West Durham.

But what stood out to me and Lizzie were three houses kinda sloping on a hill on North Alston Avenue in North Durham. Alston Avenue stretched for miles, from the county line on the southern end, running north past East Main Street (which led to Downtown), and cutting through the center of North Durham, passing Geer Street, flowing into an East/West Road.

Silently, Lizzie was looking for a place of her own. We both agreed that having your own home gave a sense of worth, and it would eventually be yours in full. Each of the houses had a living room, two bedrooms, a large kitchen, an inside bathroom, and an extra room for storage or pantry use. We were excited that each house had a backyard of its own.

The best part was the affordable price. Each house was priced at three thousand dollars. The mortgage loan agreement was three hundred dollars for the down payment and thirty-five dollars each month for fifteen years.

Buster wanted to go hunting and needed an area to put a dog pen for his future hunting dogs. Lizzie longed for a sewing room designed just for sewing. Boot—me—just wanted a house to make into a home for Buster and James, Jr. The great news came that Lizzie and Mack were approved for the first house on their own. Mack was a veteran, and that made a difference. The next thrilling message came from First Federal Bank that me and Buster qualified to buy the second house!

A quick rewind—Buster had talked to his boss at L&M about me working there after I bore James, Jr. They were hiring extra people. I was actually hired and worked there for three nights. I kept falling asleep. One of the White bosses saw me nodding and came by and said, "Wake up before you cut your knee off." I left at shift's end and didn't go back. I told my sister-in-law, Launa, about the job. She went with Buster to work and got hired on the spot. She worked at L&M for close to forty years.

Thus, she and Budja were both working at L&M. Mama Olivia was still living on Moline Street with Budja and Launa, cooking for the family, keeping all our children, and keeping the house clean. I wanted Mama Olivia closer to us so that the childcare arrangement would still work and she could help keep up our new home.

After our mortgage loan approval, I went to talk to Launa. I asked if she wanted to get the third house up on the hill next to me and Buster? Launa didn't hesitate for a hot second. She went to see the house, applied with Budja for the loan, put down the down payment, and received their acceptance notice within a few days!

How great was this magnificent miracle? Lizzie, me, and Budja, all living side by side in our homes that we were purchasing for our families! I could see Papa jumping up and down in heaven with praises and shouts of joy that his offspring were doing for their families what he had done for our family. If you want to know how a—deep-down-to-your-core—mountain of gratitude feels, imagine how we all felt in the spring of 1948! God is great and greatly to be praised!

Lizzie and Mack combined to own 1307 North Alston Avenue for a total of sixty-nine years. My time at 1309 North Alston Avenue, added with Buster's, for a total of seventy-one years, and Budja and Launa combined for forty-four years at 1311 North Alston Avenue, in Greater Durham, NC.

On Easter Monday, March 29, 1948, me and Buster went to our new home and painted the walls to make them look fresh and new. The next day we brought all that we had, along with our eleven-year-old son, James, Jr., and moved into our new home in North Durham—our first home-sweet-home!

CHAPTER 9
Tip Top Beauty Shop/McLeod's Beauty Nook

Back before I was born, in 1913, a saying—*Keeping Up with the Joneses*—came out from a New York comic strip. A cartoonist named Arthur Ragland "Pop" Momand created it based on the experience that he and his wife had living in a high-class area in New York, called Nassau County. How the story is told, Momand married May Harding, and they moved to Nassau County. It was such a well-to-do, rich county that Momand was unable to afford the Nassau County lifestyle, and they moved back to Manhattan, NY.

Even in 2012, an article by Forbes Magazine reported Nassau County "as the most expensive county and one of the highest-income counties in the United States, and the most affluent in the state of New York." It is easy to understand how Mr. and Mrs. "Pop" Momand may have certainly outclassed themselves and why the comic strip became so popular. It depicted a family trying to climb the social ladder, attempting to duplicate or "keep up" the lifestyles of their fictitious neighbors, the Joneses, who are often talked about in the comic strip but never seen. The comic strip lasted till a couple of years after me and Buster had married. The comic strip, itself, may not be well remembered, but the saying, "Keeping up with the Joneses," remains an old adage up through the twenty-first century.

Well, we were the Joneses, and we (me, my sister Lizzie, and my brother Budja with our families) had moved into our three new homes on the sloped hill of North Alston Avenue. And we heard the talk rumored about us buying up the houses on the whole street and folks asking where did we come from, who were our people, and what did the Joneses do? We were not trying to keep up with anybody and had no aspirations of folks trying to keep up with us. We were a combination of a beautician, a seamstress, a veteran, and tobacco workers trying to better ourselves in life.

As we settled into our new home, Buster learned to take care more of the outside duties and overall maintenance, and I was happy taking care of home decorations and housekeeping. Mama Olivia cooked most all the meals for breakfast, lunch, and dinner during the week. I was off Tuesday and Sunday, so Sunday dinner was my specialty. Buster couldn't boil an egg. I guess some of the things that I learned in Mrs. Forte's domestic class had stayed with me.

James, Jr. made friends with other boys in the neighborhood. He liked that we lived by the railroad tracks. He and his friends would jump on the back of a train and ride it down the track for a short spell and run all the way back home. Somehow, he got the nickname "Pepsi" from his friends. That's the only nickname I remember him ever having. They called him "Pepsi" after a left fielder who played for the Pittsburg Pirates.

Budja and Launa had the challenge of gathering sixteen years of family belongings from Moline Street and finding enough space at the new residence. They relished that challenge! Pearline (who heard that our street was in a bad part of town) and Catherline (who didn't mind if it was) stayed in the same school to finish out the school year. Mama Olivia continued to watch the girls and James, Jr. She expressed how proud and thankful she was to God for all His blessings to our family!

Lizzie was so content and at peace with her cozy home. She had so much joy in having her own sewing room! Not often did she speak of missing Burt, but she remarked that it would be different if he were here to share in the joy.

Mack had begun working with the city paving department. He was courting Ethelean "Pete" Robertson from the Wendell community. They had met in high school. She promised him that she would wait for his return from the military. She did, and he asked for her hand in marriage. Now that he was co-buying a home with his mother, he felt that he could provide for a wife. The date was set, and we all were thrilled that Mack had found his lifelong partner. She, Pete, would become my closest friend!

On Saturday, October 30, 1948, Mack, who normally was a low-keyed, quiet, and serious-natured guy, was happy, smiling, and upbeat as the family welcomed the new Mrs. Matthew Dunn. Yes, Mack was the byname for Matthew.

A few months after moving into our home, Buster had gotten our first rotary home telephone with Durham Telephone Company (DTC), which started in the 1930s. A couple of decades later (1955), General Telephone Company (GTE) bought them out. Now, James, Jr. would celebrate his twelfth birthday the Sunday before Thanksgiving, and we called family and friends to have them wish him a Happy Birthday and make sure that they were coming for Thanksgiving.

Thanksgiving had come quickly upon us, and what an amazing Thanksgiving it was! Being together, side-by-side as adults, as family, and as neighbors, magnified the holiday! All the brothers and sisters came to celebrate—Yi, Buddy, Chick, Cete, Clelly, Mozelle, and Christine—and there were plenty of husbands and wives, nephews and nieces, cousins, and welcomed friends.

It was an enthusiastic and exciting Thanksgiving gathering. I hope you can feel it even as you read about it. Inside, I missed Papa, Big Baby, and Honey; but I felt their presence even in their absence. That first 1948 Thanksgiving on North Alston Avenue was epic, and like a volcano, we were bursting with gratitude! It was only the first of many more Dunn, Jones, McLeod celebrations to come!

All was still going strong at Berma's. Six years had passed so swiftly, and we were a skintight, thicker-than-thieves team by then. As couples, we would do different activities together. We celebrated each other's birthdays and anniversaries and special occasions together. Many fond memories and fun times are centered around being with Dot, Elsie, and/or Mo and their husbands—T.C., Brown, and Fred. One particular occasion that Brown, Elsie, me, and Buster enjoyed being together was at James, Jr.'s senior play. They had gone with us to Hillside High School to fellowship and support our soon-to-be graduate of the Class of 1954.

James, Jr. always made good grades in school. He was an honor-roll student. Not one time can I remember that me or

Buster had to get on him for not completing his school assignments or school projects. He wasn't even supposed to be in the class play; however, a classmate named Pratt decided at the last minute that he couldn't do it. So, James, Jr. was selected to carry out the part.

"My part in the class play was being a fortune teller. I was the class poet and had to tell students their fortunes," James, Jr. recollected. He said that it wasn't so hard learning the script; it was having to get information on students in less than a week's time. He did an excellent job in the class play. Buster beamed with pride, and me, too. Brown and Elsie felt like James, Jr. was their son, too, and were offering high accolades and congratulations to him for his performance.

Buster was working the second shift, still, at L&M, from 4:00 p.m. until midnight. The night after the class play, I got a call around midnight. In an accelerated, high-pitched voice, Elsie screeched on the other end of the phone, "Taylor was making a funny noise, and he's on the way to the hospital!" I sat up straight in the bed, "Taylor, Taylor! Elsie, Elsie!" I managed to speak out loud. I knew Buster would be home a little after midnight, so I got dressed and waited for him to come through the back door.

When we moved to North Durham, we had no car for transportation. We caught the bus, caught a ride, or walked. A few years later, Buster had bought a used, fix-it-as-you-go Buick. I clearly remember Luzelia's mother, Ms. Maude, saying something to the effect of, "Buster done bit off more than he can chew; buying a house, a car, and who knows what else!" As I sat there waiting for the old Buick and Buster to arrive, I whispered a prayer for Taylor and Elsie, and I thanked God for Buster; I loved him deeply!

Just as the clock struck 12:30 a.m. Buster pulled up. He took one look at me and knew something was wrong. Tears started gushing from my eyes as I murmured that Taylor had been taken to the hospital. We rushed over to their house on Chautauqua Street, finding Elsie's brother there alone. He told us that the ambulance had just left, and Elsie was with Taylor. I had called Mo before we left home, and she asked if we'd come pick up her and Fred.

We went to pick them up on Mt. Vernon Street, en route to Duke hospital. Fred could not stop repeating, "We were just on the telephone talking about the fight." "We talked thru the fight until the fight was over." "I just talked to him a few minutes ago." "He was fine when we were talking about the fight!" All the way there, we listened to Fred as we fervently prayed that Taylor was alright.

The fight that Fred bellowed about was June 17, 1954, the Boxing Title Fight between Rocky Marciano and Ezzard Charles. Unanimously, Rocky beat Ezzard. This was his third-world heavyweight boxing title defense. Boxing records credited Marciano with a 49-0 perfect reputation when he retired the first time. Taylor, Fred, and most all the L&M guys liked boxing and watched it faithfully. Boxing wasn't Buster's, nor my, main sport.

When we pulled up to the hospital, Berma was already there, and Dot was on the way. There was no need to ask, "How is Taylor?" Gloomy expressions, swollen faces, and tear-filled eyes let us know that Taylor was gone! Taylor, Taylor! Elsie, Elsie! Those were the words that my heart echoed repeatedly. Elsie came from behind the curtain. She immediately locked eyes with me and cried out, "McLeod, my Taylor is gone!" I was heartbroken for Elsie!

Buster took Gladys and Fred back home, and we went and spent the night with Elsie. We talked all through the night. Elsie talked about how they had celebrated their eighth wedding anniversary in February and how he turned only thirty-five years old on the day before the senior play. It was an unforgettable night for Elsie and for us.

There were two homegoing services for Taylor. One was in Durham at Rev. J.H. Peppers' church, St. Paul Baptist Church, which me and Buster attended. The second one was below Charlotte, NC. I had never been to Anson County. That's where Polkton, Taylor's hometown, was located. James, Jr. drove Dot, me, and Mo as we followed Elsie and her family in procession to the homegoing service of PFC John Brown Taylor, United States Army.

Elsie said that Brown didn't talk a whole lot about his time in the Army. We knew that he was a military police (MP) officer and discovered that he received the American Campaign Medal, the Good Conduct Medal, and the World War II Victory Medal. He was a good husband, a good man, a good soldier, and a good friend. We said our farewell to Brown and saluted PFC Taylor!

Elsie spent a short while grieving and getting things taken care of before she returned to work. At work, however, Elsie couldn't keep her mind focused. At night, she would call and want to talk till Buster got home from work. I knew she was lonely and sad. After a while, Elsie concluded that she would leave Durham and head to New Jersey, where one of her sisters lived. It was a good decision. Although we would miss her, we knew that would probably be best for her. Our work circle was broken, as we bided her so long and God's speed.

Soon after Elsie left, something strange started happening at Berma's. At first, we didn't pay that much attention to it, but the situation kept occurring. We were getting notices that the rent had not been paid to Mr. McNeil, our landlord. We knew that could not be the case because we paid Berma every week. Our booth rent was six dollars a week. Mr. McNeil owned the pressing club next door to us, and he threatened that he was going to put us out! What in the ham sandwich was going on?

In the same block that Berma's salon was located, Mr. Lehman was renting out a space for fifteen dollars a month. He owned Beverly's Dress Shop in downtown Durham, named after his daughter. Since Berma left me in charge during the times that she was absent, I guess I was in charge of speaking with Mr. Lehman about his rental space.

I went to inquire about the location that was available for rent. He was surprisingly nice, and first, he confirmed the rent amount; and secondly, he confirmed that we could use the space as a beauty salon. I reported directly back to Dot and Mo. Yes, we could pay five dollars apiece each month instead of twenty-four to thirty dollars each, monthly.

We weighed our options—less rent, rent paid on time, our own shop that we started, and a new beginning. All the options appealed to us. Dot and Mo asked the same question, literally at the same time, "Why would we stay here and Burma won't pay the rent on time?" I think it was her habit more so than not wanting to pay on time. She would buy a dress and not make those payments on time. We all have our strengths and weaknesses.

To this day, I don't know whose idea it was to call our new business, *Tip Top Beauty Shop*, but it had a great ring to it. We had gotten tired of being threatened by Mr. McNeil, especially when we knew we had paid on time. It was time to step out on faith, once again, and see what God had in store for us.

We were grateful to Berma for hiring us and teaching us the details of the business. I sowed twelve years into Berma Pretty's Beauty Salon. It was my time to sow seeds into my own soil and reap the harvest. We talked with Berma about our decision. She understood, and when she knew it for sure, we were moving down the block to *Tip Top*.

Tip Top Beauty Shop was something extra special! We carried the great chemistry over to our salon. We shared the leadership roles and made business decisions together. If a three-way decision couldn't be made, Dot and Gladys would look at each other and then look at me and say, "Let McLeod decide." I guess like President Harry S. Truman's slogan—"The buck stops here," undecided matters stopped at my desk. Truman, our 33rd President, was Vice President to President Franklin D. Roosevelt, who died suddenly while in office at his Warm Springs, GA home, called Little White House.

There was a long list of necessary items needed to start our salon. Mr. Page, from the grocery store, handmade our desks. We had to get a salon business license from the city and the State Department of Cosmetology. We had to order equipment like—brushes, combs, chairs, curling irons, drapes, hair dryers, mirrors, razors, a register for money, shears, straightening irons, towels, and a telephone. No, we didn't have a telephone at Bermas; but in 1955, it was a necessary business tool! That year, Buster bought our first new Buick car. From then on, he only bought new vehicles. That might not have been a decision for the business; it might have been more of a Buster-preference decision. (Smile)

We needed supplies like—hair conditioner, hair grease, hair rollers, hair sprays, shampoo, shampoo caps, snacks, and toilet items. One main thing needed was a system to record appointment times and log our completed customers. We each purchased an appointment logbook that was divided up by the months, days, and hours. That kept us organized and professional. We wore white uniforms, stockings, and comfortable white shoes. We set the standard for all the new trainees that followed.

Each new addition to *Tip Top Beauty Shop* made us a unique and diverse salon. Buster's sister, Rebecca "Becca" McLeod King, joined us not long after we opened. Becca was good with hair coloring and updos, and that opened another avenue to serve our customers.

Ethelean "Pete" had worked with Lizzie at the laundry for a short time after her wedding until she decided to get her beauty license. She studied, passed the cosmetology exam, and came to work at our shop. Pete was younger and knew many of the latest hair styles and added another modern aspect to our team. We grew closer as friends and business partners.

Several other great beauticians were trained thru the *Tip Top* system. At our fullest point, we had booths for nine stylists. We had been truly blessed with quality, professional hair stylists. We all took pride in our calling as cosmetologists, and it showed in our work.

I fondly reminisce about Shirley Hargrove Lennon Abdullah, Julia Flowers Bullock, Sis Holeman, Brookie Middleton, Doris Monroe, Martha Rowland, and Nannie Walker. Martha worked with *Tip Top* for nearly ten years before she moved to Ohio and married; Dot, one of the original founders, had some issues with her husband, T.C., and to keep the peace at home, she, later, moved to another salon.

I could share memorable bits and pieces about each lady that I had the privilege to hire, train and get to know; but, let me tell you about Shirley! (lol) Shirley came to us in 1963, ready to conquer the world. She was fun-loving, hard-working, and youthful, of course. By that time, me and Mo had been doing hair for over twenty years.

Shirley declared, "I ain't doing hair that long, for twenty years, no way!" We laughed at her and her innocent declaration. I am proud to tell you that Shirley Abdullah is my beautician, she did my hair a few days ago, and in 2021, she is celebrating her fifty-eighth year as a licensed cosmetologist! Innocence turned into longevity! Not only is she continuing to grow and prosper, her son, Eric, is the third generation of our *Tip Top* legacy!

Most people have heard of a song entitled "Everything Must Change." Dozens of artists, musicians, and singers have added their rendition to the prophetic lyrics of this ballad. As great as all was going on Black Wall Street, in the Hayti District, and at *Tip Top Beauty Shop*, things changed right before our very eyes.

It was called urban renewal. The famous author and novelist James Baldwin (1963) labeled it as "Negro Removal" because of the way that it targeted sectors of the American communities that were mainly disadvantaged, impoverished, and/or Negro.

Urban renewal was a term included in the American Housing Act of 1949. Yes, our 33rd President, Harry S. Truman, presented his policy statement on housing addressing the need for "more public housing, slum clearance, and lower-priced housing." It was part of legislation named the Fair Deal.

We received letters at the beauty shop about different meetings set up for business owners to hear and understand what was about to happen. Negro leaders were told that the buildings and houses would be torn down, and with the money furnished from the government, they would be rebuilt and replaced.

Even Mr. Lehman reassured us that when the urban renewal was completed, and the community was reestablished, we would still be able to have our *Tip Top Beauty Salon*. I listened at meeting after meeting, and deep within, I didn't feel comfortable with what I was hearing and what was happening.

Something was telling me that they just wanted to tear down Hayti. Why? Because Blacks/Negros didn't have to go downtown for *nothing*. I believe I mentioned that Hayti had everything! We were self-sufficient in terms of daily living.

Just to be clear, the Hayti District consisted of: an appliance service, a bakery, a bank, barber shops, a beauty college, beauty salons, a boarding house, a butcher shop, cafés, clothing stores, a doctor's office, a drugstore, a filling station, a fish market, funeral homes, a furniture store, a grill, a grocery store, a hospital, a hotel, an ice cream parlor, a library, a music company, a notions shop, a newspaper publisher, a pressing club, a realty, restaurants, a self-service laundry, shoe shine parlors, a sports shop, a training school, two churches, three movie theaters, and a watch repair store. Hopefully, that gives a realistic outline of the depth and width of Hayti!

The United States government, between 1949-1973, bull-dozed twenty-five hundred neighborhoods in nine hundred and ninety-three American cities through the urban renewal disguise. A million people were displaced by the program.

When we look at Durham, specifically, urban renewal and the Durham freeway project displaced over four thousand families and five hundred businesses. Much was destroyed, and little was replaced, and the promise of a redeveloped Hayti never was fulfilled.

As you have already reckoned, *Tip Top Beauty Shop* would be a part of that destruction. In 1965, Buster offered me an option. "Why don't you come on home, and I'll build you your own beauty salon on the back of the house," he asked? Sounded like a great plan. I agreed with that option.

I'm not certain if Mechanics and Farmers couldn't approve the loan because it was considered a second mortgage; I know Buster went to First Federal Savings and Loan at Durham's Five Points, got a loan for fifteen thousand dollars, and had a beauty salon plus two extra rooms built onto our home. The loan agreement was reasonable. He'd pay fifty dollars a month on a ten-year plan. He couldn't get it for fifteen years, but he was satisfied with the contract.

Within a few months, in May 1965, I had a home-based business. Becca and Pete came with me from *Tip Top*. We had three beauty stations set up. Gladys and Shirley, and some of the other ladies stayed as long as they could before having to relocate to other locations. This time, I knew who had to create a name for the beauty salon, I did! I don't know how long it took, but I called it *McLeod's Beauty Nook*.

There, I was blessed to serve my customers for nearly five more decades. The exact date that I said goodbye to my last customer is not certain. It was hard because each time that I said that would be my last hair service, someone would call, asking, "Mrs. McLeod, may I come tomorrow?" I'd say, "Yes, see you tomorrow."

CHAPTER 10
From Civil Rights

I was in my early fifties when *The Autobiography of Miss Jane Pittman* by Ernest J. Gaines was published in 1971. I share with you that I didn't read the book but had heard about it and the powerful message that it delivered to our American society. When the movie was produced three years later, in 1974, I do know that I paid more attention to what I had heard about the book, and as I watched the televised version, I agreed that it was an eye-opener for our nation, our America.

The story from the book and the movie about the life of Miss Jane Pittman and her family reflected a time from slavery days to the ending of the American Civil War, right thru to the Civil Rights movement in the nineteen sixties. Even if my starting point of this chapter began at the Civil Rights door and continued to the present, it would take thousands and perhaps tens of more thousands of pages to try to chronicle what occurrences have happened in the last sixty years in the United States of America with the African American/Black/Brown/Negro/People of Color.

I am not afraid to address any of the true-life stories that I know about and have lived beyond, but my humble efforts would just leave out so many, many other devastating episodes, distressful experiences, and dreadful realities that I couldn't find an exit door to close on them all. It would be an insurmountable challenge!

Allow me to continue in the vein of my life story. It's different from Miss Jane Pittman and her family, but it still covers a century+ of living over time periods consisting of brutality, civil unrest, human tragedies, inequalities, injustices, and heartbreaking pains.

We, the Junious Jones family, were blessed because Papa was a preacher man, and somehow there was a hedge around us—shielding us from the crucial harms of the world outside of us. We were sheltered. We had a modified awareness of the multitude of struggles facing our people.

Yet, when I think about our family roots, thanks to Alex Haley's book and movie series, *Roots*, Mama Olivia's parents, Andrew and Lizzie Young, and Papa's parents, Jeff and Sally Dunn Jones, my maternal and paternal grandparents, were all slaves. We don't have as many details about the lives of my grandparents, Jeff and Sally. Papa never talked about them, ever.

But when grandparents, Andrew and Lizzie, became among the freed men and women, they wanted more for themselves and their offspring. They purposed in their minds to set an example for their family. It started when they bought a few acres of land near the Macedonia Church area, a few miles from Raleigh, NC. Neither one of them could read or write. They had God-given wisdom and some business sense about them. To sign their names, they both put their X marks on the deed. We have a copy of that deed in our family archives. Countless

Negros were determined to have something when they came out of slavery, even if it was nothing but a little one-acre plot.

I remember that one day back in the country, Mama Olivia's sister, Aunt Lula came by. They were just talking in general, and then they began talking about slavery. Me and Christine were playing together in our living/bedroom. Christine instantly started boo-hoo crying and sobbing out loud like she knew the people personally who were in slavery. Mama Olivia and Aunt Lula couldn't understand why the topic provoked such sorrowful emotions from Christine. They stopped talking about slavery!

At another time, the same unexpected crying spell happened with Christine when some of the men from church were talking to Papa about the Ku Klux Klan (KKK) threatening colored folks and whipping up on them for nearly any reason. They used Mr. Chris Rogers as an example. Mr. Rogers ran a "hoochie-coochie" house where he sold liquor, moonshine, and whiskey, plus he had dancing girls. His wife was a nice lady who played the accordion at church. I think she went to Riley Hill Baptist.

Anyhow, the story was that the KKK said that Rogers wasn't living right and was attracting young people, leading them astray. Back then, Budja was one of those young people, and he would visit there whenever he desired to do so. They threatened to whip Mr. Rogers nearly to death. Mr. Rogers sent word for them to come on out to his place. He got under his house with his shotgun. He had planned to take one or two of them out before they got to him. For whatever reason, the KKK didn't go there messing with Mr. Rogers, and he did not close down his business.

Now, a White man named Mr. Dollie Jones got in trouble with the KKK because they speculated that he liked Negro women. He owned a grocery store in the Neuse River area and treated the Negro customers with respect. He was threatened by the KKK, as well, and was beaten. He pulled thru and survived the ordeal.

But they messed up by targeting Mr. Dollie Jones. He ended up suing them and kept them in court for years. He had the money. The KKK got highly exposed as a result of Mr. Jones's case. It was discovered that Klan members were bankers, business owners, doctors, lawyers, policemen, teachers, and other big folks in the community, like upright Dr. J.R. Hester, from the Knightdale community, who was found to be a Klansman; they were hiding behind masks and looking for an excuse to hurt others!

Needless said, White people in general, and the KKK, specifically, never bothered Papa or his family. Yes, he was the preacher man, and we were kind of private, staying to ourselves on that old county road leading to Jones Chapel. Besides going to the store on the highway, we didn't have any reason to associate with Whites. We were, literally, segregated.

Papa and Mama Olivia never really had a conversation with us about slavery or their parents' lives during those years before slaves were freed, and no conversations about civil rights, integration, or racism. Papa just tried to get along with everybody—Whites, Blacks, and all shades in between. He wasn't an "Uncle Tom;" he was a man of God who believed in doing right by humans and having humans do right by him.

There are different definitions of the label, "Uncle Tom," with each carrying a negative undertone. It's often used to describe a Black man who is considered to be excessively and/or overeager to win the approval of White people. Papa had God's approval, and he had inner strength. He didn't crave the approval of Negroes or Whites. He taught us to believe and know that no one was better than us because of her/his skin color and that we were not better than no one else, skin color as a factor or not. God created us all in His image!

Yet, as children, we noticed differences, like the White children rode buses to school and we had to walk. We never mentioned to Papa and Mama Olivia that when the buses passed by us, the kids would spit out of the windows and holler at us, calling us the "n" word. We were little girls and just ran to get away from the bus. We didn't throw rocks like boys; we just didn't want spit flying in our faces.

Remember Mr. Hence Watkins, the man who sold Papa the hundred acres farm? He had some mean boys. We had to pass the edge of their yard to get to the store up on the highway. We didn't go often, like every day or every week. But, when we did, as soon as they saw Clelly, Mozelle, me, and/or Christine coming, they started throwing rocks at us. Maybe they were just being boys or just having fun, or perhaps they had hidden hostility toward us. We never asked. They never explained.

Earlier, I mentioned that Mr. Paul Robertson ran the local country store. Well, his cousin, Mr. George Robertson, ran another country store. His younger brother, Mr. Eddie Robertson, was the one who Burt and Lizzie farmed for and worked with when they came back to the country.

Mr. Eddie had a son, Proctor, a few years older than Mack. Mack and Proctor played together from the time Mack was old enough to play. When they got older, Proctor was becoming a teenager, Mr. Eddie stopped them from playing together. Mack didn't understand why he and his friend couldn't play together any longer.

Burt understood. He had heard Mrs. Robertson ask the question to Mr. Eddie, "How would it look if his friends from school came over and saw him playing with him?" So even without a formal discussion from Papa and Mama Olivia, life's little incidents made us aware that we were treated and viewed differently by many White Americans.

Getting back to Mr. Paul, when their dad, Mr. Jim Robertson, died, he sold the country store and started buying up people's land. That's what happened to our hundred acres farm. When we left the country, Yi took over the farm, and he worked it for a couple of years. Then, Papa died. Yi had planned to move to Durham to be closer to the family.

It was up to Yi to get a proper settlement for Mama Olivia on the land. He was being smart, and somehow, he didn't put Mama Olivia's name on the land contract, or he took it off and was negotiating with Mr. Paul to sell some of the acres. Whatever really happened, Mr. Paul, being more understanding of land contracts, bought our entire farm. It was sold, and Yi didn't even know it. It was nothing Mama Olivia could do, so she was told. It hurt our family to know how Papa, my brothers, and my uncles had worked so hard to cultivate and develop the land, grow and produce crops, and provide for us for all those years and that our homestead was gone in a blinking of an eye.

We were not alone. It is documented that of the fifteen million acres of land that freed slaves and their descendants accumulated after the Civil War, most in the South, that eighty percent was lost through partition sales. That's all I'll say about that.

CHAPTER 11
Love of Baseball, Fishing, Pinochle, and Buster

Baseball was the only sports game that I ever played during my childhood days. I loved it from the first time that I played with my friends. There was another Robertson Family that lived not too far from our farm, the Negro Robertsons. I didn't know their family tree or if they were related to Mr. Jim or were connected to descendants of his ancestors. I just knew that their boys could play baseball, and they treated me like a ball player, not like a girl!

Their Dad was Mr. Willie, and Mrs. Jane Ellen was their Mama. They had two older sisters, Leatha Mae and Dorothy. Clarence was the oldest boy. When I was ten, he was around fifteen. The next son, James, was a couple of years ahead of me; Archie and Christine were born the same year. Their baby boy, Ardis, was a little baby in 1928.

When the Robertsons boys came over—Clarence, James and Archie, and the Perry crew—we usually had enough to play baseball; if not, we played catball. You've never heard of catball? It was played with five players—the pitcher, two hitters, and a catcher. We rotated between hitting and catching. James, the one closest to my age, always tried to outdo me, and anything James would do, I tried to do it, too. If he wore overalls, I wanted to wear a pair. If he hit a home run, I knew that I was going to hit one, too!

We made our own balls and made them out of string. We took cotton and kept wrapping the string around the cotton. It was the tobacco thread string that we used to make the ball. Papa used to make balls for us before we learned to make them for ourselves. His ball was much harder than ours. Remember that all of our toys were homemade from using strings, old tires, or wheels that came off the buggies.

When we were in school, we didn't have to work in the fields every day. We had more time to play than when school was out. We looked forward to playing after school. Mama Olivia made the bases. They were stuffed with cotton, thickly padded. Whether it was baseball or catball, the fun was in making the hits, sliding into the bases, or even hitting the home runs. It was no fun getting out! Christine and Archie were smaller, but both of them played "good enough" to keep up with us, the bigger players.

Clarence always pitched, even though he couldn't pitch a lick. He thought because he was the oldest, that he should be the pitcher. In fact, Clarence thought he could tell us all what to do. Papa and Mama Olivia had to go away for an evening, and they left Mozelle, me and Christine with Mrs. Robertson.

Of course, Clarence thought he was in charge. We had played a great game of catball. We were, then, rolling the different wheels out in the yard. Some came off buggies, cars, toys, tricycles, and wheelbarrows. It was getting close to nighttime, but the moon was shining so brightly that we could still see clearly. Somebody hit Mozelle by mistake, and she started crying. Clarence made us all come into their house and lay down on pallets until Papa and Mama Olivia came to get us. Not too long afterward, Clarence moved to New York, married Gertie Mae, who was a Robertson from Marks Creek in Wake County, and he served in World War II.

After me and Buster had married and went back home to visit Jones Chapel, we saw Clarence. He looked good, and he started teasing me and asking why he didn't try to talk to me and Christine back in the day. I told him, "You were too busy trying to be our Daddy and telling us what to do." We both had a belly laugh. He knew what I said was true.

Each church in the country had a baseball team. Jones Chapel had a big baseball field down a block from the church. All the churches competed with the other local churches. People are different now than during my growing up years. I say that because a guy came to our area, and he didn't have anywhere to stay. Papa didn't really know him, but he extended hospitality to him, and he stayed at our house the whole winter. He worked and helped around the farm. That was an understood principle to stay at our home.

Nobody remembered his name, but he bragged all winter long to Budja and Big Baby that he was a pitcher and was going to play professional baseball. They were excited, thinking that they had a real pitcher for the Jones Chapel Baseball Team. When spring came, and baseball fever was in the air, the big boys began practicing for the upcoming season.

Budja said the guy would pitch, and all the players hit the balls far out into the field. He didn't have a fast or curve ball.

He didn't strike anybody out! Budja and Big Baby finally concluded that the guy was not professional at all. I think Budja was really disappointed about the guy because he thought we had a pitcher staying with us at the house all winter long.

In our early years, baseball was the greatest common bond between me and Buster. The Brooklyn Dodgers was our favorite team. We loved to listen to games on the radio and, later, watch them on television together. It didn't matter whether it was spring training, exhibition games, regular season, or play-offs leading to the World Series. We were on it. Even Buster and some of the guys that he worked with had baseball games every Saturday at the local parks.

It was in the 1940s that the Dodgers began to emerge as a mighty team. They won their first National League pennant in 1941. They won one-hundred games that year. Me and Buster had been married five years. Before that season, they had not won a pennant in twenty-one years. The new manager was called Leo, and he seemed to be more aggressive in getting the guys to play harder.

The Dodgers had a good season the next year, winning more games but finishing number two behind the St. Louis Cardinals in 1942. World War II had its effect on everything in this country, and baseball was no exception. Many of the Dodgers' players and League players across the nation had to fulfill and serve their military obligations.

The absence of men ball players gave way to the creation of the first USA formal women's professional baseball league, called the All-American Girls Professional Baseball League (AAGPBL). Me and Buster were celebrating our seventh wedding anniversary when the potential lady baseball players went to the first tryouts in the spring of 1943.

The tryouts were held in Chicago, IL, with nearly three hundred ladies arriving from various US states and from Canada. I remember thinking, *here are women doing something that has always been done by men; how amazing and extraordinary!* My thoughts quickly envisioned me competing with James Robertson for hits and home runs. It certainly could be done!

In 1946, the Dodgers came back after WWII had ended in 1945 to have a winning season. They actually tied for first place with their archrival, the St. Louis Cardinals. Me and Buster, plus the world, witnessed the historic first playoff series between those two teams, with the Cardinals pulling out the victorious World Series Championship.

Something else quite historic was happening with the Brooklyn Dodgers in the 1947 season. First, they did win the National League pennant over the Cardinals. Secondly, never before in the professional major league had a general manager done what Branch Rickey was about to do. He went against the American grain. He signed a baseball contract with a Negro baseball player!

In 2021, it's easy to think, "that's no big deal." Certainly, from hindsight, it is common and expected to have a combination of players from different ethnic and racial backgrounds. But a rewind time machine would have to take us back seventy-six years to the 1945 signing of the very *first* African American in Major League Baseball, Jackie Robinson. Can you feel the vile atmosphere? It was thick enough to cut with a butcher knife.

Jackie Robinson lived through hatred, hostility, and humiliation. He was called names, cursed at, threatened, thrown at, and yelled at, among other acts of resentment and retaliation. He had to take it and taste it and swallow it and try to digest this unhealthy meal of racism, both among the fans and the players. Yet, he stood strong, and he "had the guts not to fight back"—which was the question that Branch Rickey asked him before offering him the contract.

In the 2013 biographical motion picture movie *42*, Robinson replied to Rickey, "Give me a uniform, give me a number on my back, I'll give you the guts." Jackie Robinson was portrayed by the late Chadwick Boseman and Branch Rickey by Harrison Ford. Epic performances were anchored by both of these incredible actors. Infamous words were spoken by Jackie Robinson to his on-screen wife as she expressed concern about what he would be facing as he got closer to the Brooklyn Dodgers roster from the Montreal Royals AAA team. She encouraged him to "not let them get to you." His response was, "I won't. God built me to last." When Jackie was being confronted by a Manager from the Philadelphia team with derogatory remarks, Branch Rickey declared that Jackie would be fine, and he used some of his same words, "Don't worry, he can take it. God built him to last." Indeed, he lasted thru a remarkable ten-year career.

We had been Dodgers fans, undoubtedly, and when Mr. Rickey added Jackie Robinson to the team, our joy, happiness, and pride were heightened. There was a Negro man playing on our favorite team. And he did not disappoint his supporters. His talent could not be denied. In his first year, he received the first-ever Rookie of the Year award. He won the National League's Most Valuable Player award the next year.

Jackie continued to thrill us as we watched him excel, capping off his legacy with the 1955 World Series title against the New York Yankees. That was the year that we started *Tip Top Beauty Shop*, and the television was certainly on the baseball games. Jackie Robinson retired the year following the World Championship pinnacle. Our beloved Brooklyn Dodgers moved to California around 1958 and became the Los Angeles Dodgers.

As we still loved the game of baseball, me and Buster started following the Braves, who were originally in Boston, MA. The team moved to Milwaukee, WI, and became the Milwaukee Braves. They actually won the 1957 World Series against the New York Yankees. By the time urban renewal had taken place in Durham and Buster had created McLeod's Beauty Nook for me, the Milwaukee Braves had changed to the Atlanta Braves, located in Georgia. They were a great team for years, managing to win another championship in 1995.

In addition to baseball's love, there was another love of our lives, the joy of fishing. Boy, did we love fishing! We caught bass, bluegill, bowfins, bream, carp, catfish, crappie, flounder, perch, pike, and trout, just to name a few types. Occasionally we would catch eels and turtles. We never had to buy fish from a fish market or store because the freezers were always full of recently caught and cleaned fish.

We went fishing every week. The salon was closed on Tuesdays, and that was our fishing day. We had our own fishing boat and a 7.5 hp motor—black with a blue stripe down the center. Budja and Launa, Catherline and Christine, George and Lucille, and/or Lizzie, Pete, and Becca would join us any time; the more, the merrier. Except, you had to be serious about staying out on the fishing bank or lake all day and not running your mouth too much. Fishing is a peaceful sport, to a certain degree. It's a practice of patience, learning to embrace the silence and the stillness.

We fished in different locations—a pond off of Angier Ave. in Durham, Creedmoor Lake in Creedmoor, NC, Jordan Lake in Durham, and Lake Michie, near Bahama, NC. The pond off Angier Ave belonged to a White lady that knew Catherline. She gave her consent for us to come fish whenever we wanted. It was a private, small pond that was close to home. If we were limited on time, we would head straight to Angier Ave. It was full of catfish, bluegill, and white bass.

In Creedmoor, Lake Rogers Park was the main recreational spot in that area. It was not as modern back when we would go as it is now, but it was always welcoming to local and visiting fishermen. It had an attractive and pictorial lake that stretched for miles along the boundary of the city limits. You could see all the way across the lake. It offered boat launching, boat rentals, and pier fishing. We had an annual boat pass to launch our boat.

One of my great memories at Creedmoor was the day that I lost my line, sinker, and almost my reel. A big one jumped on my hook, and I fought hard to bring him up. He got hung up under a root and took my line and sinker. We were at the end of the day, so we let him go on his way. The next day, I took off at lunch and went to the Ace Hardware store and bought me a hundred-pound test line. I didn't plan on letting another one get away from me!

The City of Creedmoor has, in the last few years, invested into the park's natural beautification and promotes it as a destination, "for those wanting to spend an afternoon fishing, go for a paddle on the tranquil water, sit on the boardwalk and watch the sunset, enjoy a picnic and a day at the playground, or a quiet walk through the woods." We went for the bowfins, carps, pikes, and perches!

We didn't fish at the Jordan Lake as often as Lake Michie, but it was, and still is, a huge combination of waters extending around a fourteen thousand-acre reservoir. It stretches from Apex, NC, through Durham and Chapel Hill and past Pittsboro, NC. Bass and crappie reigned as the most common catch. However, there was a variety of other fish. The lake had largemouth, small-mouth, striped and white bass; crappies came in colors—black and white; perches were yellow, and the catfish came in every color—black, brown, gray, red, light and dark yellow, and white. Jordan Lake had great fishing accommodations, also including boat ramps, boat rentals, and shore fishing.

Our favorite fishing spot was at Lake Michie! Lake Michie is located in Durham County, close to the town called Bahama. It feeds off the Flat River and is the main reservoir for the entire city of Durham. It had a log clubhouse. Now, this was catfish hotel (smile). They were stocked with blue catfish, bull catfish, channel catfish, flathead catfish, and mud catfish. Lake Michie had plenty of largemouth bass, giant crappie, longnose gar fish, chain pickerel, and northern pike. The crappies were large as both of my hands put together. When we launched our boat at the boathouse, we knew where our spots were, and we headed in that direction.

Sometimes, me and Buster would stay out so long that one of the workers would come looking for us. Even if it was threatening a storm, Buster didn't want to leave. He wanted us to weather it out. Calvin was one of the young men who worked at Lake Michie and always helped us. He kept the boat for us, secured it in a special place till we returned the next week. One day we didn't come in when they broadcasted a pending storm. Calvin told me later, "fishing is going to be the death of you and Buster if you two keep staying out there in a storm!"

One sunny day at Lake Michie, every fish we caught was a catfish, nothing but catfish! We had two large foot tubs full of catfish. We thought about Mr. Washington Daye, Denise's father-in-law, who lived up above Lake Michie. We carried the foot tubs to Mr. Daye, and he couldn't believe his own eyes. Mrs. Daye had a huge basin, and we dumped the mass of fish into it. He immediately started to clean the catfish, telling us, "Put them over there; I'll clean them." He and his wife were so excited. He cleaned almost all night long. It made our day to make their day!

One day, me and Buster had a frightening experience at Lake Michie. The weather forecast projected a clear and mild temperature day. As usual, we got a boat; this was before we had our own boat. We went to one of our key fishing spots and set up. We noticed that it was a little windy, but nothing too dramatic. Within a couple of hours, the wind was so high that we were being hurled and slung like bowling pins falling from a strike.

The wind picked up speed and relocated us to another area of the lake. We landed across a boulder at the base of a hill. The boat was beaten up pretty badly, and we managed to exit it with mild bumps and bruises. When we got to the top of the hill, a street sign marked that the boathouse was two miles ahead. A nice, White man, going to the boathouse, gave us a lift back there. We had rented that boat for one dollar a day. That might have been its last day rented. We were thankful to be alive!

Back in the country, not only did we play ball with Clarence, James, and Archie, we went fishing together, also. We caught crappie, catfish, and perch. When we didn't want to dig up worms from the ground, we used flathead worms. They were the little white worms that you find under the bark of a log or piece of wood.

One day little Ardis came with us fishing. For a moment, we weren't paying him any attention, and he started sliding down the bank into the water. Clarence ran to grab him and me, James and Archie helped pull him up. I think about how God saved Ardis that day, saved me and Buster when we crashed on the boulder, and has kept us all through so many of life's episodes. We have lots for which to be thankful.

Now then, my biggest catch was at Lake Michie. It was early in the day. We had gotten up around 4:00 a.m. to make sure we had everything. I even left a note, *"Gone Fishing. Be back tonight."* We headed to the bait house to pick up minnows and red worms. Daylight was just cracking the sky when we pulled into the parking area at Lake Michie. I could say that I had a *good feeling* that day, but I had a good feeling every time I headed to a fishing hole.

Buster had caught a few crappies when all of a sudden, a fish snatched my pole right out of the socket; that one had a minnow on it. I grabbed the pole before it went sailing down the lake. Buster shouted, "Hold him, Boot! Hold him, Boot!" Had the boat not been tied to a bush on the bank, the fish would have pulled us for miles.

I fought him like Joe Louis fought all his opponents, with a determination to win. I wore him down and got him to the edge of the boat. Buster picked him up with the net. That fish didn't even swallow the hook; the hook got him around his lip. At day's end, they weighed him at the boathouse and took my picture for the newspaper. I was holding a thirteen-pound largemouth bass. That might not have been big for someone else, but it was my big catch! The newspaper caption could have been, *"Mrs. Cora Jones "Boot" McLeod and her Bucketmouth."*

James, Jr. had gone fishing with us as a lad. When he got older, he had made other plans. One time, he went out to the lake with Buster and came home puffed up. "I'm not going fishing with Daddy no more, 'cause I told him that I had a date before we left, and when it was time to leave, he didn't want to go." I laughed and smiled to myself; I knew the fishing routine. Buster was never ready to go.

When he retired from L&M, he fished every day. He ran the freezer over with fish. Rev. and Mrs. Lawrence lived across the street from us on North Alston Avenue. They had twin grand-girls, Karen and Sharon, a little younger than Denise. Buster would get a bucket of fish and take it to them. He'd take fish to Brother Perry, who was in his Sunday School class, and Brother Vereen, who worked as a janitor at Mount Vernon with Brother Perry. Basically, for anyone who wanted fish, Buster thought of it as his civic duty to get them some freshly caught fish.

All the fishing that I've shared about has been fresh-water fishing. Some folks may say if you haven't been deep-sea fishing, you haven't been fishing. Well, that's a saying that I might have to debate about. Some fellows from work talked Buster into going deep-sea fishing, and in turn, Buster talked me into going with him. Budja and Lizzie came along, so did George and Lucille.

I didn't know what to expect since this deep-sea experience was new to me. Couldn't be too bad, could it? Well, it was bad!! I caught two fish before I got so sick that I couldn't stand on my feet. I had slumped down in a corner of the charter boat. I was sick to my stomach the rest of the day. Buster was catching and slinging fish all over my head. The more he slung, the sicker I got.

Lizzie had brought drinks and food to make sandwiches, but I couldn't eat anything. By the end of the day, whatever was in my stomach got deposited out in the deep blue sea. I didn't die that day, yet I felt like it could have been the "big one," like Fred Sanford used to say on the television show *Sanford and Son*.

I lived thru that sickly exploration, only for Lizzie to suggest a little while later that we go back again. She declared, "Boot, let's try it again; you're not going to get sick again next time." I agreed with her on part of her declaration. I simply confirmed, "I'm not going to get sick again because I ain't never going back!" That was the debut and end of my deep-sea fishing journey!

My life with Buster was full of gains and growths, likes and loves, with blotches of pains and problems, and sicknesses and sorrows. Let me add one more love point before we uncover the blotches. We loved playing cards. Yes, our game was pinochle! We played Bid Whist, too. But we actually had a Pinochle Club. When we lived in West Durham, we played with their Pinochle

Club, and when we moved to North Alston Avenue, we started our own North Durham Pinochle Club!

We had serious, playing folks in our club: me and Buster, Mack and Pete, Cat and John, Yi and Budja or Johnny Hamm (a neighbor beside Budja). Sometimes, Christine played, getting excited one time and mad another time. John might've had a drink or something before he got to the house. He would agitate and pick at Christine. Launa, Lizzie, and Willie didn't play, but they came and watched many games. It was like a Hollywood reality show. We had some big bluffing, card slapping, loud talking, and tons of laughing. We served a repast of chips and dips, lemonade, punch and soda pop, and no whiskey.

We met and played twice every week, Wednesday and Friday nights. John Rhodes was a lucky player. He and Catherline (Cat) had married in March, 1969. He was a real bluffer, even if he didn't have anything in his hand. Cat could play. He'd make crazy bids, and the funny part was somehow they would make their bids, even though he didn't have a good hand at all! Cat would pull him out and fuss at him about his bid!

We played against other clubs. A lady named Lillie and her sister stayed down on Drew Street, and they had their own club. We played them. But those folks on the West End could really play, too, and we had playoff tournaments with them, like the MLB! They would beat us some kind of bad! We were their best and main competitors. What good recreation and great times! *Those Were the Days, My Friend,* as sung by Mary Hopkin (1968).

Fifty-four years of my life were shared with Buster and his life with me. And there were a few times when we questioned the glue that held us together. One of those blotched times was early in our marriage when my sister-in-law, Lucille, found a note in George's pocket, which read, "You and Buster meet me and Mamie tonight, Love, Irene." They were my friends, or so I thought. Lucille caught a cab to my house on Gurley Street; she was so hurt. George always had his women on the side. Not to mention that he would beat Lucille like she was his child.

You know how you feel when you feel betrayed, when you find out that your husband, too, is courting on the side? I felt a hurt so deep in the pit of my heart that a backhoe loader (good name for digging equipment) couldn't dig it out. Buster couldn't convince me of nothing, even though he tried. To back up the finding, Mrs. Louise, our landlord, had one daughter named Elsie. Elsie would frequent the pinochle house on the Southside. Somehow, Elsie and Mamie got in a fight about "who knows what," and Mamie yelled out that, "Yes, I love Buster."

Maximum hurt and pain that I had never felt before consumed me, not like when Otis passed or Papa left. It was like a dagger sword cutting my heart right out of my breastplate. I thought my heart would fall out on the floor, and I'd watch myself bleed to death. I packed up my baby and my clothes and went straight back to Budja, Launa, and Mama Olivia.

One night, Budja sat down and gave me "the talk." It was probably the talk that many women heard back in the day. It was a talk of how the woman holds the family together, how the children need both of their parents, how you don't leave your husband for practical reasons—like clothes, food, and shelter, and how your marriage vows mentioned, "for better or worse." Did that only apply to the woman, I wondered?

I listened to my older brother. Yet, I thought about how Becca's husband, James, had a woman over on Drew Street, how George flaunted around town with Irene and "anything," and how Budja never hid his courting. When Papa died, Budja and Honey were at the other end of Moline Street at the liquor house with his girl, Ms. Lena. Mama Olivia sent me and Christine there. "Go tell Budja to come home," she instructed us. We did. He was there. He came home. When me and Buster married, Budja was going with a female on Wheeler Street. Buster took me there, and I met her. He was a good brother, a good father, a good provider, and a smooth player.

I listened to my older brother, and I knew and understood "the talk." I looked at those beautiful brown eyes of James, Jr., and I decided two things: one, I'm going back home to my husband; two, I'm going to get a job to take care of myself and our son, if ever Buster headed for the door. He'd have to walk out, not me. I had made a vow.

Buster didn't know that I had fixed my mind to return home. He came to the house and was saying anything to get me back home. Budja was saying anything to get me out of his house. I let Buster know what I had decided, and he was agreeing with everything. I then told him, "Your wife is younger than you, and if you are going to run around, then she can get a boyfriend and do the same thing." I felt guilty even for saying that. But the devil told me I was paying him back. Buster accepted the ungodly proposition but said, "Don't let me catch you with him." I replied, "You won't." He knew that I was just trying to hurt him and that my heart had been broken.

Buster still worked from 4:00 p.m. until midnight. There was plenty of time to play around if I chose to do so. He said nothing much when I came back home. He knew me, and he figured that I had said what I said for meanness. And I had.

Things seemed better in our relationship. A short while later, however, I was tested. For about a week, the phone would ring around 7:00 a.m. Note that he got home after midnight and hadn't had much sleep after winding down. He would answer the phone, get up, go out, and return home shortly afterward. The week had passed, and the next day, same time, the phone rang, and he got up. I got up, too. He went to the car; I went and sat in the car with him. I spoke kindly to him, "Please tell whoever is calling you every morning that you ain't no cab service." That nipped that blotch of a problem in the bud.

One of my fondest and most vivid memories is the day that Buster quit drinking. We had been married for twenty-five years. For twenty-five years, I had been praying for my husband. From the day that I became aware of his drinking habit, I put it in the hands of the Lord. I'm not saying that it didn't bother me, because it did. But it was not my battle; it was the Lord's.

Not only did he drink liquor, but he also sold it in our early days. He bargained with Walter McKinney and made a deal. McKinney would buy the liquor by the truckload, and Buster would sell it down the street at our house. This was during the time that we lived back on Dunstan Ave. Mrs. McKinney fussed at me about Buster's resell business. I told her, "You're talking like that's my house! It's Buster's house, and I don't work, and besides, it's your son that's buying the booze."

Mack, my nephew who was in the service, came home and fussed at me, too. He would buy a drink from Buster, get drunk and then, get mad at me. I couldn't figure that one out. In a drunken stupor, he snarled, "Buster's nothing but a floozy for Walter McKinney. Got him peddling for him." Mack didn't know the arrangement between Buster and Walter or how much he was making, but he was probably right. McKinney had loaned him money, and Buster ended up in debt to him. Buster finally stopped selling.

It was June 1961, a week and days before his birthday, that Buster came home from work somewhat jittery. He looked puzzled, although he looked straight into my eyes and spluttered out these words, "Something happened to me at work. Something told me to pray!" "Did you pray?" I asked. "No," he replied, "I don't know how to pray." I responded, "Buster, the Bible says, if you open your mouth to pray, it will come out, with God's help." I couldn't quote the Bible exactly, but I had heard Papa preach those words all through my life.

Buster kneeled down and began to pray. I had not ever heard a prayer from my husband's lips. Like Papa on that Sunday that we joined Mount Vernon, Buster lifted up supplications to God Almighty in a sincere and touching manner. It was one of the best prayers I had ever heard. Me and Denise were down on the floor with him. I was praising and thanking God and weeping unto the Lord. His Holy Spirit was present in the midst of that powerful transformation.

Buster got off of his knees and simply stated, "I'm not drinking anymore." And just like that, he didn't drink anymore. Hallelujah! The "just like that" was God answering twenty-five years of fervent prayer. It took his family and friends two or more years before they even believed him. Joe Louis, his nephew in DC, and all his kinfolk in Lumberton circulated the news, "Uncle Buster's not drinking anymore."

James, Jr. had brought him a fifth of foreign alcohol from Japan when he was overseas. Do you know that Buster never opened it? James, Jr. came back a year or two later and got it, took it home and probably drank it himself. George and Budja were in shock! George begged him for days to drink with him, for old times' sake. Buster wouldn't. George commented to me, "You must be married to a preacher, now." With a soft answer, I stated boldly, "He's not a preacher, but he's not drinking anymore." Buster's sobriety was a gain and growth milestone for us!

Speaking of brother George, he was a strong influence on Buster. Buster always wanted to please him and do for him and help him out even when he got himself into trouble. For example, George liked to gamble. He would work all week and then gamble away his earning, knowing he had bills to pay and nine children with nothing to eat.

Buster didn't gamble. I give credit where credit is due; that was not one of his vices. But when George would lose all his money and come asking Buster to bail him out, Buster couldn't say no. He would give him the shirt off of his back. That was his brother. He never got independent from George until he stopped drinking. When he got sober, he could say no!

It took those twenty-five years for me and Buster to learn to live together in harmony and peace. It's hard when one spouse is pulling one way, and the other spouse is pulling another way. The following years became the happiest days of my life, his life, and of our lives as one. We started talking, one with another, and listening to each other, and maturing as a couple. We still enjoyed our activities of watching baseball, fishing, and playing cards. Now, as spouses, we were on the same sheet of music, marching to the same drummer and walking in rhythm.

The question is asked often, "What's the secret to a happy, lifelong marriage. I may not have a 100% certified answer, but may I suggest—perhaps we give up too soon on one another. I can hear the thoughts, *Twenty-five years, heck no, that's too long to put up with—and the lists of complaints and dislikes get written.* I'd ask this question, "What's the advantage of seven years with one person; ten years with another person; and eight years with yet, someone else?" It's still a quarter of a century of your life, isn't it? Don't detest me for sharing my reflections. We all have our own reflections, yes?

Anyway, everyone has her/his own decisions to make. I am thankful for the strength to make the ones that I did make. Me and Buster started going to church together. He joined the J.E. Best Men's Sunday School Class. One Sunday, Buster and Mama Olivia had walked to Mount Vernon. It was Easter morning, and he joined our church. Papa would have been so happy. I was so excited.

Then the blotches of sickness spotted our lives. Buster had two light stokes. After the first one, he was still drinking. But God didn't give up on him, and neither did I. The second stroke caused him to retire in 1972; he was sixty. Sorrow hit when in 1980, Buster's brother, George C. McLeod, was called on home to glory. I could see the lost-felt feelings all over Buster's face.

His brother was closer than a friend. He passed that last day in December, at age seventy-two.

Ten years after Buster's last stroke, he was confronted with another health challenge. The doctors diagnosed him with poor circulation. The recommendation was the removal of his right leg. It was a hard reality. Buster had always been active, agile, and independent. The mere image of losing those abilities was more than a burden on his mind. We prayed and even got a second opinion. Dr. White, at Lincoln Hospital, had suggested that we go to Duke Hospital. The prognosis was the same. My husband would lose his leg.

Tears welled up in my eyes, and I bit my lip; and I thanked the Lord for keeping him strong for seventy years. I pledged in my heart to be his shoulder to lean on and his support system to get him through this ordeal. The operation had me on pins and needles. We were at Duke, one of the best hospitals. The doctors kept me updated as things went along. I waited for hours, pacing back and forth in the family room. When it was over, Buster had come through like a champ!

Buster received an artificial leg, and he learned to walk on it. He really loved his crutches and would rather get around on them. He could take his crutches and almost run. He even went back to fishing and enjoying a normal life.

However, he was self-conscious around people other than family. I remember one Sunday that we went to church, and Buster wouldn't get out of the car. When I went into the church, I saw Brother Frank McCrae and asked him to go get Buster out of the car. McCrae assisted him, and they ended up in the same Sunday School class. Buster just needed some male bonding, I believed. McCrae was one of Durham's first African American police officers, known as the Hayti Police. He remembered me from working at Berma's and opening Tip Top Beauty Shop.

One fact was for certain, me and Buster grew to love one another with an everlasting love. We realized it more and more as we approached and prepared for our fiftieth wedding anniversary in April 1986. We have heard the old saying that time flies by so swiftly, and it does. Back in 1936, when Buster magically added years to that marriage license, neither one of us could have predicted how our lives would have changed, developed, and progressed in fifty years! Despite the blotches of sicknesses and sorrows, the twenty-five years after he quit drinking were absolutely the best! I must give God all the glory and the praise. He is worthy!

James, Jr. and Denise planned a spectacular gathering for us. It was held out in the backyard of our home, where we had lived for thirty-eight years at that time. They put food all around the garage. It was spread out like a banquet fit for a king and queen. Mack barbequed a whole pig; Pete made the best BBQ sauce, loaded with so much butter. John Rhodes painted a room for us, and he cooked the whole week prior to the event. He cooked beef roast, chicken, and pig feet along with collards, macaroni and cheese, potato salad, and string beans. So many people were present to celebrate with us—brothers and sisters, nephews and nieces, grandchildren, in-laws, church members, pastor, and friends. Hope I've included them all:

Aldonia "Chick" Young—Atlantic City, NJ
Mary "Mae" Ruby —Atlantic City, NJ
Clelly Gailes—Asheboro, NC

Clyde Foust, Sr. and Family—Asheboro, NC
James and Mary "Sis" Deberry—Parkton, NC
Hattie Mozelle Jones—Raleigh, NC

Durham Locals:
Matthew and Ethelean "Pete" Dunn
James, Jr., Barbara, and LaKishia McLeod
Robert, Denise, and Karleshia Daye
The Daye and Deberry Families
James and Rebecca "Becca" McLeod King
Budja and Launa Jones and Larry Keith
Willie and Christine Jones Johnson
Allan and Pearline Jones Summers
John and Catherine "Cat" Jones Rhodes
Clarence, Syvil, Cedric, and Mia Burke
Pastor and Mrs. Percy L. High-MVBC
J.E. Best's Sunday School Class—MVBC
People-Davis Men's Bible Class—MVBC

Clarence took tons of pictures. We played cards and games and laughed and sang. Our hearts were joyful and thankful for such a gala gathering.

Life was being good to me and Buster. Early the next year, January 1987, we welcomed a new granddaughter, Krystal. Only God would have known that she would be the one to care for me as I lived into my hundreds! A couple of years later, we had to experience the same trauma with the amputation of Buster's left leg. "My God, My God," I cried out, "Why, Buster? Why so much agony and pain?" Immediately, my mind took me to the cross of Calvary and the pain that Jesus suffered for me and you. I never asked again!

This second surgery took a toll on Buster. He stayed in the hospital longer than anticipated. He didn't snap back as he had done in the past. His frame of mind seemed to be different and distant. He wasn't thinking toward positive improvements. He was tiring, and I could see it in his eyes. I was trying to keep him strong by preparing his meals each day, as I had done for over a half-century. He was seventy-seven.

The day before Valentine's Day, 1990, Buster sat at the kitchen table eating his breakfast. We both loved breakfast! Abruptly, Buster felt a pain in his stomach. He wanted to go lie down on the bed. I helped him back to the bedroom. He was holding tightly to the bed post. I tried to remove his hand from the post, but he wouldn't let go. Peacefully, he slept the rest of the day. I called his nurse, who had been coming every week for about a year. She came and stayed with me the entire day. At 9:00 p.m., the love of my life slipped away into eternity. My Buster fought the good fight and finished his race!

CHAPTER 12
Loving My Lord, My Church, and Mama Olivia

My love for the Lord has been an integral part of my life since I was a little girl. It's embedded in my heart, the soul realm of my spirit. It helped that Papa was a preacher man, I'm sure. It made a difference that Mama Olivia lived humbly and uprightly before God and her family. True religion gets real, though, when you, as a person, individually, have a personal relationship with the Lord Jesus Christ.

In the country, we had a family pond where Papa baptized every first Sunday. Mama Olivia would tell us not to go to the pond when they'd leave home. Papa would say, "Don't tell them not to go to the pond; let's teach them how to swim." That was how Papa was, a teacher. He was the same way about the Bible and teaching us how to live for Christ. He wanted us to learn and understand so that we could swim through life's deep waters and not drown in sin and Satan's traps. Papa taught every one of his children how to swim!

Papa lived the life that he preached about, and he taught us the core values of fellowship, forgiveness, grace, humility, love, patience, prayer, and worship—just to name a few of them. Back then, everybody in the country came to church, whether they stayed outside, drank whiskey and shot the breeze, or came inside to hear the Word. Drunks, pimps, prostitutes, saints, sinners, and sugar daddies, alike, made their way to church on Sunday morning. Especially at Jones Chapel, Papa and Mama Olivia welcomed everyone. Papa would say, "We don't know the day nor the hour that the Lord will touch someone's heart.

So don't throw this book down and stop reading now, not because I brought up the conversation about a personal relationship, or redemption, and salvation. Let's talk about it. It may be that your beliefs are different than mine. Or you may be without beliefs at all. It's correct to assume that down through a hundred-plus years of living that I've met people from all different faiths and backgrounds. When someone knocked on our door in Durham and wanted to talk about their faith, I would invite the person in when time permitted, and I'd listen. Then I'd share what I've learned and lived to believe.

Uncle Bill Roberson was an example of a man that I would see every Sunday outside of Jones Chapel. He lived across the branch from the church. He had ten or twelve children, and he never shaved. His beard was long and white, like his hair, and he looked like Santa Claus. If he belonged to a church, it was probably Riley Hill, but every Sunday, he'd be on our church grounds until one Sunday, he came on in and surrendered his life to the Lord. No, he wasn't our real uncle.

Look at another example, my granddaughter, Krystal, who God prepared to be my helper in my senior life, has married a young man from Africa, Bai. He's kind, has a pleasant personality, and I love to hear him call me "Granny" in his native tongue. He was brought up with a different religion. His wife has taken on his culture and beliefs. Would I not welcome him into our family because of our differing upbringings? Of course not. I will love him with the love that God has placed in my heart for all people; he will love me as his Granny-in-law out of the depths of his heart. God is the author and finisher of our faith.

I joined the church when I was eleven years old. That was in 1929, the same year the great depression began. I'm pretty certain that my joining the church was not a result of that occurrence, just a coincidental fact. Revival happened every fall. Papa would get a guest preacher to come for a week, and each night of that week, we would be in church. There were strict rules in church—no chewing gum, no playing, no running out to the bathroom, no sleeping, and no talking. We all sat together in the Amen corner with Mama Olivia. I can see her now, in my hall of fond memories, waving her white handkerchief in the air and praising God.

If I had not mentioned, there were a good fifty children at Jones Chapel in my young days. We, the preacher's children, had to be good examples of how to act. For the most part, we were. So, during the revival, the preacher would invite anyone to come to the mourner's bench who wanted to pray, reconcile with God, receive forgiveness, repent of sins, and turn toward the path leading to eternal life. It was a once-a-year opportunity; if you didn't confess salvation then, you'd have to wait till next year.

I went to the mourner's bench. I was ready to give my life away to God and accept His son Jesus Christ as my Lord and Savior. I wanted to live right and be a Christian girl. I wanted God to change me and make me more Christ-like. That might've seemed like a tall order for an eleven-year-old, but I knew it was my time. As I surrendered my life to God on that mourner's bench, shedding tears of joy, I felt light and uplifted. I felt like I was going to float away. Had it not been for Sister Myrtle Haywood putting her arms around me and holding me down, I would have elevated right there at Jones Chapel.

Sister Myrtle weighed about three hundred pounds, and there was no way that I was going anywhere from under her arms of protection. Sister Myrtle was married to Brother Charlie, a faithful man at our church. They both were faithful along with their children—Percy, Annie-called Bessie, David, Robert, Lula Mae, and Lucile. They, too, were our friends.

All of us who had confessed Christ at the revival had to go to church on Saturday to meet with Papa. Mozelle had gone to the mourner's bench that same night. Papa asked us about the genuineness of our decision. He asked me did I feel changed. I answered, "Papa, I don't even remember leaving the mourner's bench, and the next thing I knew, I was across on the other side of the church. Yes, Sir, something happened, and I've been changed." He told us that we would be baptized on the first Sunday. Me, Mozelle, and Lula Mae, Sister Myrtle's girl, were excited!

Our excitement was, first, because baptism was the outward acknowledgment of the inward transformation in our lives. Secondly, we were excited because we would get to wear a newly made swagger suit, specially made for baptism. It was a green flowery coat and skirt with a white blouse made to wear with it. Mama Olivia and Lizzie crafted the outfits for me and Mozelle. Haven't I bragged that they could sew anything! No brag, "just the facts, ma'am," as spoken by Sgt. Joe Friday on the 1967 television show *Dragnet*.

It was a beautiful fall Sunday, October 6th, as we went to the pond. There were twelve of us, quietly walking in processional style. The Jones' children only had one pair of Sunday shoes and one pair of everyday shoes. The girl's Sunday shoes were patent leather. We polished them on Saturday night with a homemade biscuit. So, our shoes were shining in the bright morning sun. Papa led the way, followed by the deacons and church officers. The choir and church members sang the ceremonial hymn, *Take Me to the Water:*

Take me to the water,
Take me to the water,
Take me to the water,
to be baptized.
None but the righteous,
None but the righteous,
None but the righteous,
shall see God.
I love Jesus,
I love Jesus,
I love Jesus,
Yes, I do.
Glory, hallelujah,
Glory, hallelujah,
Glory, hallelujah,
to be baptized.

Mama and the deaconesses were arrayed in all white, and they had their white handkerchiefs. We were nervous. But Papa made us feel better, and he took his time with each candidate. After the baptism, we had a feast of appetizing foods prepared by the ladies of the church. It was a special day. It's a day that will live on forever. It's the day I began my new walk with Christ.

Make no mistake, when you become committed to living for the Lord, tests and trials will come to try your commitment. One test for me came quickly after my baptism. Remember that we had hundreds of chickens on the farm? I had a particular purple biddy that was incredibly special to me.

Out of the blue, Clelly decided to get a chick and cook it. Of all of the chicks, she had to kill my purple biddy. At first, I was so outdone with her, not even wanting to talk to her. But after reading God's Word, I forgave her. In the sixth chapter of Matthew, we are instructed to forgive those that do us wrong, as we are forgiven when we do wrong. That was a growth test for me. I read the Bible many times a week.

It's false to think, however, that Christians, those who follow and live for Christ, are mistake-free and living perfectly. Truly, false. We have the promise of eternal life, are forgiven and saved, and are striving each day to be more like our Savior. Yet, within the church family, there are discords, issues, problems, and scandals.

There were definitely scandals in our personal families and the neighboring churches. On Papa's side of the family, Grandmother Sally had eighteen children. A story from cousin Evelyn, one of the Pepper's offspring, had it that fifteen of the children were with Grandfather Jeff, while three of them were from her live-in, supposed-to-be nephew, who had an additional family in another county. He was kind to Grandfather Jeff, but no one knew how he got into the family. Remember that Papa *never* spoke of his mother and father. It had to be a reason!

On Mama Olivia's side of the family, Grandpa Andrew and Grandma Lizzie had seven sons and two daughters. Mama Olivia was the knee-baby girl, just like me. Uncle Broady was her oldest brother and was married to Aunt Lillie. They had eight children of their own. Uncle Broady had, what was called, dropsy—an old-school term for the accumulation of excess water in the body, causing the swelling of the soft tissues. It was a long-term illness, and Mama Olivia would go take care of him. Why? Because Uncle Charlie came and took Aunt Lillie from Uncle Broady and put her up on his farm.

This Uncle Charlie was not the brother next to Mama Olivia, but he was the brother-in-law who was married to Aunt Lula, the baby sister in Mama Olivia's family. The scandalous aspect concerning the church was because Uncle Charlie—the brother-in-law—was going with another woman at Macedonia Baptist, Sister Minnie Hodges. Can you believe Aunt Lillie and Sister Minnie got in a fight right there at church? It was a big stink in the community.

Aunt Lula was sick over the fact that Uncle Charlie wasn't treating Lillie right, either! She was hurt for herself, too. He was supposed to be a deacon at Macedonia Baptist Church, setting an example to the church congregation. Even his children were angry with him and were pretty bitter toward Aunt Lillie. Aunt Lula didn't ever leave him, and neither did Aunt Lillie. Don't know how Uncle Charlie reckoned within himself his situation with his wife, and with the Lord.

But that's the part of being a Christian that's sometimes hard to understand. Each person is accountable to the Lord for her/his actions and activities that are done while we are alive here on our earthly journey. We look at others and judge lots of times based on what we do or don't do. But the roadmap for our Christian paths is in His Holy Word. By that standard, "we all have sinned and fallen short of the glory of God" (Romans 3:23).

What makes my heart so happy to share is there was never, ever chatter, gossip, rumors, scandal, shame, tittle-tattle, or whispers about my Papa. Yes, I may be stretching the words, but out of all the churches in the community, the churches that he pastored, and all the years that he was in the ministry, Papa stood firmly on the Word of God as his anchor and battle-ax. I know that he wasn't perfect, none of us human beings are, but I know that the example that Papa set was one of high and holy standards. Our home in the country was a refuge for anyone needing shelter, strength, and support. Thanks to my Papa and my Mama Olivia, that's where I learned to love the Lord.

Our church, Jones Chapel, was the foundation for my loving and respecting the church. It's true that it's "just" a building. We, God's people, are the church, but there's more. It's the establishment by God as a place of fellowship, a safety net for deliverance and healing, the storehouse for giving, and it's the tabernacle of worship. Writers have written many things about the church. Let me share a few:

The church is a hospital, and not a courtroom. She does not condemn on behalf of sins, but grants remission of sins.

—St. John Chrysostom

I see the church as a field hospital after battle. It is useless to ask a seriously injured person if he has high cholesterol and about the level of his blood sugars. You have to heal his wounds. THEN we can talk about everything else.

—Pope Francis

As a leader, it is your responsibility to see to it that the church under your care continues as a gathering of people in process; a place where the curious, the unconvinced, the skeptical, the used-to-believe and the broken, as well as the committed, informed, and sold-out come together around Peter's declaration that Jesus is the Christ, the Son of the living God.

—Andy Stanley

The task of the church after Jesus' resurrection and ascension was to proclaim the forgiveness of sins to all nations.

—Charles Stanley

A church is a hospital for sinners, not a museum for saints.

—Abigail Van Buren

The power of the church is not a parade of flawless people, but of a flawless Christ who embraces our flaws. The church is not made up of whole people, rather of the broken people who find wholeness in a Christ who was broken for us

—Mike Yaconelli

When Papa took the family to Mount Vernon in 1934 and put us in the care of the church family, I had no problem committing to it as my church home. I was a young girl and not as faithful in my Christian walk, but I never stopped going to church.

We have been blessed as a church to have had great leaders as great pastors. We, the church family, have grown spiritually under the leadership of them all. I can confirm that for myself, starting with my first leader:

Pastor W. C. Williamson, who cared for and covered our family after Papa died.

Pastor J. H. Thomas, who led the church from 304 S. Queen Street up to the hill on S. Roxboro Street.

Pastor E. T. Brown and Mrs. Rose Butler Brown, who added the educational building and stressed academic and spiritual education to youth and adults.

Pastor and Mrs. Percy L. High, who led us for thirty-four years, six months, and one day into deeper depths and higher heights in the Word of God.

And presently,

Pastor Jerome Washington, who preaches and teaches with great power and who is facilitating the new renovation of our church thru 2021.

There was a supply pastor, Rev. F.O. Bass, and an interim pastor, Rev. L. Thomas. I have served under these pastors over the last eighty-seven years. It's easy to change churches like changing a pair of shoes, But I've wondered why "church hop" and what is the advantage or purpose of doing it? Tell me, please?

Biblical teachings from my pastors and Sunday School teachers have helped me in many of my life situations-like: when I was faced with Buster's drinking for a quarter of a century, when dealing with my decision to go to beauty school, when my marriage was on the line, and when I decided to get fully involved in my church. Lots of times, I was trying to fix things on my own, or I didn't have unconditional love, or I didn't have a real commitment to the work of the church. I was a good churchgoer.

No one convinced me to adjust my life and sell out to the Lord; I made up my mind that I was going to get right with the Lord and do it "right now." I didn't want to join any organization at Mount Vernon until my heart was committed to living the life like Papa and Mama Olivia did.

I started ushering at Mount Vernon in 1955, not long after we opened up *Tip Top* and after Buster had stopped selling booze. I didn't want to be ushering and hear someone whispering, "That's the lady whose husband is the bootlegger." Lizzie joined the usher board soon after I did. We loved serving and welcoming members and visitors.

Brother Elwood McNair was the President of the usher board and had been for years. He had asked me for nearly a year to take over the secretary position for the usher board. Sister Owens had carried the secretary book for many years, and I would replace her. I finally agreed to accept that calling.

Sadly, Brother McNair's heart failed, and he passed away a short while after I accepted. He left a lovely wife, Sister Carrie, and a son and daughter. Mrs. Carrie McNair celebrated her centenarian birthday in April 2021. Another Mount Vernon member to reach that milestone birthday!

The reason that I phrased the secretary position as a calling is because it became one for me. I took a special joy and pride in being dependable, faithful, and steady. That secretary book was with me for over fifty years. I served thru many presidents after Brother McNair. They included Brother Chester Spells, Brother Joseph Sims, Brother Johnny Philyaw, and current president Brother James Morris.

I tried several times to pass the book over to a younger person, but to no avail. I finally told President Morris that it was time. I had fulfilled my calling, and someone else could carry that torch. I was honored and recognized for my decades of service. I was even crowned as a lifetime honorary member of the usher board. Together, me and Lizzie served close to eighty years!

Remember when I shared that Mama Olivia had joined the Missionary Group and really enjoyed it? Well, I followed in her footsteps and joined, too. Really, we learned in church that all Baptists are missionaries. I started attending the monthly meetings under Sister Lydia Vanhook's leadership. Sister Annie Filmore had been the dedicated head of the Missionary Group. She had answered the heavenly call prior to my joining, but her influence lived on through the members.

After Buster passed, Sister Vanhook asked me to consider joining Senior Choir #2. I took it into consideration and decided to join. We sang on the first Sunday of the month. Sister E. H. Fogle, well-known for her musical talents, had been the choir director. After her death and homegoing, my friend from high school, Sister Ruth McCollum, became the new director.

It was more jubilant than I thought it would be. I couldn't lead a solo, but I sure could make a joyful sound.

The more that I became committed to working in my church, the more committed I became. I was elected as President of the Lady's Department. I served in that leadership role for many years. The lady's meeting was coordinated with the Sunday that we ushered. First Sunday—the men ushered; children—the second Sunday; women—third Sunday; and young adult—fourth Sunday. The Lady's meeting was at 3:00 p.m. on the third Sunday evening. It was a great group of Christian ladies. We got along well and stayed focused on our mission of serving the church family. I love my church!

Thinking back, me and Mama Olivia got closer when I got involved in the church. Her life had taken a turn when an accident occurred at the Upchurch house. She loved working with the Upchurch Family after Papa passed. One day the sons were killing hogs, she was watching, and accidentally fell on a knife that stabbed her in the fat part of her calf. The incident stopped her from being able to work and cut off her income.

That was when she began keeping our place in the mornings and watching the grands—Pearline, Catherline, and James, Jr., while me, Buster, Budja, and Launa worked. She was still staying with Budja and Launa. Then, Launa's mother, Della Thompson, got sick and had to be given care. So, Mama Olivia came to stay with me and Buster.

As Mama Olivia began to talk more openly with me, I learned so much more about her and the family. Growing up, the Youngs were a staunchly religious family in Macedonia Baptist Church. They attended services each Sunday and Bible

Study on Wednesday night. Mama Olivia loved the Lord from a little girl, just like me, and she loved her church. She knew that it was a great probability that she would be a preacher's wife. She was prepared for that challenge.

I began to understand Mama Olivia's 'heart and soul.' She had pledged her life early to be a consecrated, devoted, faithful, and surrendered vessel for the Lord. She was firm and strict because that was the way she had conditioned her body and mind. I sat listening and realizing what a jewel of a mother that we had.

Mama Olivia made it clear that she loved Papa, and Papa only. "No one else could ever measure up to his qualities," she expressed, "He was my only love." She was different from Papa, of course. How so? She told us not to fight; Papa said, "If anybody hits you, you take up for yourself and hit back." Mama Olivia didn't want us drinking sodas; Papa said, "Go on and drink sodas; they make your liver hard." She taught us to be quiet and not talk so much; Papa preached, "If somebody talks all the time, there's bound to be some telling of lies."

Certainly, Mama Olivia believed the proverb of 'sparing the rod, spoiling the child.' She did not have any spoiled children; she did not spare the rod! Whereas Papa, in lieu of spanking, would lecture for an hour or so on "why we should not have done" such and such or "how we knew better to have done" a different such and such, and we had to sit and listen.

Papa had lots of saying that, I know now, were words of wisdom. One of my favorites that I shared with Karleshia and Krystal, our grand-girls, was, "The more you stir a turd, the worse it stinks." When they would argue and fight, the more they fussed, the worse that it got; I told them to stop stirring the stinky situations. Growing up, Mama Olivia nipped our arguing and fighting in the bud, which was not on her agenda for the Jones children.

Every chance that I got to spend time with Mama Olivia, I'd take it. She bought her dresses from The Wee Shop, downtown Durham, corner of Main and Corcoran Street. I enjoyed taking her shopping and watching how particular she was in her buying. We laughed and talked about many good things, like when me and Christine went to a girl's party who lived right next door to us on Moline Street. Mama Olivia said she didn't know that we had gone or what we were doing. I reassured her that there was only punch and chips served and that we were just dancing.

One thing that I learned from Mama Olivia, and it has stuck with me all these years, is she always taught us from the Bible. In addition, she took us to church, and she taught us right from wrong. Many times when we'd do something wrong, we'd hear, "For the wages of sin is death, but the gift of God is eternal life through Jesus Christ our Lord." She lived by the Word.

The last Sunday that Mama Olivia was able to go to church, Budja joined Mount Vernon, and she shouted all the way home. We thought that she'd never stop praising the Lord. She prayed so hard for all her children after Papa died, but especially hard for Budja! I can hear her voice saying, "If children have a strong foundation, they have something to fall back on." I loved Mama Olivia. She was that solid foundation for Papa and for our family!

The Jones Family

The McLeod Family

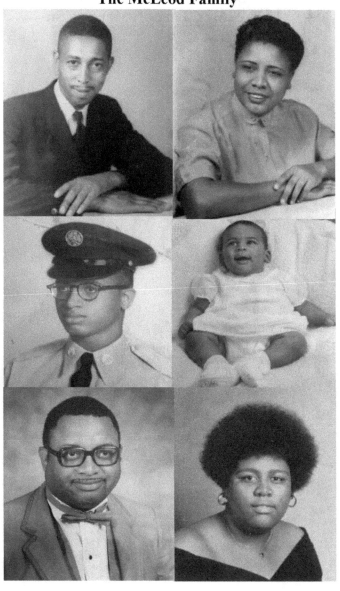

50th Wedding Anniversary
Mr. & Mrs. James F. McLeod, Sr.

Family Gathering • Asheboro, NC

Thanksgiving Family Dinner in
Asheboro, NC

Younger
days of
Cora
Jones
Boot
McLeod

Gone
Fishing!

The Love
of Fishing!

Tip
Top
Beauty
Shop
&
#1
Beauty
Club

Capitol
City
Visit
2018

100th Birthday Celebration
Friday, August 3, 2018

Sheraton Imperial Hotel • Durham, North Carolina

101st Birthday Celebration 2019 ● Golden Corral

102nd Birthday Celebration • 2020 Pandemic Year

103rd Birthday Drive-by Celebration
Sunday, August 1, 2021

103rd Birthday
Tuesday, August 3, 2021

103rd Birthday Facetimes and Visits 2021

Mount Vernon Baptist & Beacon Light Church;
My Nieces & Friends

Mrs. Cora Jones 'Boot' McLeod and Offspring

CHAPTER 13
Birthing and Burying Our Daughter, Denise

Beforehand, I mentioned that the ladies at Tip Top Beauty Shop worked well together. We grew as a business and as a team. At first, it was just Dot, me, and Mo. We were happily married women, and neither of us had young children, although Mo had a young girl to come live with her, and she told us that the young girl was her brother's child. It might have been that Mo had her prior to coming to Durham. Mo wouldn't let on, and the story behind the story wasn't released or revealed. So, we were all without young ones. That changed faster than lighting strikes.

The ball started rolling when Fred and Mo purchased a house down on Lee Street, off North Alston Avenue, near our home. They weren't in the house a year before Mo came up pregnant. We, the ladies of Tip Top Beauty Shop, were all so excited. Mo worked thru her pregnancy with no issues, and she proved to be a pillar of strength.

In February 1956, we welcomed a precious Ava Darlene as the first of the Tip Top babies. Dot eagerly and proudly came up with her name. Fred and Mo loved it. They were proud parents! Unfortunately, Dot and TC, byname for Thomas Clifton, had been married for five years without any success in the baby department. She longed so strongly to be a mother. Ironically, I had no longings or notions about birthing another baby.

As life would have it, I was the next one in line getting prepared to have a Tip Top newborn! I wasn't rejecting the idea. It was the fact that I hadn't had a baby in twenty years, me and Buster hadn't had any plans to have one, and I was thirty-eight years old, not a spring chicken!

Understand my thinking, James, Jr. had graduated with honors from Hillside High, Class of 1954. He had started working at a mechanic shop out on Hwy 70, only miles from Raleigh, NC. However, he had made up his mind that he wanted to go in the military, the Air Force!

He sent me down to the recruiting office because he was at work and wanted me to find out when he could come in to enlist. They informed me that they had a crew getting ready in the next few days, and if he could be there in the morning, he could ship out with that crew. The next morning, we headed to the office, and, sure enough, they had James, Jr. fill out the necessary paperwork, had me to sign for him to join, and he was enlisted into the United States Air Force. He was an Airman Basic, and he was a ripe seventeen-year young man. He left us that August 1954.

His first desire was to do mechanic work. They had offered him a career in Auto Mechanic, but it never came to pass. James, Jr. shared, "I had taken three years of typing in high school, and when the Master Sergeant found out that I could type one hundred words per minute, that was the end of my auto mechanic career." He became an office administrator/typist.

His basic training was at Lackland Air Force Base in Bexar County, Texas, built thirteen years before James, Jr. arrived. The base is a reserved area around San Antonio, Texas, and it was then and still is the only site in the USA for Air Force enlisted Basic Military Training (BMT). After the eight-week training, James, Jr. left for his first duty station at Alexandria Air Force Base in Louisiana.

We missed him. Thought about him quite a bit. I remembered how much he loved graham crackers and wished that he were home to eat a handful of them. But the military did well for our son. It broadened his perspective and shaped his thinking. Serving in the Air Force gave him focus, independence, inner strength, and maturity. He acquired a whole new outlook on his future and his life. He stopped confiding in me as much and felt that he had to be the strong one. All his duty tours and the places that he got to see helped him realize that there was a big, wide world awaiting to be discovered.

James, Jr. met a lot of great people during his career. One was a beautiful, special young lady from Florida, Barbara Jean Clark. I'm proud to share that in 1963, Barbara Jean became Mrs. James F. McLeod, Jr. and has been my amazing daughter-in-law for fifty-eight years. James, Jr. completed his military service after twenty-one years and four months. God brought our son home safe and sound and unharmed. We were very proud of his accolades and accomplishments. He had served our country diligently!

He began working at the VA Hospital in Durham after his retirement and spent another twenty-four years in service there. We were so excited when James, Jr. and Barbara Jean brought home their beautiful daughter, LaKishia Olivia, in March 1980, our first grandchild. She has grown up to be an attractive, intelligent, and kind young lady. She uses her many skills and talents as a middle school teacher and a fun-loving cheerleading coach. So immensely proud of her!

This is a good point to share with you about our other son George. I claim him, too, although he's Buster's older son. Before we met, Buster had been courting a young lady back home in Lumberton. He had come to Durham for some form of employment in order to go back and ask for her hand in marriage. In the meantime, their baby boy, George Green, came into the world.

It took Buster three years to get on at Liggett & Myers. When he finally got established and went back to keep his promise, the young lady was keeping company with someone else. She had moved on, and Buster had to move on, too. But he never forgot about little George.

He loved and provided for his son by the young lady. He told me about him when we started dating. He was three years older than James, Jr. He was a smart little fellow, and he knew that Buster's oldest sister, "Sis," was his Auntie. He was grown, though, when I finally got to meet him and his family.

George called and asked "Sis" if she would call Buster and see if he could come to visit us. "Of course, he could come," we declared! Buster had gotten his first leg amputated when George and his family came to spend some time with him. He came and fit right in the family. Denise and James, Jr. bonded with him, and he called me Mama Cora. He reminded me a lot of Buster.

George shared that he had a son who had been killed, and that was a hard time for him and the family. George had a good spirit about him, and I was glad that he reached out to connect with his other side of the family. I did get to meet the young lady, his mother, when Buster passed. She was the mother of thirteen children, we were told. She, George, and one of his sisters came to be with us during the homegoing wake service. Buster has been gone for thirty-one years, and I can expect a call or visit from George any day of the week! God bless our son, George!

I am aware that I was about to explain my twenty-year later pregnancy, when I updated you on James, Jr. and George. We will get back to that surprising time. But since we're here, let's continue on with updates on more of Papa and Mama Olivia's grands.

For Papa and Mama Olivia to have had fifteen children, twelve that they raised, you would think that they might have fifty or more grandchildren, wouldn't you? For some reason, none of the Jones' children had more than three offspring. Isn't that quite interesting? Plus, we had no knowledge of why some of us had a nickname and some of us didn't, no clue!

Here's the breakdown of grandchildren as best that I know, listed by our birth order:

Leroy "Yi" and Luzelia had two,
Katie Olivia and Junious Jones.
William "Buddy" and Lonie had two,
Johnny "Jeff" and Etta Mae Jones.
Nathaniel "Honey" and Millie had one daughter,

Frances Jones. Pearl by a friend.
Lizzie and Lonnie Burt had one son,
Matthew "Mack" Dunn.
Aldonia "Chick" and Otha "Buddy" had one son,
Irving Lee Lucas.
Annie Dora "Cete" and John had two,
Mary Ruby and Ramona High.
Lennon "Budja" and Launa had two,
Pearline and Catherline Jones.
Jimmy Lamont by a friend.
Otis, Clelly, Hattie Mozelle and Christine,
did not have children.
Cora "Boot" and James "Buster" had two,
James, Jr. and Denise Olivia McLeod.
George by a friend.

Mama Olivia was blessed to have lived long enough to know and love all her grandchildren, as well as some of the great-grands. Wish Papa had, too, but God has the final say, Amen? Amen.

So, we are back to 1956, twenty years after James, Jr. arrived. So, I was next, pregnant, following in line after Mo. We were teased by our customers and were asked, "How many more Tip Top babies are arriving?" My question was, "what did I need to do to have a healthy baby and not fall all to pieces after all these years?" I waited three months before I went back to Duke, where we had found Dr. Easley, hoping to find the right doctor.

We found Dr. Parker, head of the OBGYN department, who took a keen interest in me. He assured me, "If you do what I tell you to do, Cora, you won't have any problems, and you'll have this baby like a sixteen-year-old." I didn't know about the sixteen-year-old part, but I trusted him, saying that I wouldn't have any problems. One of his first requirements was he didn't want me to gain more than fifteen pounds. I complied with his requirement.

One customer from Creedmoor got mad because she didn't know I was having a baby; she said I should have told her. Some customers didn't like a pregnant lady fixing their hair, perhaps because of a myth or an old-fogey tale. So, we really didn't talk about my pregnancy while working. I wore bigger-sized uniforms; they covered my irreplaceable status.

From September to May, I followed Dr. Parker's guidelines. My eating habits adjusted to the new, healthier regiment, and I got the proper amount of sleep. As time progressed quickly, I got excited about our new arrival. Buster seemed in tune with me and the reality of his pending fatherhood role. We didn't discuss the desire of a boy or girl. It really didn't matter. We were starting back over again as new parents of a newborn.

Buster was strong-willed about naming James, Jr. after him. He left the name of our upcoming baby to me. There were no baby showers, or gender reveal parties. We had to wait and find out the sex of our baby. Dot gave me a book of baby names; I chose the name Denise for a girl. I had two or three optional names for a boy. Naturally, if the baby were a girl, her middle name would be named after Mama Olivia.

I fixed a lady's hair, got my hair done, and went on to the hospital to have our baby. Dr. Parker had been out of town for a short while. He returned the same day that I was admitted to the hospital. Entering my room, he said cheerfully, "Cora, I knew you were going to be here today! Everything will be fine." This go-round, I was able to get a shot to help with the labor pains.

They put a gas mask on me; I slept between pains. The labor wasn't too long, and out scurried our Denise Olivia, born in May 1957. She weighed eight pounds and a few ounces. She came only fifteen months after Ava Darlene arrived. That was a happy day and a happy time for me and Buster. It was a great day for our Tip Top Beauty Shop, adding and celebrating another Tip Top baby girl!

Denise was born on a Thursday. I was able to go home mid-morning on Sunday. Dr. Parker was completing his rounds when he came to my room. He verified that all was well, and we could leave. Then he said, "See you next year, Cora!" I kindly but smartly replied, "Not if I can help it!" With that being said, I went home with no intentions of returning any of the next years.

Mama Olivia was waiting to meet her namesake. She had made a giant pot of vegetable soup. I inquired why she had made such a huge pot of soup. "That's what you make for someone when they're sick," she answered. I shook my head, "I'm not sick, Mama Olivia, I just had a baby!" We laughed. Clelly had decorated Denise's bassinet with a flowery pink, handcrafted crimped skirt; and also crocheted a rainbow-colored blanket. Quite pretty, it was!

Budja and Launa, Willie and Christine, Lizzie, Mack and Pete, and Mozelle filed in and out throughout that Sunday. William and Clelly came from Asheboro; Ruby "Honey" and Ruth "Sis," my double first cousins on the Peppers' side of the family, visited from Raleigh, and Buddy and Lonie, who had reunited after thirty-plus years, stopped by—all to meet our new McLeod addition, Denise Olivia, prettier than the North Carolina state flower, the flowering dogwood!

Absolutely, I do believe in miracles; I hope you do, too. After Denise was born, we witnessed two miracles at Tip Top Beauty Shop. Nannie Walker, just like Dot, had longed to be a mother and have a child of her own to care for, love, and raise. That was McNeil 'Mack,' her husband, and Nannie's prayer. A year swiftly passed. Denise had already begun walking as we celebrated her first birthday; she was plump as a biscuit pudding!

One day at the shop, we were talking about babies, as usual. Nannie was doing the hair of a young lady named Wilhelmina. "I wish I had a baby of my own," Nannie lamented. Wilhelmina quickly spoke up, "You can have this one, patting her stomach. We could see that she was carrying. She had five or six other children, and the one on the way was an "unexpected surprise." Nannie didn't think that she was serious, and no further discussions were had.

Three months later, Nannie received a call from a nurse at Lincoln Hospital instructing her to come and pick up her baby son. "What?" exclaimed Nannie! After the initial shock, we all began scrambling and trying to get necessities—a bassinet, bottles, clothes, diapers, and whatever else was needed for a newborn baby. Nannie was excited beyond words and highly unprepared. Her sister lived on Fayetteville Street and had several children of her own. Some of the items needed were picked up from her on the way to the hospital. God had answered Nannie's prayers, and she was, overnight, becoming a mother.

Shaking and nervous, Nannie arrived at the hospital on that warm September day, 1958, to meet her new son. Mack met her there with his arms open wide. Wilhelmina and the baby were doing fine. She was the vessel God used to make Nannie's dream of being a mother come true. That made Mack an overnight father. The next month would be their twentieth wedding anniversary. What a blessed anniversary gift, parenthood! They brought their stunning son home, named him Dwight L. Walker, and Tip Top added another infant to the roster!

The second miracle happened for Dot and TC. They had rejoiced with the births of Ava, Denise, and Dwight. It was as if God was saying to them, "You have been faithful and patient, now is your time." Their long wait turned into another answered prayer. Dot's doctor had told her mother that, medically, Dot couldn't have any babies. Well, surprise, surprise, surprise! God has the final say, Amen? Amen.

Dot realized that she had symptoms of pregnancy in late spring 1958. She didn't want to say anything to anyone until she was sure that she could go to full term. When we found out, the ladies at Tip Top Beauty Shop, we could hardly believe what our ears were hearing!! "Dot's having a baby! Dot's having a baby," we screamed and shouted. The sheer joy and praises to God were lifted up high and nearly non-stop!

Dot was seven years younger than me and was able to handle her pregnancy with few to no restrictions. She went through the hot days of summer, the cool autumn days of fall, and quite a bit of the freezing cold winter days. Then, the first week of February 1959. Dot and TC happily welcomed their bright-eyed, darling daughter, Heir Fleur Steele, into this world. They beamed with gratitude and pride. After nearly a decade, The

Steeles could proudly say they added a pretty newborn to the Tip Top baby club!

There was a baby break at Tip Top for a few years. That is, until Shirley came along. Yes, we counted on Shirley for her enthusiasm and excitement, as you can imagine. When Shirley first came to Tip Top, she was a single young lady. A couple of years afterward, she jumped the broom into marriage. One year later, her oldest son, Derrick, joined our baby roster, and three years thereafter, little Eric came bouncing on the scene.

With Eric, the score was even. We, the ladies of Tip Top Beauty shop, had brought forth three Tip Top girls and three Tip Top boys. The last newborn was the final of the Tip Top babies born before urban renewal descended upon us and completely ended our Tip Top Beauty Shop legacy and our booming baby reign!

Now, when Denise was born, I had planned on staying out of work for a month, enjoying our bonding time. However, Mo called me and said, "Your two little girls are here. The daddy just dropped them off, kept going, and nobody here is available to do their hair. Can you come in?" They were regular customers, but the daddy never called or made an appointment. They just showed up. Both were sweet little girls, about ten and twelve years old. I'd wash their hair and either straighten and curl it or give them double pigtails. I didn't mind coming in.

That was a Saturday morning that Mo called. I asked Buster and Mama Olivia if they would keep Denise for a few hours. They agreed. So, three weeks into my maternity leave, I headed back to Tip Top and continued on working full-time. I laughed when I got back home that afternoon. I walked in the house thinking I was going to fix Buster's lunch for him to carry to work. I cried out, "Y'all ain't cook no dinner?" Both Buster and Mama Olivia looked frozen. I asked what they had been doing. Both spoke up, "Watching Denise!" They were so captivated by Denise that they forgot to cook dinner. LOL! I cooked dinner for the family.

Denise, like all the Tip Top babies, went to Scarborough Nursery School when they became potty trained. That usually occurred between the ages of three and four. Prior to birthday number three, Denise was kept by Ms. McNeil, who ran an in-home nursery for babies on Pettigrew Street. She kept a house full of babies, and she was affordable. She loved Denise and hated to see her leave.

Denise was ready for the daycare school environment. She was a fast learner and had sharp retentive skills. The Scarborough Nursery School, Inc. began in 1925 and is recognized as the oldest daycare organization in North Carolina. It was founded by legendary John C. Scarborough, Sr.

Mr. Scarborough was a pioneer in the Durham Hayti community. He was one of the owners of Scarborough and Hargett Memorial Gardens, which was started in 1871 in Kinston, NC, moving to Durham in 1905. It is now named Scarborough and Hargett Celebration of Life Center. He is recorded as the first African American to receive his mortuary science license in NC. The year was 1906.

Both his Nursery School and Funeral Home have been and are strong, unwavering pillars in our Durham districts. Five generations of The Scarborough Family have carried on the vision of Mr. J. C. Scarborough, Sr., including his son John

C. Scarborough, Jr., his grandson, John C. "Skeepie" Scarborough, III, and now Queen M. Bass Scarborough, the widow of "Skeepie." The city of Durham mourned the loss of a great leader, John C. "Skeepie" Scarborough, III, and celebrated his life in November 2020. He served local families for over sixty years, including our family.

Having mentioned Scarborough, it would be remiss of me not to quickly acknowledge the longevity of other Hayti Memorial businesses that survived urban renewal and continued to proudly serve our communities:

Amey Funeral Home started in 1933 as Carolina Funeral Home, by William Amey and E. G. Spaulding. Provided services for forty-eight years until the passing of Mr. Amey. Started on Pine/Roxboro Street.

Ellis D. Jones & Sons Funeral Directors, founded in 1935 by Ellis D. Jones, Sr., and continues to provide quality services for eighty-six years; now, by the third generation of Jones descendants, with care and dignity. Original and present location—Dowd Street in North Durham.

Burthey Funeral Services commencing in 1947 by Groover C. Burthey, Sr. Providing continuous services for seventy-four years, proudly, by the second generation—with benevolence and compassion. Located on Fayetteville Street. They will be in charge of my Homegoing Service.

Holloway Memorial Funeral Home originated in 1954 by the Holloway Brothers—James, George, and William. Having a strong reputation for professional services for sixty-seven years. The offspring of the Holloways give their best to serve the community on the corner of Apex Hwy 55 and Riddle Road.

Fisher Memorial Funeral Parlor was the vision of Elijah John "Pookey" Fisher, III, which came to fruition in 1963. With caring and personal service, he and staff served families for fifty-three years, up to the farewell of "Pookey" in 2016. The baton was picked up by Fisher progenies, adding to the years of service. Urban renewal displaced them to South Fayetteville Street.

This was important for me to impart because over five hundred African American businesses were closed or displaced as a result of urban renewal. Yes, it was shared earlier, but it still hurts after nearly sixty years.

It's a wonderful feeling to know and share that many businesses like the Memorial industry readjusted, reemerged, or relocated and are still vibrant in our community. They have inspired other new businesses in the industry like Hanes Funeral Service, founded by Bishop Franklin O. Hanes in 1997, ministering to families with sincerity and sympathy here in Durham and the surrounding areas. Located in East Durham.

I was so proud of Denise and how she shined so brightly at Scarborough Nursery. She had so much fun learning and playing with the other children. She was a great baby, not finicky or whiney. Her appetite was always hardy, and she laughed and smiled at the drop of a hat. She was walking around ten months, and being with the Tip Top bunch helped her to develop her motor skills quickly.

I dropped Denise off at the Nursery on the way to work, and the other ladies dropped off their child on the way to Tip Top, too. There was a guy that hung around Tip Top every day. He was called "Monkey Britches." Buster and Fred knew him, and he turned out to be a decent guy with more time on this hand than money in his pocket. He had electrical skills and helped the local electrician whenever help was needed. He knew the electrical business; he just didn't have any certification papers or a verifiable license.

Monkey Britches enjoyed being around Tip Top and especially being around the children. Well, we gave him an assignment that made him so very thrilled. Scarborough Nursery closed daily at 6 p.m., and it was within walking distance. We had Monkey Britches pick up Ava, Denise, Dwight, and Fleur and walk them back to the beauty shop. They enjoyed him, and he certainly enjoyed his assignment! Ever so often, Buster and Fred would come by the shop, pick up Ava and Denise and take them home, spending daddy/daughter time.

By 1963, Denise was following Ava to East End Elementary School for first grade. She was a plump little first grader, and Lizzie made all her clothes from infancy thru high school and college, and she even made her beautiful wedding dress for her wedding day! Lizzie never had a daughter, so Denise was her girl. She made many of my dresses, also. She made our MVBC usher's uniforms and ended up making the uniforms for all the ushers. Did I mention that all Lizzie had to do was see an article of clothing, and she could sew it instantly? Her sewing talent was "a cut above," and it was hard to find a good seamstress, so she was in demand!

Elementary School helped bring out Denise's personality. She joined the local girl scout troop, sang with the music class, and was a teacher's helper each year. Because of her love of music, Denise started taking piano lessons in the fifth grade, under the tutorial leadership of Mrs. Hallie Lawson Reeves. Sister Reeves was the daughter of Rev. Andrew Lawson, who preached at the Holiness Church, and the wife of Rev. William Alphonza Reeves, founder and funeral director of House of Reeves (1970s–1980s). Sister Reeves had many students, including Pearline's daughter, Syvil. Denise continued piano lessons up till high school.

Academically, she was in the top rankings of all her classes and was promoted every year. East End Elementary School went from first grade thru sixth grade. Junior High was seventh thru ninth grade. Ava had gone to Carr Junior High when Denise entered Holton Junior High. Denise arrived with great expectations for her middle years of learning. She discovered her love of science, and somewhere along the way, she decided that science would be her field of expertise. Those years went by quicker than quick, and with the blinking of an eye, she was entering the tenth grade at Durham High School (DHS) in fall of 1972.

Durham High ranked as a high-level school, meaning it was acclaimed for academics, athletics, and extra-curricular opportunities. Originally, it was opened under the name Central High School in 1906, only open to White high school students in the city of Durham. In 1922, Central High became Durham High School (DHS). The school was on property once owned by none other than the Duke Family. Credit was bestowed upon the Superintendent of Schools for integrating the Durham School

System, which included Durham High, in the 1959-1960 school year. That was during peak times of the Civil Rights movement.

The Superintendent was Mr. Lew Hannen, and the students who integrated the Durham School System included Anita and Claudette Brame, Lucy Jones, Andree and Joycelyn McKissick, Larry Scurlock, and Henry Vickers. Most Durhamites knew well of Atty. Floyd McKissick, Sr., and his wife, Mrs. Evelyn. Both were civil rights activists and advocates of equal education through desegregation of schools.

Their daughter, Joycelyn, became the first African American young lady to graduate from Durham High (1960). Daughter Andree, along with Henry, were the first students of color to enroll in Carr Junior High in the 1959 school year. They paved the way for Ava to follow. Lastly, their daughter, Charmaine, and son, Floyd, Jr., were among the first to integrate the elementary level by attending North Durham Elementary School in 1963.

In fact, Atty. Floyd McKissick, Sr. attended North Carolina College (NCC) Law School in Durham, after being denied entrance into the School of Law at the University of North Carolina (UNC)—Chapel Hill because of his race; only later to be accepted and was in the first group of African American students to be admitted to the UNC School of Law. The change in his admission (along with a few others) was a result of Atty. Thurgood Marshall and the NAACP. Despite these early landmark entrances into the Durham School Systems, "previously white-only school's complete desegregation did not occur until the courts ordered it in 1970."

The diversity at Durham High enhanced Denise's stamina and studying habits. She migrated to others who were interested in science and excelled in the college preparatory courses. Her passion for doing well in school seemed to grow each year.

She was a member of a club called The Parnassians. It wasn't a science-related club, but she enjoyed it. The essence of the club was for students who were interested in reading, understanding, and writing fine poetry and prose. The group's main project was the publication of the *Teleidescope,* a magazine expressing artistic drawings, photography, and poetry. "This project gives us experience in editing and appreciation of the processes of publication," according to the club's mission statement. Mrs. Ernestine Jones, a well-respected English teacher, was the advisor.

It was time for our baby girl, Denise, to graduate from high school. We could hardly believe that one day she was a Tip Top infant, and now she'd be getting her diploma, throwing her tassel, and heading to college. She chose North Carolina Central University (NCCU). Ava and Denise had reconnected at Durham High. Ava had already graduated the year before and started her freshman year at NCCU.

Graduation for the Class of 1975 was at the Durham County Stadium. Most of our family came to congratulate Denise. Buster had turned sixty-three, and I was fifty-six. We may have been older parents, but we were the proudest. When I heard over the microphone, "With honors, Denise Olivia McLeod," I could feel the teardrops slowly gliding down my cheeks, one after the other. Never would have made it without the Lord on our side!

NCCU had already sent Denise her welcome letter for August orientation. She and Buster had previously discussed her college decision. If she stayed local, he would pay all of her tuition. She would graduate without debt and student loans to repay.

Deal and deal, they agreed. She chose biology as her major and chemistry as her minor. She was ready for this new chapter in her life and her freshman year began without a wrinkle.

College life harmonized quite well with Denise. Her classes were mainly in the morning, and she studied all evening long. She had labs several days out of the week, and they took up a good portion of her open time. I never heard her complain about school. I got the impression that she was progressing at her own speed and was marching to the beat of her own drum, in a positive way. Ava also attended NCCU in music, and they were able to continue their friendship.

Denise started playing for the Sunday School Department at our church, Mount Vernon Baptist, when she was still in elementary school. She continued to play through high school and college. Back then, Sister Fogle had come to each Sunday School class asking did anyone know how to play the piano. Ralph Judd and Denise were the only two youthful ones who could play. Ralph suggested that Denise take that position because he might not be there each Sunday. I told Sister Fogle that Denise hadn't been taking lessons long. She needed a pianist and said it was okay because she'd only be playing hymns; so, that's how she started that mission.

Denise had successfully completed her freshman, sophomore, and junior years of her college program when she met a nice young man at a friend's home. She asked me and Buster could she bring him to the house for us to meet him. We both agreed, "yes!" They came on a Thursday night. We ate a great supper meal and enjoyed meeting Robert Daye. He was a country guy from Granville County, born to Washington and Georgia

Hawley Daye. He was the second oldest of four daughters and four sons. He was humble and polite. We liked him.

Denise found time to pledge a sorority. She became an initiated pledgee of the Alpha Kappa Alpha (AKA) Sorority, which was the first African American historically college-based sorority. It was founded in 1908 at the famous Howard University in Washington, DC.

By establishing this sorority, barriers were broken for African American women offering opportunities in areas that had previously lacked access, authority, or power for minorities and women in the early 20th century. The sorority was created based on five important principles that attracted Denise to join. They were:

> To cultivate and encourage high scholastic and ethical standards, to promote unity and friendship among college women, to study and help alleviate problems concerning girls and women in order to improve their social stature, to maintain a progressive interest in college life, and to be of "Service to All Mankind."
>
> (Alpha Kappa Alpha Sorority)

Denise had a heavy load of courses, even though it was her senior year. Plus, she had to do an internship at NIH in the Research Triangle Park (RTP); it was one of the animal laboratories owned by Duke. It was for the entire school year. I can't imagine how hard it was for her those last two semesters—classes, dating, and working. All I know is she made it through it with flying colors!

On a brilliant Sunday morning, May 20, 1979, we experienced another milestone day when our Denise Olivia received her Bachelor of Science degree, with honors, from North Carolina Central University (NCCU).

Life seemed so right for both James, Jr., and Denise, and me and Buster couldn't have been more thankful. Denise and Robert started plans for their wedding for the next year. Denise continued to work at NIH after graduation. She studied to take the professional teacher's exam that fall. She passed the first time taking it. She was planning a career in education. I was happy that she was so happy. Robert really loved her!

The wedding was set for springtime, May 1980. It was held at Mount Vernon. Our pastor, Rev. High, officiated. Not only did Lizzie make Denise's beautiful wedding dress, but she also made all the dresses for the bridesmaids; and she did all of that while still working at the same laundromat on Angier Ave that she had started thirty-eight years prior. Amazing, right?

There were five lovely bridesmaids and five handsome groomsmen. The groomsmen rented their attire and tuxedos for this special occasion. Buster looked mighty dapper to me as he escorted his grown-up baby girl down the aisle. Denise celebrated her birthday the day before the wedding, and the wedding just happened to be on Pastor High's birthday!

Robert and Denise had gotten their place a few weeks before the marriage. They settled in well and began their happy life together. Denise received calls from schools far and near. One offer to teach came in from Louisiana; she turned it down, not wanting to relocate from Durham, NC. She was home-grown and wanted to stay that way!

Then a call came from the Durham Public School System. They had a teaching position open in Biology for the approaching school year. Guess where? At her alma mater, Durham High School (DHS). She was eager and totally excited! To give back and go back to the school that set her on the path to achieving her long-term goals was a dream coming true! She accepted the offer and started the fall semester after becoming the lovely Mrs. Robert Daye!

Many of the teachers who taught Denise were still at Durham High and were proud to have her on the staff roster! There were many new and newer teachers that she met and became their colleague. Mr. Earl R. Hedrick, the principal when she graduated, was still in charge. Unfortunately, Mr. Hedrick passed two years later, spring of 1982.

After the untimely loss, Durham High was privileged to get Mr. John W. Thompson as its new head principal. He came in and helped turn DHS around as it was battling and experiencing major problems at that time. He was compared to Principal Joe L. Clark of Eastside High School in Patterson, NJ, who was the inspiration for the 1989 high school movie, *Lean on Me*. The staff and teachers appreciated Principal Thompson's no-nonsense approach.

Denise got acclimated to teaching as if it were her calling. She was nominated for teacher of the year after her third year of teaching. Her student's science test grades improved each year. Before they were married, Robert had started working at the First Presbyterian Church on East Main Street, downtown. He was doing exceptionally well and enjoyed being the caretaker of the church. He spent over four decades with them, retiring in 2021.

With their careers established, Denise and Robert started the conversation about their future family. They celebrated their third wedding anniversary and began planning for a new little Daye to arrive the next year. Our second, sweet granddaughter, Karleshia Chere Daye, graced our lives with happiness and jubilation in April 1984. She was an alert, bright-eyed and bubbly doll-baby. Buster had retired from L&M after about forty-five years, so he enjoyed taking care of Karleshia. She was just a toddler at our fiftieth wedding anniversary celebration.

Soon after that wonderful anniversary celebration in 1986, Denise received the great news that she was having another little treasure. Robert "flipped his wig," so to speak in excitement. Coming from his medium to large-size family, he was looking forward to a nest full of little ones.

For Denise, all went well with the second pregnancy, just as smoothly as the first. The Happy New Year had come in with fireworks and new resolutions. Days later, in January 1987, our third granddaughter arrived with a beautiful smile on her face. We had a happy, healthy, and high-spirited Krystal Lynn Daye, a radiant little doll-baby number two.

From the outside looking in, all appeared to be the makings of a happy family and a happy home for the Dayes. Yet, with most all marriages, changes occur, and children add responsibility and, to some degree, stress, and struggle. No one actually knows what goes on behind closed doors except the people behind those closed doors. It wasn't a long stretch of time before airborne stories floated that a certain catty Caucasian lady was in pursuit of Robert and vice versa. Denise found out the—who, when, and where. The next thing I knew, Buster's pistol was missing, and the children were left behind with us.

That was a hard night to sleep or think or even cry out to God for help. Denise was a gentle spirit most all the time. The thought of her in pain and in rage at the same time had my heart fluttering with anxiety. Buster was getting weaker, and this was around the time that his second leg needed to be removed. I remember pacing the floor—from the front room to the back room to the beauty shop through the kitchen to the bedroom to the den—one room after the other, wondering if she could really hurt Robert. She loved him, undoubtedly. She'd had a couple of friends in high school, but none that passed the test of time. Robert was her choice, and all I could hope was that she wouldn't choose to end his life or someone else's!

Daylight broke the sky the next morning, shining through a clear, glazed-like horizon presenting a cloudless new day. I hadn't slept a wink. Finally, near noontime, Denise came to the house. She didn't say much. Her quietness was chilling. It was not like her. She normally started talking from time of entrance to time of exit. She was hurting to her core. She had found her husband at the "where" location, had escorted him back home with a pistol to his head, and they talked all night. "Will things get better, Mom," she asked, "or will they get worse?" I couldn't answer definitely. My comforting words were, "We all make choices and have to live with them. Only God knows." I was thankful that no lives had been lost in the heat of the night.

Buster had struggled thru his last surgery, lived a while afterward, and had gone on to glory in February 1990. For Denise, losing her daddy—her hero—was an insurmountable peak of heartbreaking pain. She and Robert had already separated, and he'd moved out of their place. A short time after Buster's service, by May, they were no longer married. The girls were five and three. I was minus a husband, a son-in-law, and fearful of our daughter not being able to stand strong during that stormy season.

Denise did regain her sense of being. She continued teaching and tutoring to keep herself grounded. The girls were fun, growing like wildflowers, and very smart. Denise began communicating with a friend she had known from high school—her first boyfriend. Tony, the byname for Anthony, was an interesting young man, stayed on the West-End. He seemed to care for Denise and the girls. He had fathered two sons and a daughter from another friend from high school. As he and Denise spent more time together, the decision was made. They became united, and our daughter became Mrs. Denise McMillian-Liles.

Tony had a heavy influence on Denise. Soon after marriage, the piano that we gave Denise for her sixteenth birthday got missing, along with her computer and game boy system, with no explanation. He guided Denise down a path that was not healthy or positive for her well-being. That bleak, dim path affected her job, her life, her parenting, and her self-worth.

It affected Tony just as bad—or worse! He would get so sick and swollen up until the medical doctor told Denise that if he continued on that same pathway, it would jeopardize his life. He continued on. Unfortunately, in April 1993, the doctor's forecast was forthcoming, and Tony slipped into eternity, with only thirty-seven short years under his belt. Denise and Tony didn't have a chance to celebrate their second anniversary. But his passing helped bring his bride back to a reality awakening. Rest on, Tony!

Denise still believed in love. She wanted what she saw that me and Buster had, especially in those last twenty-five years, and what Barbara Jean and James, Jr. had and still have—love that stands the test of time. She didn't give up on having that forever amour and believed that she had found it when a young man, Michael Batts, found her, and asked her to be his bride. She said "yes" one more time.

Michael was different. He was an aspiring, enterprising kind of business guy, a smooth talker with a great sense of humor. At first, for Denise, it was a joyride being Mrs. Batts. There were big, bubbly dreams, hyped hypothetical plans, and promised projections for the future.

Quickly, spotlights turned into busted-out streetlights. Night drives turned into nightmares, and the shining halo turned into burning hades. There were too many people hanging around at all times of the days and nights, mostly men. The girls slept in the bathroom on the floor all night, on more than one occasion, because there was no place for them to lay down to rest. That was the last straw for me! That's when they came to live with me on North Alston Avenue, one of the best decisions for them. Karleshia was in the fifth grade, and Krystal was in the second grade.

I don't know all that was going on in terms of lifestyle at the Batts home. I could only use my imagination, especially with the influx of people trailing in and out on a regular routine. But it got deep and dirty when domestic harm got served as the daily menu! Things were rougher than I visioned, and when violence was added into the discombobulated equation, it was past time for action!

Me and the girls hadn't heard from Denise in over a week. One time, prior, she had ended up in the emergency room, and we didn't even know that she was harmed and injured. Krystal found her in the restroom in the emergency area. She wasn't willing to speak of her situation at that time, but we learned that her pinkie finger had been broken by a sledgehammer by her spouse.

This time, it was different. Her husband had hurt her badly, kept her locked up for days, and then took her over his brother's place to keep her hidden from family. Somehow, she escaped out of the back door, went to the nearest neighbor's house, and called Karleshia to come and rescue her. Instantaneously, Karleshia rushed to the address. Upon arriving, she was horrified, in shock, to see her mother in such a battered and bruised condition.

Denise was transported to the hospital and spent the necessary time for her recuperation. The accumulation of injuries had the doctors baffled as to how someone could suffer such agonizing, painful hurt and remain conscience. There were black eyes, both arms broken, broken ribs, and numerous lacerations, welts, and wounds. Mr. Batts served a few months for that incident and received probation. Their marriage was never dissolved.

Denise had retired from the Durham Public School System, and after getting released from the hospital, she came to live back home on North Alston Avenue with me and her girls. The year 2008 had been an extremely difficult one for her. On top of all the other occurrences, Denise was involved in a terrible vehicular collision a few months before year's end. A drunken driver in a F150 pick-up truck swerved into the lane that Denise, with Aunt Idell, was driving in, crashing head-on into them, totally demolishing Denise's 1997 Dodge Intrepid and putting all three involved in the hospital—either for concussions, injuries, or surgeries. Thankfully, they all lived!

Aunt Idell, Denise's mother-in-law's sister, had broken ribs and punctured lungs, needing a drain tube. One of the surgeries that Denise endured was an eight-hour skin flap, a type of wound closure procedure. It allows for skin to be taken from another area of your body and used to surgically fill the defected or deeply damaged injured body part. A skin flap differs from a skin graft in that the flap is transferred with the blood supply intact and still connected to its original source, whereas a grafted tissue is completely removed from its source and therefore has no blood supply. Her ankle had snapped!

Denise spent three months, combined, in the hospital and in rehabilitation. It was the first Thanksgiving and Christmas holidays that she didn't cook for the family since her adulthood. Krystal took on the challenge for Thanksgiving dinner and did an incredible and stellar job. I cooked the Christmas dinner. Both dinners were not quite the same without our Denise present.

She had multiple other procedures and surgeries. Doctors confided to her daughters that they were concerned if she would ever walk again. When Denise was told the news, it saddened her to think of the possibility of not walking. However, prayers were lifted up for her from the Clergy, the church, family members, friends, and saints from all around. God is a faithful God, and He answered those fervent prayers. Denise gained more endurance, progressed in rehab, and walked out of the facility on her own two feet, with healing power from on High!

I got so much enjoyment from Denise being back at home. I hated that she had experienced such agonies, calamities, and sorrows. Parents want the best life and good outcomes for their children. It hurt my heart and Buster's to know that our daughter went through so much. Psalms 46:1 was a scripture that I believed to be foundational with regards to her trials and all of our trials. It is written, *"God is our refuge and strength, a very present help in trouble."* There's no way that she or we could have survived without the very presence of the hand of God.

It was a blessing for me, also, that Denise moved back home. She took over the driving, and I decided to cease driving. Karleshia had graduated from Durham School of Arts in 2002 with honors, and Krystal graduated from the same school with honors in 2005. Before their graduations and Denise's retirement, I would normally take Karleshia to work after school, drop Denise off at work in the mornings, and Krystal was the last one that I took to school if Robert didn't take her. Also, I was the PTA chairperson for several years. Well, in August 2008, I had reached ninety in age, and it was a good time to relinquish the wheels.

I didn't mention that during all of the pains of 2008, there was a happy blessing in my honor. Denise gave me a beautiful and delightful ninetieth birthday gathering at Mount Vernon Baptist Church in the fellowship hall, full of church members, family, and friends. The Usher Board helped sponsor it and served as hostesses. Minnie and the McLeod family came from

Lumberton, NC. Donna, Sylvia, and Tanya brought in the New Jersey circle. Willie and Beverly attended from Georgia.

Local family members, like Mack and Willie; Allan, Pearline and family, James, Jr. and Barbara Jean, and the three grand-daughters, LaKishia, Karleshia and Krystal, and Karleshia's new son, Kassan, who was born earlier in January that year—all showered love upon me. Willie, my brother-in-law, Christine's husband, sang a solo; he had a deep, great voice, and had sung in the MVBC male chorus for decades! All of my brothers and sisters had gone on; my best friend, Pete, had passed away, and I was still blessed to be alive. I was thankful to the mighty God we serve!

After healing and getting released from her doctors, Denise started going back to church at MVBC. She rededicated her life back to Christ and rejoined the fellowship of believers. She carried her grand-boys to church each Sunday. Khalid, the newest addition, was born in 2009. She played piano, once again, for the Sunday School department, sang in the choir, and worked with the children's department.

Physically, Denise had healed; emotionally, she was slowly and steadily pulling herself together. Her focus was on the girls and the grands. She found peace in the God that she knew about early in life, but now, she had begun knowing Him in a real, personal way. At different times, she'd look straight at me, expressing the words, "Thank you for bringing me up in the church and giving me that foundation to return to, when I needed it the most." You know, my thanks went straight back to Papa and Mama Olivia for giving me and my siblings that foundation to pass to the next generations!

In addition to enjoying church events, one of our other enjoyments came on early Saturday mornings. We loved to go to yard sales. We got up quite early on Saturdays, around 5:00 a.m. My friend Margaret (from the usher board at MVBC church), me, Denise, and a nice couple, who were friends of Margaret, all rode together. The husband's friend actually drove the van that we all rode in.

By the time it started getting light outside, we were on our way. Me and Margaret had been doing this for a while. It was great to have Denise join in. We'd go from one yard sale to another, probably six or seven per morning. I literally clothed Karleshia and Krystal when they were young, with nice and new apparel and designer outfits on our yard sale sprees. Margaret had two sons and twin grand-girls, and she was able to do the same for her offspring. We were back home by noon or no later than 1:00 p.m., fully exhausted from our exuberating Saturday venture.

Time spun by; year after year fleeted right along. Denise was blessed with two more grands—Kayla was born to Krystal and her husband, Moses, in February 2011, and Kaiden came in August 2011 to Karleshia and her husband, James. I enjoyed all my great-grands. I got them hooked on chocolate with cornflakes and chocolate on sugar cones. All the great-grands love chocolate ice cream because of me. Krystal reminded me of the chocolate hash that I'd always make after Thanksgiving. I remember, vividly, the Christmas of 2012 because everyone in our family got sick; we were sick for days! We had no idea if our sickness was from the food that we had eaten or a virus from the air; we just suffered thru it until the new year rolled in.

We were all quite excited about getting well and starting a fresh 2013 new year. I hadn't seen Denise so full of great expectations since her college graduation. Now, James, Jr. and Barbara Jean were doing well and ready for a prosperous year. One particular day, James, Jr. had called me, and we talked for a good while. However, he failed to mention that he had fallen at his home and couldn't get up. The next day when his daughter and the rescue squad arrived, they got him the care that he required. For a short time, he resided at a nursing facility for physical therapy and rehabilitation. LaKishia discussed with him and her mother about the possibility that they come to stay with her so that she could be a closer caretaker and guardian. The conversation was tabled until the next year.

One of Denise's close friends, Charlene, lost her brother, James "Jay" Marshall Rogers, Jr. right after the beginning of the year on Saturday, January 5th. Denise was close to the entire Rogers Family. Mr. Rogers had been Denise's history teacher at Durham High her freshman year. That was the same year that he was named Teacher of the Year on the local, state, and national levels. He became the first African American Teacher to earn that distinction. His prestigious recognition stuck with Denise and inspired her to strive for that honor when she began teaching.

Charlene was one of her bridesmaids on her original wedding day. They grew up in Mount Vernon together, had sleepovers together, and were like sisters. Denise attended the homegoing service for Mr. Rogers that next week, spent time with Charlene and the family, and returned home. We talked briefly about the service. She was ready for bed and slept all night like a baby.

The next morning, Denise got up saying that she felt refreshed, cooked us breakfast, and went into the bathroom. Shortly thereafter, I heard her fall. It was a loud collapse—crash—crumple! She was lying horizontal across the door. I screamed, trying to push the bathroom door open, "Denise, are you alright? What happened?" She couldn't respond. I called the 911 rescue squad. I called Karleshia and Krystal. I called on my God!

Within minutes the emergency medical service (EMS) team hurried in, barging in the bathroom door. They were able to get to her. She regained consciousness. They assisted her up and relocated her to the bedroom on the side of her bed. They realized that she had hit her head on the bathtub, breaking two vertebrates in her neck, and she ended up with a neck brace. It was not optional whether Denise would go to the hospital. She was certainly going. She was carefully placed on the stretcher and transported to Durham Regional Hospital. The girls arrived after she had been taken away. They went on to the hospital to be with their mother, where she stayed about four days.

The doctors performed multiple tests. The results were coming back favorably until the last test was taken. Unexpectedly, the last test was the dagger. It revealed a spot on her liver; it was confirmed as cancer. She came home and was to go back in two weeks to find out how extensive the disease was. On her return doctor's visit, she learned that the spot was the size of a dime on the outside but was all over the liver on the inside. The expert doctors deemed that the cancerous liver was inoperative. Our Denise was facing the greatest challenge of her life; I wished Buster had been here for both of us!

All January and February, Denise was back and forth to the hospital. She was not getting better. Something was wrong with her stomach; it was hurting, pulsating, and swollen all the time. She wouldn't eat, and when she did, the food kept coming back up. Her cancer doctor ordered an abdominal ultrasound, unfortunately, to discover a ten-centimeter tumor. Krystal confided in me that "Mom did not tell me that she had been given one year to live." Prior to her sickness, Denise always affirmed, "I don't ever want to be suffering long." She reaffirmed, "Do not let me suffer." All I could do was pray that God heard her affirmation.

Denise ended up at Duke Hospital with a new, younger doctor who encouraged her that he might be able to operate on the tumor. She told him, "I got the faith; you got the know-how," and he proceeded in drawing out the plan to operate. The night before the surgery, Denise sat on the edge of the bed and commented, "I guess it's too much to want to be cancer-free and bug-free." We were battling with bed bugs. The scheduled date for her surgery was "love day," Thursday, February 14th, and along with Denise, we were all hopeful for the best results.

Contrary to our hopefulness, the plan for the operation failed. The tumor was so big that the doctor could not risk her life trying to remove it. The whole objective had been to cut the tumor out to save her life. He was terribly disappointed. He was able, however, to insert a chemo pump inside of her that emitted chemotherapy directly to the liver. After the surgery, when she came back home, she still couldn't keep anything on her stomach. The next alternative was to send Denise to a rest home where she would have around-the-clock attention and medical services.

The first arrangement was for her to go to the Brian Center Health and Rehabilitation on Fayetteville Road in Southern Durham. Denise wanted a private room and didn't want to share a room because of her deteriorating condition. The cancer was spreading. It had expanded inside her stomach and to her lung. It was in her bile ducts. The bile ducts are a "series of thin tubes that go from the liver to the small intestines." Their main function is to allow the fluid, called bile, to go from the liver and gallbladder into the small intestines, helping to digest the fats in our food. As the cancer spread, it was destroying her liver. We found out that a human being needs at least one-fourth of the liver to survive.

The first arrangement didn't happen for Denise because of insurance issues. The Carver Rehabilitation & Living Center, located on East Carver Street in Northern Durham, was the only facility that accepted her insurance. We were in the month of March, and as spring brings in new, renewed life, the flowers begin to bloom, and the days get longer and warmer, yet the curtain of life was slowly being drawn on our Denise Olivia.

She didn't complain, but gradually, she started pulling back. She didn't want to do physical therapy; she stopped using the bathroom on her own; and she didn't attempt to give responses to the caretakers. Her blood pressure had gotten so low that it wasn't registering on the monitor. She had to get a PICC line (peripherally inserted central catheter). Her blood pressure continued to drop, and there was a leak in the PICC line. Fluid backed up in her lungs. She went into crisis mode and had to be rushed to the intensive care unit.

At one point, Denise didn't even know who Krystal was. According to Krystal, she just didn't seem right, and her skin changed its color; looked like it was yellow instead of brown. She was on five different blood pressure medicines, in addition to the chemo and the other drugs that were given to her to help keep her alive. Krystal checked on her mother later; "She was staring out of the window, not making any eye contact," Krystal reported. For any question that Krystal asked, her answers were "uh-huh, okay, uh-huh, okay." Then, her mother snapped out of "it" (whatever "it" was) and told her, "I love you."

Of course, I had the great-grandchildren so that Karleshia and Krystal could spend as much time as they wanted to at their mother's bedside. On Tuesday before Easter, I went to see my daughter—my grown baby girl. Sister Bennie Daye, one of the missionary helpers from MVBC, carried me to Carver. The girls had called Mike. He and his mother, Ruth, were there. Denise was dozing in and out of sleep; they had her on sedatives. Denise saw me and cheerfully said to the attending therapist, "That's my mommy!" Ruth thought that she might have been hurting and asked if she should get the doctor, but Denise told her, "I'm not hurting. I'm fine." I was happy to see Denise. I missed her and enjoyed spending that time with her, hoping and praying that a miracle would bring her home again soon.

I knew it was hard for Karleshia and Krystal to call Mike. They still held in their hearts the scars from how he mistreated Denise. Through the passing years, Mike would come to see Denise. On different occasions, he would bring her food, funds, and gifts; and they would sit and talk and even laugh together.

She forgave him, and I think he forgave himself. He was still her lawful husband; she was still his wife.

On that Thursday after I visited, Krystal and Moses were at Carver with Denise. She told them that she was hungry. Moses fed her soft mashed potatoes. She seemed to enjoy them, and they stayed down. She was watching entertainment tonight on television, which was featuring the singer Dionne Warwick. Karleshia had visited often during that week, also. She felt like Denise had quit fighting and had given up. On Good Friday morning, we received a call from Carver. Denise had a bad night and was struggling to breathe.

The girls headed back to Carver. I chose to stay home and watch the little ones. Sister Bennie had come over that morning to sit with me and help with the great-grandchildren. She stayed the entire day. She was a true missionary; and was head of a church missionary group.

By midday, there was no good news about Denise's improvement. Krystal said that she heard her mother breathing hard from outside the room. They called Mike at the latter part of the day. He zoomed to Carver with an urgency. As soon as Mike arrived there and walked into the room, around 7:00 p.m., March 29th, 2013, Denise took her last breath. She went home to be with her Lord. When they called to tell me, my heart ached with sorrow, and I spoke out loud, "There comes a time when you quit fighting and accept His will."

Thousands of teardrops fell for our Denise. Calls, cards, flowers, letters, and visits came from every corner of the community. Her church family, classmates, colleagues, extended family, and friends poured out sympathy by the barrels. I felt the caring, loving expressions all around me. James, Jr. had to reckon with his only sibling, his younger sister, leaving before him. The girls were strong, considering all the pain that they felt. They knew that their mother wasn't coming back. The year that the doctor gave her to live turned into only a few short weeks. Her darling grandchildren were still young, the oldest was only five, and they didn't know, realize, nor understand it all.

Her Homegoing Service was at the only church that Denise had ever attended, where she got baptized, joined the children's choir, loved the Easter egg hunts and picnics on the church farm, played the piano, said her first vows, and where she was being funeralized. Mount Vernon was the one staple throughout her life. The service was simple and sweet, just like she would have liked it. When I thought about it, I really had said goodbye to Denise on that Tuesday when I visited her—just in case I didn't get to see her again. I had hoped that she'd come home to North Alston Avenue, but God's plan was for her to have a new home, a new address in eternity.

The nucleus family members were asked to share one of their most memorable times with Denise. Here is what was shared:

James, Jr.—Party time at Denise and Tony's with loud music and children dancing and entertaining the adults!

Barbara Jean—Denise jumping in bed with me and watching TV while James, Jr. was overseas—soap operas and Tom Jones!

LaKishia—Riding in her red hatchback car, running errands, meeting her AKA sisters, and my chocolate birthday cakes!

Karleshia—Mom excited about cooking for the holidays and getting the menu together!

Krystal—Mom dancing and playing the record player, listening to *Earth, Wind and Fire* and getting us to come dance with her!

"Boot"—For me, it was me and Denise watching baseball games together, and if I asked her what she wanted for Christmas, it was always a kitchen gadget. She loved cooking!

No parent expects to bid farewell and bury one of her/his children. Doing so has a pausing, penetrating, and permanent effect, different than any other life tribulation. Anyone that has gone through it knows what I mean. For those who haven't gone through it, I sincerely hope that you never do. Life is never the same, yet it is necessary to go on, resume living, and trust that each day will get better and less painful.

This chapter was the hardest to talk about, the hardest to write, and the hardest to read—for me. I know it's a mini book within this book. But Denise was a mini-me. We were different, of course. We were from different generations and had different mindsets, and we chose different walks of life, but she was more like me than I realized. God gave her to me and Buster in our latter years. Lizzie said she was my "change of life" baby. She was our last born and our first gone. She will forever be in the depths of my heart. Now, I'm calling James, Jr. to tell him how much I love him, while I still have that chance!

CHAPTER 14
I Didn't Expect to Live This Long

No way did I expect to live this long! Who does? I'm sure that someone, somewhere does, but it wasn't me. No one in the family had ever lived over one hundred years. I take that back. Cousin Moselle Freeman White, one of Mama Olivia's nieces, lived to be one hundred and five, passing away in 2016, six months from her one hundred-sixth birthday. She was Aunt Lula and Uncle Charlie's baby girl. I thought that was amazing, but still, you could not have convinced me that I'd crack the one hundred ceiling, even though I was close to ninety-eight when she was called home!

God has brought me a mighty long way. I think about the midwives that brought me and my siblings into this world. Aunt Narcisse Dunn delivered most of us. She lived in the Knightdale community. Evidently, she didn't send in any of our birth certificate information to the State. Aunt Harriett Robertson got to deliver Mozelle and maybe one or more babies. There was a baby born between Big Baby and Clelly; and another one was born between Clelly and Mozelle. I don't think the midwives really had formal training. They learned through errors, observations, and practice. I'm not sure if they could read and write. They did their best in name spelling and accurate documenting. Again, that's why me and Mozelle had to pick a date for our birthdays. It was grace that brought me into this world and grace that has kept me this long.

When I think back to the country and how our home didn't have any closets, it's hard to believe, isn't it? We all had different nails to hang our clothes on. And you best believe that our clothes were hung up every day—after church, playtime, school, and working in the field. We've seen folks who took off their clothes and, on the floor—they landed *and* stayed there! Great googly-moogly! There's no way on planet earth that Papa or Mama Olivia would have allowed such a travesty! The nails were our lifesavers. They taught us organizational skills.

Think about something else, we didn't go to the store to get our shoes. It was Mama Olivia who measured everyone's foot with a tape measure and went to town to buy our shoes. One time, she brought shoes back for me, size 5; but I wore a size 6. I didn't want Mama Olivia to have to go back to town, so I told her that the shoes felt fine. What a mess I had made for myself. I had to walk around with too little shoes. For all I knew, I could've gotten a blood clot, foot ulcers, long-lasting pains in my legs, hips, and back, or poor blood circulation. Mama Olivia observed me and realized that the shoes were too little and took them back. The Lord looks after us when we are adolescents and "wet behind the ears."

Speaking of being naïve, this story that could have dampened my longevity happened after Yi had married Luzelia in 1926. He carried her back with him to NY as he continued to work for Mr. Roosevelt. Coming from our little country area, Luzelia didn't fit in the big city atmosphere and was uncomfortable being there. Yi bought her back home, and she stayed with us until baby Katie was born in March the next year. Always remember that our home was that anchor!

The part that involved me was that Luzelia dipped Tuberose snuff, and I tried to learn how to dip snuff, too. She put some snuff in my mouth and told me to suck on it. I did what I thought was sucking on it, and I got so terribly sick that I thought I was going to die. We couldn't tell Mama Olivia, so I suffered dizziness, stomach pains, and vomiting in solitude. I was lying in the grass, couldn't get up. I don't know if I was drunk and sick, or just sick and drunk! At the unripe age of nine, dipping snuff could have carried me on out! Believe me, I didn't dip "no mo'!"

It's funny, now that I think about it after all these years, me and Buster were living on Dunstan Avenue, and a man came by selling snuff. He asked, "Anybody dip snuff?" and I quickly replied, "No, no-one, not at all," but Buster said, "yes, me," and he bought some snuff. Well, just because you smoke doesn't mean that you can dip. That night, Buster got himself sick as a dog, about as sick as I had been at nine years old. I had learned my lesson back then. Buster learned his lesson that sick-filled night. I could probably think of hundreds of times that my life was in jeopardy of missing longevity, and yet, I am blessed to say that God has given me more time to do His will!

When I think about all my family members who were called home before me, it fills my heart with mixed emotions. Our family had a number of cancer battles but mainly have fought a lot of heart issues. Annie Dora "Cete" left us in 1960, before

Mama Olivia, from heart disease. She was a quiet spirit. When she left Durham and headed to Atlantic City, her life got established there, and she didn't come back home very often. We talked occasionally on the phone. Like Lizzie, she began working as a presser there. When she went North, she didn't turn back.

My fondest memory of my dear sister, Cete, was when she let me, all by myself, come stay with her and Uncle John after they got married on Christmas Eve of December 1923. I went a few months later after school was out. I had never before stayed away from home. I was going on six years old, then. They lived in Knightdale, where Uncle John worked for the railroad. He had a niece named Josephine, who was about my age, and she came to visit, too, and we played together. To add sweetness to this dear memory, Uncle John took us to get ice cream cones at the ice cream parlor.

Cete and Uncle John got along great (as far as a kid could see), and you may have wondered, "Why did Cete leave her husband and move back to the country with Papa and Mama Olivia?" From what I had heard, it was an "in-law" issue. She wasn't getting along with John's sister, Hattie. When they first got married and stayed in Raleigh, either they stayed with Hattie or Hattie stayed with them. Whichever way the cookie crumbled, it had a crumbling effect on their marriage.

Sometime after Cete came back home to the country, John moved to Durham and worked at Liggett & Myers with Budja and Buster until he passed away in 1967. Early on, he had joined Mount Vernon Baptist and actually lived across the street from the church. Even though he wasn't blood-related, a heart issue was his health problem. Cete had met and married Adolphus

Davis in New Jersey after their break-up. But Uncle John never ever remarried. Surprisingly, listed on his death record is my sister, Cete, as his wife, as informed by his sister, Hattie Mclean!

When Cete was sick, she stayed in the New Jersey hospital for over a month. All my siblings went to visit her. I couldn't go because at that time, Mama Olivia had been sick for over a year, and I was her caregiver. Mama Olivia couldn't walk. Because she was bedridden, I had to pick her up and carry her to the bathroom. Clelly's husband, William, made her a bottomless chair to sit next to her bed. He took an older wooden chair and cut out the seat, lined it with soft foam all around, and found a pee pot to sit underneath it. What a major help that was for me and her!

When Cete succumbed to her illness on an autumn, midweek, September morning, Launa stayed with Mama Olivia so that I could attend her Homegoing service. As we traveled in several cars, single file up interstate 95 to Atlantic City, my thoughts were of our broken family circle. I could see Otis's handsome, young face smiling at me, Papa's calm, cool demeanor nodding his head in approval to our processional, and Honey in his free-spirited mood—relaxing, singing, and walking around heaven. Yet, again, we were heading to say farewell to another broken link. Although it had been eighteen years between our last sibling goodbye, it was still an agonizing and heartbreaking ride. Her Homegoing was a touching service. The Joneses and extended family stood together in loving memorial of Annie Dora "Cete" Jones High Davis. We loved her dearly!

You already know how much I loved Mama Olivia. It was painful to see her bedridden and frail, fighting each day to make it to another day. It was especially hard because it was nothing that I could do to change her downturn. It began one day when she was hanging out clothes on the clothesline; she collapsed to the ground. Launa was home that day, thank goodness, and saw her lying in the dirt. Instinctively, Launa got her up and into the house; she called me, and I instantly came home. She seemed weak, but nothing serious enough for medical treatment. I began to arrange my appointments so that I could be there for her, in and out, throughout the day. Buster was there, sleeping before his work schedule. Lizzie got home after 4:00 p.m. and checked in on her. Christine came by every day to aid in her care. We shared the load.

Slowly her health deteriorated. Catherline and her first husband, Robert Earl, had married and moved to New Jersey. Budja and Allan, Pearline's second husband, went to get Catherline and bring her and her daughter back home. Things didn't work out up there, and she was three months expecting when she got home. It was perfect timing that she returned because as Mama Olivia got weaker and weaker, she needed more constant care; with Catherline back home, she provided the daily attention and nourishing that Mama Olivia needed.

When Mama Olivia got where she couldn't swallow, we'd beat up food, like eggs, potatoes, and vegetables, and put it in milk, making it like a milkshake so then she could sip it down slowly. Her mind was sharp, and she wasn't in pain, but gradually, her days were winding down. Her doctor, Dr. Thompson, put it in a simple sentence, "She is giving out." He made me think of a car running out of gas and going no further. He actually joked that the doctor's book didn't go past the age of eighty! She was going to turn eighty-four on the next Christmas day.

One of my fond memories of Mama Olivia in her latter years is how happy she was when her brother, Uncle Joe, came to see her. Joseph "Joe" Young was one of the last boys born into the Young Family. Grandfather Andrew was half of a century when Joe was born in 1880. They were so happy to see each other. It had been many years since their last time together. Mama Olivia was so excited that she called downtown for a photographer to come to the house and take their picture. It was a great picture taking and one of the few best pictures that I still have of her. Nearly three years after Cete's passing, on a warm, June Friday evening, Mama Olivia heard the angels calling her name. She answered the call. She went to her heavenly home to be with her Savior and to see her lifelong love, Papa.

After Mama Olivia took her heavenly flight, Lizzie assumed the role of the Jones' matriarch. She always wanted to tell us what to do, anyway, so now she was in that position by default. I never was able to hold a grudge toward her, so anytime Lizzie would get on my nerves, or I on hers, I'd take a break from the situation, take a deep breath and let it out; and rather quickly, I was over the situation and kept on as if nothing had happened. If Lizzie could, she'd keep the matter going.

For most of her life, Lizzie was healthy and strong. However, one doctor's visit, about a decade after Mama Olivia was gone, revealed that Lizzie had uterine cancer. It frightened her! Fear was knocking at my door, too, but faith answered, and I told Lizzie not to worry and that God would take care of her. Her doctor recommended a hysterectomy. She consented, and the operation was successful.

I don't want to give any accolades to cancer because it is such an ugly, unwanted disease. The survival rate is better than it's ever been due to check-ups, earlier detections, and research. But many times, it is still a battle to be fought. Lizzie had recuperated well from her surgery and carried on like a brand-new person.

Little did she know that the ugly, unwanted culprit would rise up again, near another decade later. This time, it took its toll on my sister. I tried exercising my faith and believing for a miracle, yet she remained in the hospital for a couple of months. She would say to me, "I'm suffering now." Rev. High would call and ask, "Where you at, Sister McLeod?" knowing that I was at the hospital with Lizzie.

I didn't want to leave her side. I sat there watching her day after day, until one day, I saw a calm come over her face. She had made peace with her fate. It was her time. Everyone came to the hospital to say goodbyes. Siblings—from the oldest to the youngest—Yi, Buddy, Chick, Budja, Clelly, Mozelle, me and Christine, nephews, nieces, aunts, uncles, cousins, in-laws, friends, co-workers, and church members, all came from far and near.

God allowed a special time for Mack and Pete to embrace the fleeting time with their mother and mother-in-law. Mack had lost his father, Bert, before enlisting in the military. As an only child, he had no one that felt what he felt saying farewell to Lizzie, his mother. I knew the pain so very well, but I had the rest of my family to share my sorrow! Lizzie put on her wings and flew away on the last day of November 1983.

Two of my fondest reminiscences of Lizzie are etched in my thoughts. First, she was so happy to be named after Grandmother Lizzie. That was such an honor for her to carry that name into another generation. She proudly wore that name like a noble peacock! Secondly, I can recall all the family reunions in the country that we attended together. She absolutely loved going back to the Jones Chapel community and seeing the new relatives—but mainly, the older legends that were still around who had known Papa and Mama Olivia, The Dunn Family, and other neighbors in the surrounding districts. A side thought—Lizzie liked being the "Boss," and she thought that we all should listen and respect her. The truth is—I did listen to, love, and respect Lizzie Alma Jones Dunn.

The 1980 decade would strip from us several more family members. The next year after Lizzie departed, Yi started feeling a little nauseated every so often. He thought nothing much about it. He had been doing quite well. After his wife, Luzelia, passed in April of 1967, Yi continued being faithful at his beloved church, Gethsemane Baptist Church, which was a block down the street from Mount Vernon. He, too, served as an usher, was Superintendent of Sunday School, and served on the deacon board for nearly fifty years.

Yi made up his mind to remarry. He headed back to the country to find another country lady. If you recall the Perry Family, who were our close friends, the oldest sister was called Sis. Her name was Queenie Perry, and she became my new sister-in-law. She made Yi happy, we believed, and I was glad he had found another love in his later days.

It made me sad when Queenie called me on Thursday, December 6th of 1984, to let me know that our beloved brother, Yi, had made his eternal journey home. He departed at his home, peacefully, surrounded by his wife and offspring. His heart had worked long enough, and it ceased. Five of the Jones sisters and two of the Jones brothers were left to pay respect to the life of our eldest sibling, to a life well-lived.

At age eighty-eight, Yi was still honored and proud to have served as the personal valet of the late President Franklin D. Roosevelt. It was one of his greatest accolades. One thing for sure, I shall always remember the sermon that his pastor, Rev. Dr. V. E. Brown, preached about my brother. It was titled "Steps of a Good Man." Leroy "Yi" Jones was a God-fearing, good man, like our Papa.

I love sharing my fondest memories of my family. I hope that you like reading about them. With Yi, I have the most vivid memory of him driving up to our country home in a brand-spanking-new, 1927 black-on-black, T-Model Ford! We, the Jones family without a vehicle, were so shocked; we couldn't believe it! You can imagine how sophisticated he looked—with his shoulders squared back, his head perpendicular to the steering wheel, and his tall frame almost touching the top of the inside? It was a two-sitter, and there were no windows; Yi had gotten the snap-in plastic side window curtains to use when it rained. Mr. Henry Ford enriched my brother's life, and Yi enriched Mr. Ford's wealth.

The history of Henry Ford and the world-changing invention of the car is known all over the world. From 1908–1927, over 15 million cars were produced, which was a record that stood for forty-five years. We learned in high school that Mr. Ford, a visionary, was determined to make the highest quality product, in the most efficient manner humanly possible, to sell at an affordable, competitive price that any working person could afford. Yi was one of those working persons who could afford one. Yes, he rode me and my sisters around, going nowhere, just around!

Another fond memory of my brother, Yi, was remembering the many things that he would send to Papa and Mama Olivia and the family. Because he traveled on his job as personal valet for Mr. Roosevelt, he saw things and went places that we were never exposed to as a family in the country. I told you that he sent Mama Olivia a Victoria record player that she truly loved. Well, he sent an ice cream maker that thrilled the whole family. Who remembers the hand-cranked, old-fashioned ice cream maker?

Man, did we love helping Mama Olivia put the can of Pet milk, a cup of sugar, teaspoons of vanilla flavoring, and a pinch of salt in a pot on the stove, letting it come to a boil, watching it cook for about fifteen minutes on low heat until it thickened and finally putting it in the ice cream maker's canister. We would add eight to ten pounds of crushed ice inside the wooden frame of the ice maker along with two-three cups of rock salt—first, one layer of ice and then one layer of rock salt. Then we'd put the gear-frame top on the ice cream maker, locking it tightly; we'd all take alternating turns whirling the crank in a clockwise motion. At first, it was easy to crank, so the little ones could join in the fun. After about twenty minutes or so, the cranking got harder, and the grown-ups had to finish the task. When Papa pulled the dasher from inside the canister, the end result was delicious, fresh, hand-churned, homemade ice cream! Yum, yum, yummy! Thanks, my brother, Yi, for sending that great memory.

If you agree that the ice cream maker story was a great memory, I must share about the coconut story, lol! We had seen coconuts before, and they were all furry or hairy. One day in the mailbox, there arrived a round, smooth ball-like object. Written on it were Papa's name and our address. It wasn't in a box or package; it just came like a regular letter. Papa shook it, and we could hear the liquid inside; Mama Olivia smelled it, but nobody had an idea of what it was. After Papa got tired of shaking it and Mama Olivia was tired of smelling it, Papa went and found his hammer. He came back and set that smooth thing in the middle of the front porch. Papa was strong if I hadn't told you that, and he reared back and swung a powerful blow, splitting it down the center. Coconut juice flew in multiple directions; we all realized that it was a coconut. Leave it to Yi to baffle us with a smooth coconut from Warm Springs, Georgia! We all ate it up right then and there!

The next family loss after Yi is hard for me to think about because Catherline came by to see me the same day that she passed. I don't know where she and John were coming from, but it was the day after New Year's Day 1989. She and John came on in that afternoon around 4:00 p.m.; my door was never locked during the day. I was sitting in my chair in my bedroom, Buster was in his wheelchair, and they came and sat down on my bed. Cat, as most everybody called her, was jolly as she always was; she had such a happy spirit. John looked like he had been on one of his benders; he was a little quieter and subdued than normal. No matter what situations they had, you would find Cat and John together.

Cat told me that her tastebuds were calling for some home-cooked vegetable soup, and she was going to the store to get the ingredients to make a fresh pot. They had just come by to say hi and wish me and Buster a Happy New Year. After a sweet and short visit, they went on their merry way.

The next morning my phone rang early; it was Beverly calling. "Cat had what? What did you say? Cat?" I was so shocked! I couldn't believe what my ears were hearing; I just couldn't believe it! I tried to hold back my tears; Buster was recuperating from surgery, and I didn't want him sadder than he was. But there was no floodgate on my tear ducts, and the emotions, the pain, and the sorrow all poured out intensely, overwhelmingly! "Cat, Cat, oh, Cat," I wept.

I thought about Budja and Launa, John, Pearline, and her offspring, Beverly and Lennon Earl. I had not lost a child at that time and could not imagine the hurt in the hearts of my brother and sister-in-law. John would be lost without Cat, I believed, because he loved her so and depended on her strength to sustain him. Catherline and Pearline had always been close sisters; it had to have been difficult for Pearline. A sister's love is strong; I knew so well.

I mentioned that Catherline was three months pregnant when she came back home to Durham. Her son, Lennon Earl, was born in May 1960. He was twenty-eight, her daughter, Beverly, was thirty-three, and Cat was only fifty-four when she suffered the heart attack and died. Because of Buster's health and surgery, I couldn't attend her Homegoing Service. It hurt not to be there. I stood in our side door and watched as the processional left 1311 North Alston Avenue with Scarborough and Hargett carrying my niece, Cat, to Mount Vernon and onward to Glenview Memorial Park. A knot was in my throat and a hole in my heart.

I talked to Budja afterward, he said Cat looked pretty, like herself. John told me later that she had made the vegetable soup, ate a bowl of it, and laid down. Then, he said that she got up and started throwing up. When she laid back on the bed, her eyes rolled backward, and he called the ambulance. The EMT arrived and worked on Cat for nearly an hour, he shared, but when the siren lights flashed as they drove away, John said he knew that his wife was gone forever.

I have so many fond memories of Cat—from fishing and playing cards to her invaluable help in taking care of Mama Olivia. I do fondly recall the time that we wanted to get a swing set so that Beverly and Denise and Lennon Earl could have a little playground in the backyard. Me and Cat went uptown to a local furniture store and picked out a nice red set with two swings and a sliding board. The store clerk asked me where did my husband work. I told him, Liggett & Myers. That's all that was asked of us, and they delivered the swing set the same day. Buster came home that afternoon and asked me what had I bought using his name? Cat was there; we fell out laughing because we had gone to buy the swing set ourselves, not put it in Buster's name; like James Brown sang his song in 1965, it must have been a *Man's Man's Man's World*, cause the bill came to Mr. McLeod.

Now when I think back on the year 1989, I had to agree with my great-niece, Beverly; it was a challenging, difficult, and heartbreaking year. Twenty days after Cat left us, we endured another force of bereavement. Me and Buster were in the den watching television when Mack came in the side door. He sat down, which was strange. Mack wasn't the visiting type. He normally stayed at 1307 North Alston Avenue, minding his own business.

The look on his face gave me alarm. He quietly stated, "I think we lost Budja." I shrieked out, again, "What? Budja?" Mack was coming from Budja and Launa's house where the ambulance had arrived, unknowingly to me. Trying not to upset Buster, I calmly said to Mack, "Stay here with Buster," as I rushed to go out of the door. As soon as I ran in next door and got to the kitchen, I saw the frame of my handsome, smooth, tall brother sprawled out on the living room floor.

With urgency, the EMTs were doing all that they could do to revive Budja. Tears welled up in my eyes. I felt so sad for Launa–losing her baby daughter, now-her husband. How could it be? Pearline was there; Allan had gone to see his sister, Josephine, who lived right in back of me on Hanover Street. Pearline must have called Mack and told him to come get me. She exclaimed in agony, "That's the same way Catherline went. One minute she was fine, and the next, she's gone." My heart was torn for Pearline—saying farewell to her sister, now her Daddy. How, Lord, could it be?

Budja, Launa, and Pearline had been sitting in the living room laughing and talking. Budja did have a good sense of humor! What I recall from Launa and Pearline was that he was talking about a guy back in the country, Pittman Hinton. We knew his family; they didn't live too far from us. Pittman had a sister named Ada and a brother we called Buddy, who actually married our cousin, Burt Dunn's sister. Anyway, Pittman was special, and he'd roam the country visiting from house to house, hanging sometimes with the guys. Keep in mind; no inside toilets existed, never had seen toilet paper, so instead of going to the outhouse, guys would go around the building to let it out. Budja said, Pittman saw a guy doing such and shouted, "Ain't you got no manners?" and Budja threw back his head, laughing so joyfully as he remembered Pittman. His next breath was his last. His head slumped down on his shoulder without notice or warning.

Even though the EMTs had worked fiercely without any response, they told Launa that they were taking Budja to the hospital. She jumped up, telling Pearline to get her clothes so that she could get ready to meet Budja at the hospital. Launa was a petite lady who I thought moved gracefully, like a swan. At that moment, she could have been a speedy cheetah, trying to get to where her husband was going to be!

One of the EMTs said caringly and slowly, "there's no need to rush." I knew what he was saying. I knew that my dearly beloved brother was only a body, with his ashes going back to ashes and his dust back to dust. His spirit had been set free! He'd dealt with previous heart issues, and like the majority of the Joneses, his heart gave Budja his final curtain call.

Exactly three weeks from our family visiting Glenview Memorial Park with the burial of his daughter, Catherline, Budja made that same trip for himself. Scarborough and Hargett led the same processional from 1311 North Alston Avenue to Mount Vernon to Glenview Memorial Park. Buster was getting stronger, and I was able to show my last respects for Budja with the family. Our sorrow was real; our grief was reeling, like trying to catch a fish that got away. Our heartbreak couldn't be captured or hooked; it was deep and devastating, as we kissed 'so long' to Lennon 'Budja' Jones. Lord, how could it be?

Yes, I have a plethora of fond memories of Budja. The first one that popped in my head was how he declared, "Ain't no cornbread coming in my house." Mama Olivia cooked a delicious pan of cornbread, but when Budja got sick, he couldn't eat cornbread anymore! Many other memories stemmed from childhood, several from his assuming the leadership role when Papa passed; a heap of memories formed after we married our spouses, and some especially great memories came after we moved to North Alston Avenue. I knew Budja for seventy-one years and lived beside him for forty-one years.

People would marvel that our neighbors were my brother, nephew, sister, and sister, and in-law. We'd hear smart comments about how people couldn't stand to be around their siblings for more than a few minutes or no longer than a few hours. I didn't get it because we were taught that family is your backbone, where you get strength to go through life's trying times, and if you can't depend on family, who can you depend on? There's an old saying, 'To each his own" or "Each to his own,' whichever way you choose to say it. Both mean that others are free to like different things and have different views.

This may not be a specific fond memory of Budja, but I thought about this as we left Glenview. Back in the 1950s, shortly after moving to North Durham, a preacher came by selling grave plots for Glenview Cemetery. It had just begun development, and I guess that they were trying to gain working capital. A family plot of four graves was $330.00. Lizzie decided to invest for her, Mack, and Pete. I went along with Lizzie, getting a family plot for me, Buster, and James, Jr. We were among the first investors.

But Budja didn't want to think about "that," and he didn't take time to think about it. Thank God for Launa; she always had a good head on her shoulders. I believe that she acquired only two plots for herself and Budja, after Budja passed. All of our original plots were at the front of the cemetery by the white, praying hands. We used one of ours for Mama Olivia, and another one for Buster's sister, Rebecca. The only one left is mine.

Someone needs to read this message from me-someone who has lived an extended time:

Plan for your life and also—

Plan for your departure.

One is happening now. A great future is ahead of you; make wise choices! The other will happen later, but it will happen. Don't leave that burden on someone else. Be respectful and responsible. I loved Cat, and I loved Budja. I think about both of them often. I'm thankful that our family had prepared for the unexpected; your family will be, too!

The year wasn't done with heartbreak and pain. I had predicted that John would have a hard time without Cat, but I was hoping that he would stay strong and make a better life for himself. Well, sadly enough, adding sorrow upon sorrow, we lost John E. Rhodes "Ba-boy" seven months after Cat expired. The reported tragedy of John's demise was that he was walking to his mother's home, Mary Rhodes, who lived on Taylor Street by the park and a wooded area.

Two young men confronted him, robbed him, and killed him. The story was told that the young men thought that he had money from his wife's death. He had twenty dollars on him. John didn't deserve to have his life taken from him in such a cruel and heartless manner. He was funny and kind, and he had a lot of life in front of him; he was only forty-three that August 15th, summer day. For our family, it was like tic-tac-toe—three special family members gone in an unreal row.

Now, Buddy was my last living brother after Budja. He was in his golden nineties and was getting along pretty well. He attended Budja's Homegoing Service and shared that he truly enjoyed being around so many family members. By the next year, he had slowed down and ended up in the nursing home on Wake Forest Hwy in Durham. He was there a little over a year. His daughter Etta Mae was in charge of his well-care after his wife, Lonie Mae, had passed away in 1981. Buddy was later transferred to Rose Manor Nursing Facility on Roxboro Road in Durham. He fell victim to pneumonia there at Rose Manor and left us in April 1992, a few days before his ninety-fifth birthday.

My fond memories of Buddy include him playing horse and buggy and sail-a-way with me, Christine and Mozelle—bouncing us on his knees and letting us flip over; and I can't forget how great of a cook that he was—probably the best in the family. He and Yi learned so many delicious recipes from working at the Washington Duke Hotel. He faithfully served at Ebenezer

Baptist Church and was president of the Men's Sunday School Class until his health declined. We, the last of the Jones sisters, were in mourning once again for a beloved sibling, our brother, William Arthur "Buddy" Jones—our family's first nonagenarian.

Christmas vibes were in the air as December of 1992 began with its advertisements and super-hyped commercials. By and large, everyone was excited to enjoy the festivities of the holiday season. I still had quite a few customers come to the beauty salon, and my appointment scheduling was booked up for the entire month. I had a conversation with Launa about her plans for Christmas, and she was planning to spend time at Allan and Pearline's home for the holidays. She was busy getting out greeting cards and helping local charities; as a missionary, she also helped with plans at church to assist needed families with food and with toys for the children.

Launa was as close to a Saint as anyone earthly that I'd known. She reminded me a lot of Mama Olivia. She cared for strangers as she did for her own family. Her patience, her piety, and her prayer life, combined with her Christ-like nature, allowed her Christian light to shine before others. I was proud to be her sister-in-law, next-door neighbor, fellow church member, and her friend. We never feuded!

Launa called down to the beauty salon a few days before Christmas, saying she didn't feel well. I was with a customer, and I asked her to call Pete, next door. I believe that she got up with Pearline instead, and she came and picked her up. Pearline shared later that Launa had been nauseated and passed out as she came out of the restroom. When the ambulance got her to the hospital, the details reminded me of Budja in that they worked on her to no avail. Pearline and her daughter, Syvil, came to my house and broke the sad news. Four days before Christmas, God called his angelic Launa home. On Christmas Eve, instead of caroling in the community or last-minute Christmas shopping, we were saying our last goodbyes to Mrs. Launa Thompson Jones.

My favorite memory of my sister-in-law, Launa, is how she glided like a ballerina and moved like a swan. Her ease in getting from one place to another was comparable to a dancer, but she didn't ever dance. She was flowing and graceful in her demeanor. I missed her calming and gentle manner. But guess who made the best strawberry pie? You guessed it; Launa made the most delicious strawberry pie. When Mama Olivia worked for the Upchurch Family, she'd bring home big, fresh, ripe strawberries, and Launa made homemade pies. Budja could eat a whole strawberry pie by himself, and I could run a close second place! My heart rejoiced thinking of Launa and Budja hanging out in heaven, together again.

Now Clelly was "Mrs. Organized," and she had everything together in business and in life. She continued to manage Gailes Funeral Home in Asheboro, fifteen years after her William suddenly deceased in 1980. She had tremendous help with a professional staff which included Clyde, Betty, Chip, Kevin, and others who were committed to excellent community service in memorial care.

All our family loved coming to Asheboro for family gatherings. Pearline, specifically, had a special place in Clelly's heart and home. After graduating from Hillside High and North Carolina College, she came to live and teach in Asheboro. She had married young and had a fine little bouncing baby boy, Larry Elliott. After gaining valuable teaching experience, she returned home to Durham.

Clelly thought of Pearline as her own daughter and said that because of her staunch determination and focus, Pearline would have a great impact in her career and on many lives. Shortly after returning home, she met and married Allan T. Summers, Sr., the spouse who would love her until the day he died; and they were blessed with a darling daughter, Syvil, and an adorable son, Allan, Jr. God blessed Pearline as Clelly had prayed for her blessings.

When Clelly got sick and her health began failing, it was hard on Pearline, as well as on Chick, me, Mozelle, and Christine. We were the end-caboose of the Jones' family train. Clyde had called me when Clelly went into the hospital for her first surgery. Brother-in-law, Willie, took us—me, Mozelle, and Christine—to see Clelly. Now, Chick had been committed to an assisted living facility in NJ. Our niece, Tanya, had taken care of her for as long as she possibly could; the burden became heavy, and she was challenged to do what was best for her Aunt Chick.

Traditionally, our Asheboro family dinners were around Thanksgiving or just before the Christmas hustle and bustle. This 1995 holiday season would be different; the family understood why. Clelly was getting close to her transition, yet she remained alert and aware of all that was happening to her. "Mrs. Organized" had every single detail planned and ready for her departure. I'm sure that by her being a funeral director for over 50 years, she didn't want to leave any burden on her sisters. We were by her side on New Year's Eve when she closed her eyes and slipped away to heaven.

I have to share that my fondest memory of Clelly was of her being my confidant. When we were growing up, she would tell me all the happenings that the grown-ups didn't convey to children; but if Clelly knew what was going on, then I was in the know-about-it, too. I laugh, now, when I think about Clelly leaving home to marry Robert and how I threw her clothes out of the window as she ran away to Virginia. None of Papa's girls had a wedding!

Let me interject that one big wedding that I recall so well, from the country, was the wedding of Paul Robertson's daughter, Pauline. It was bougie, lavish and majestic. I won't forget it because Lizzie and Mary Freeman, Uncle Joe Freeman's child, were serving the guests. They were dressed up as maids in black uniforms with white aprons, bonnets, collars, and cuffs; just a thought to take my mind off of our next family sorrow!

Since Cat and Launa had been gone, it had been tremendously hard on Lennon Earl. He was by himself. Beverly and her first husband, Chaplain Edwards, along with their children, Melody and Jonathan, had gone into the Navy, had moved to California, and had moved back on the East Coast of South Georgia. Their oldest daughter, Charmelita, was a sophomore at NCCU, and she remained in Durham. But Earl, as he was best known, was in and out of the judicial system. He had fathered two sons, Landis Strickland and Lennon Earl Royster, Jr., but didn't get to see them as often as he wanted. Charmelita, his niece, tried to keep him, as much as possible, connected to his sons.

Earl was "my boy," and he would do anything that I asked him to do. He'd come by the house and say, "Aunt Boot, loan me a dollar till I get on my feet." After I gave him a dollar, he knew that my next question would be, "What you standing on now, Earl?" We both grinned from ear to ear. He was a good young man, maybe lonely and lost—uncertain of his destiny. He wrote me long letters from his time of imprisonment. He had gotten sick and was brought to Duke Hospital. Pearline went to see him and let me know that he wasn't doing too well.

He had "the virus," and at the young age of thirty-six, Earl caught the morning train, bound for glory. It was in 1997, six days before his thirty-seventh birthday. Beverly was beyond devastated. She shared with me that the only time that she's ever fainted was when she faced her deceased brother, Lennon Earl, who was named after Budja and his father, Robert Earl. Robert Earl had remarried. His wife, Mary, was from Rocky Mount, NC, and they had two more sons, Kenneth Earl and Brian Keith. I remember Robert Earl's sadness at the intimate homegoing service for Earl that was held in Scarborough and Hargett's Memorial Chapel with close family, friends, and loved ones. Catherline's only son followed her homeward.

Like Beverly having to say goodbye to her sibling, a couple of months later, in July, it was me, Mozelle, and Christine's turn to give our parting words to our sibling, "Chick." She was quite a classy chick! She was articulate, elegant, fashionable—full of charm and poise! She had acquired the Northern accent, and I loved to hear her talk—all Jersey-like!

Chick had a good life; she often said it herself! Atlantic City had treated her quite well, and she had treated it even better. She and Lucas Young, Jr. had married in 1944. They bought a new, split-level home there and enjoyed inviting family and friends over for any occasion. Me and Buster would go up during our vacation times. Clearly, I remember that we went up to visit in 1956. Wonder how I remember that trip so well? Yes, because Denise came the next year. Chick would tease me all the time, saying, "You and Buster had fun and made Denise at my house."

She outlived her first husband, Otho "Buddy," who passed in 1970, her second husband, Lucas, who departed in 1971, and her son, Irving Lee, who also departed in May 1970. At the time of her homegoing, she was the longest living sister in our family. She lived ninety-one years, five months shy of her December 5th birthday--another family nonagenarian. Again, James, Jr. was able to drive us northbound to send her off, in her true, fabulous form, our loving sister—Aldonia "Chick" Lucas Young!

We had a short break from mourning after Chick's celebration of life service. Everyone was talking about the upcoming year of 2000, the last year of the 20th century. There was anticipation about problems that computers might have in transitioning from one century to another one. The year 2000 problem was labeled as the Millennium Bug or Y2K Bug. I didn't have good knowledge about computers—not their hardware, mainframe, or software—but from what I understood, there needed to be a way for computers to distinguish 1900 information from 2000 information, since both ended in 00. It was on the news quite a bit and on the minds of many Americans.

However, my mind in February 2000, the first Thursday, was on the passing of my great-nephew, Larry Elliott. Lots of folks in North Durham called him Keith. Larry, as I called him, was a free spirit, a happy-go-lucky kind of guy. His smooth demeanor reminded me a lot of Budja. He also had qualities like his mother, Pearline. She was practical and straightforward. Larry shared that every time she saw him, she was preaching a sermon. Ironically, I've thought that as she has gotten older, the more she sounded like Papa. She could have been a preacher woman. Larry knew to straighten up and do right around his mother.

Now, he had a young son and would bring him by to see me. Named after his daddy, Larry, Jr. had that great Jones smile and an even-keeled behavior. Big Larry was a hard worker; he served in the Navy, and when he got out, he worked over two decades at Duke. Like all of us, he made choices and had habits that affected his life and, conceivably, contributed to his demise.

My fondest memory of Larry was his love for my pig feet. He'd ask, "When you going to cook some pig feet, Aunt Boot?" By now, you know I can be funny, too; so, I'd smartly answer, "When you bring some pig feet over here for me to cook." We laughed together! Pearline's oldest offspring was only forty-nine when the family gave him our last hugs and sad sendoff with Scarborough and Hargett in charge of his touching homegoing service.

The twenty-first century came in on Monday, January 1, 2001, without a ton of drama and Y2K glitches. It was Mozelle, me and Christine hanging together as best sisters and lifelong friends. Who would have known that the turn of the century would pickpocket me of both of my family anchors? Mozelle had made quite an enjoyable and respectable life for herself. She loved teaching and career development for the special students at the School for the Blind. After retirement there, her fulfillment came from her involvement in all her church activities.

Despite her visual handicap, Mozelle had always been energetic and healthy. When I got the phone call from the Wake Medical Hospital nurse informing me that my year-older sister had been admitted, it caught me by surprise. Willie rushed me and Christine to Raleigh to be with her. The attending physician looked somewhat worried. He explained that she needed immediate heart surgery and told us what the complications could be. We prayed and believed God for her successful operation.

God brought her through the first surgical procedure, and she was able to go home for recuperation. Back and forth, Mozelle re-entered the hospital. She lived alone in her home in Raleigh; her next-door neighbors assisted in transporting her to and from the hospital. Within a few short weeks, Mozelle took a turn for the worse. Adding to our family history, congestive heart failure took its toll on Mozelle.

Angels came for her on Tuesday, January 23rd. Her church, Martin Street Baptist, and her pastor, Rev. Dr. David Forbes, Sr., honored her in such a special way at her homegoing service, prepared by Gailes Funeral Home, as they carried on in honor of William and Clelly. Me and Christine held hands and shared tears as the last two representatives of Junious and Olivia Jones.

There are many fond memories of Mozelle—from her coming with us to pick plums from our family's plum tree, to her graduating from North Carolina College, to her purchasing her dream home. We learned a lot from having a sister with a disability. We didn't look at her as being handicapped; we just knew that because her eyesight was limited, we had to treat her carefully and special. We learned how to share responsibilities in helping and teaching her certain lessons. One example would be Mozelle learning to tie her own shoes. She learned quickly.

When Mozelle, me and Christine went to pick plums, to keep Mozelle from running into the bushes and trees, we had her sit down with a bucket while me and Christine plucked the plums; we'd then announce, "Here come the plums" and plump them in her bucket. She was thrilled to be helping and beamed with pride as we carried them back to Mama Olivia for her to work her magic!

When Mozelle graduated from high school, she stayed with Budja and Launa on Moline Street while she attended NCC. She walked to class for four years. We celebrated her as the first Jones offspring to obtain a bachelor's college degree! She acquired a job in Durham quickly and soon had purchased her first home off Pettigrew Street. She was fortunate to get a teaching offer from the School of the Blind; she accepted it and planned her transition to Raleigh. She sold her home to Buddy and Lonie and bought her dream home on Cotton Place in the Capital City. Buddy and Lonie lived in that home until Urban Renewal forced them out of the area. Luckily, Buddy found a home on Walker Street, where they lived until Lonie passed. In recognition of Mozelle, local history documented our sister among the influential educators of North Carolina. Our family pride for Miss Hattie Mozelle Jones helped heal the hole that was left in our hearts by her homegoing.

No matter how large or small a family is, each relationship within the family circle is unique. Within our Jones unit, Christine was my "right-hand girl." Yes, it could have been because we were the last two children born or because we were the last two alive. Either way, we had a close and special bond. After we, The Joneses, had moved to North Alston Avenue, Willie and Christine found a quaint little house right across the railroad track from us on Union Street, later renamed Manteo Street. We were in shouting distance from one another.

Me and Christine talked every day about something; we found a reason to hear each other's voice, especially after losing Mozelle. Summer days began around the 20th of June, and Willie and Christine got the jump on me in canning and preparing their fruit preserves and vegetables. Willie and Christine usually had breakfast and lunch together each day. When I called on the last day of June to check on the number of jars that they had completed, Willie picked up the phone. They had finished eating lunch, and Christine had gone into the living room. Willie said they had completed five jars of preserves and were working on canning a new batch of corn. He called out to Christine to come back in the kitchen to help him cut the corn off the cobs.

Christine didn't answer. Willie called out the second time, "Christine, come back in here and give me a hand." I heard the silence and Willie's footsteps heading toward the living room. I heard him gasp, "I think I've lost Christine." I dropped the phone and headed to the back door.

By the time I got in the car, Karleshia was pushing me to the passenger's side and cranking up the car. Within seconds, I was across the street, up the steps, and into the front door of 1311 Manteo Street. Christine was poised gracefully in the chair by the door that separated the kitchen from the living room. She looked peaceful; she was always pretty. Denise and Rev. High arrived,

The emergency attendants raced through the front door, pushing me aside, and headed straight for Christine. They moved her to the bedroom and stretched her out on the bed as they administered CPR and chest compressions. Willie and I watched in shock. Tears rapidly rolled down our cheeks.

Moments before, Willie and Christine were having lunch, laughing and talking and canning corn; and now my precious sister, my eighty years of companionship, my secret holder of every story that I ever told her—slipped away on that very day! Another family member was plagued by heart disease-cardio-pulmonary failure.

Different than with Budja, the head EMT attendant pronounced her departed there on the scene and urged Willie to call his preferred undertaker. Like a sick puppy, Willie went thru the motions. Fisher Funeral Parlor arrived, got all the necessary information, and took my baby sister, Christine, away. Only five months after Mozelle left the two of us in painful agony, Christine left me all alone!

As most things were segregated as we grew up, cemeteries and graveyards were designated for either—colored or white. If it were not a site designated for African Americans, then we were denied burial accommodations. Well, Willie had his eyes on a huge cemetery near the Wellons Village area. It was only a short distance from where we lived, and it was very well-kept. There was no need to ask; the answer was "no" to us; they did not sell plots to coloreds. But things change, and patience is a virtue.

The Woodlawn Memorial Park was created in 1821. It was quite historical in the Durham Area. Although it had a veteran's section, Caucasian soldiers were only allowed. But new management took over, and it was a new day. The new White manager told Willie that, "color didn't matter, that money didn't have no color, and besides, dollar bills are not black or white." Willie was able to buy two gravesites. I remember Clelly messing with him, saying, "Willie Johnson done moved up and got graves in a white cemetery."

As we took Christine to her final resting place, it didn't matter to me, at all, where it was. I didn't want to be going in that direction or any direction to deposit my last, loving sister into a mausoleum. Her homegoing service was precious and treasured. Pastor High spoke of her heavenly crown, and the pearly gates opened wide for her arrival. I wish he could have spoken of the Grand Canyon-like hollowness that I felt inside. I kissed Christine Jones Johnson—goodbye, realizing that the broken Jones Family circle had only one link remaining, the knee-baby girl, me.

A tremendous volume of fond memories flooded my mind of me and Christine. The first one was how we learned to draw water from the well by alternating our hands on the rope—my right hand on top, her right hand next, my left hand, and then her left hand—as we pulled on the rope, we'd start over and continue until the full bucket of water was out of the well. Neither one of us was strong enough to pull the rope by ourselves, but together we were strong like Sampson. Mama Olivia called it a team effort!

Christine was a team player. She didn't choose to usher at Mount Vernon, like me and Lizzie, but one of her greatest joys was teaching the J. E. Best Sunday School class! Me and Lizzie were in her class. She was an excellent teacher, teaching that class for decades.

This next memory is classic for me. After summer on the farm, when it was time to reap the harvest, the family and workers went over all forty acres in the field gathering the tobacco leaves. This particular September, when it was all done, me and Christine went back into the field to find tobacco sticks that had been left. Can you believe that we found thirteen extra sticks of tobacco? We earned money for our extra work, thirteen dollars. I took my six dollars and fifty cents and hid it behind a loose board in the house, thinking that I'd have money for Christmas. Come time for Christmas, I went to my secret hiding board, and the money was gone.

I cried my eyes out, and Christine sat beside me and started crying, too. Papa saw both of his baby girls wailing, and his heart was touched. He knew how hard we had worked, and he caringly and graciously replaced my earnings. I was able to buy Christmas gifts for my whole family! Just like in that instance, during our entire lives, Christine was my "right-hand sister."

I thanked God for Ethelean "Pete" because the weeks following the life celebration of Christine were blurry, hard, and unstable. Had it not been for Pete, I'm not sure that I would have pulled through the fog. I read my Word and prayed, yet the grief overwhelmed me. Pete was my best, real, and true friend. Her comfort and support meant the world to me. I knew her as a little girl in the country. Her parents were well-respected in the Knightdale, Wake County area. Mr. Morton Robertson, folks called him Maude, and his wife, Gracie, sang so beautifully that I'm sure the angels in heaven stopped and listened. They were long-standing members of Riley Hill Baptist; that's where we would hear them "bring the house down."

Mack picked the best wife for him. Pete was quiet-natured, but coming from a larger family, she knew how to socialize with people of different age levels. She was good with children. She had lots of children as her customers, yet she and Mack never had children of their own. After a few years with McLeod's Beauty Nook, Mack added a beauty parlor onto the back of their home, and Pete became the proprietor of Dunn's Beauty Shop at 1307 North Alston Avenue. Our friendship remained solid, and we never had an ill word; we were happy for each other's growth.

Both, me and Pete smoked for a good while. I quit in 1965. My main reason centered around being a "smoking usher." It didn't seem to fit the person that I wanted to be as a representative of Christ; so, I stopped. Pete told me that I must not have been addicted to smoking because it wasn't that easy to quit. She tried several times to stop; each time was like a mountain climb—going up so far and turning around heading back down—not able to reach the peak.

At the beginning of the next year, only months after Mozelle and Christine had made their transitions, Pete made a doctor's appointment. I thought nothing of it other than a routine check-up. She wasn't feeling bad, hurting, or sick. The doctor took tests and set a time to follow up. When Mack and Pete came back from the follow-up appointment, they came with fear in their eyes. The report showed a tiny spot on her lungs. That day, Pete stopped smoking!

Unfortunately, it was too late, cancer was there, and chemotherapy began. I washed her hair after the first treatment, and all her hair came out in the sink, leaving a clean, bald head. Pete had long, pretty, thick hair, and it was gone. I went with her to a few doctor visits; I sat numb and tense. Could this be happening? Is my best friend going to be alright? "Dear Lord, Dear Lord, touch my dear, dear friend," I prayed.

I visited Pete every day. On one visit, she looked at me and said, "I'm hurting, Boot, pray for me." I got down on my knees beside her hospice bed and prayed for my forever friend. I thanked God for her life, for being her comforter, and prayed that His will be done. Her sisters, Gladys and "Mark" came and spent the last weeks with Pete. They always treated me like their adopted sister.

Only a couple of months after her diagnosis, on Monday, the 15th of April, God touched Pete with His finger of love and whispered gently, "Come on home." She suffered some, but not long. A close friend from the North Durham neighborhood, Dorothy "Dot" Kelly, came to express her sympathy and broke down like a bombed building. She was great friends with Catherline, and Pete was her loving beautician. We cried and embraced for what seemed like hours. Mack was brokenhearted—hurting and sad. A special, special lady had gone to heaven.

This was too much for me! It was like losing a sister all over again. Friends and neighbors, we were for fifty-four years. My fond memories of Pete stretch out over the decades. We worked together every day; we went nearly everywhere together. We did worship at different churches; she was a member of Greater St. Paul Missionary Baptist on Juniper Street. Other than that, we shared each other's lives on a regular basis.

What I think most fondly about when remembering Pete are all the Cosmetologist Conventions that we attended. Our local club was Cosmetology Club #1. Mrs. Margaret Minor was the president when we joined, but not long afterward, the club members voted her out. Me and Pete "walked on eggshells" as we became more involved. We traveled to different cities and states and enjoyed meeting fellow beauticians from all over the country. We both served in various Club positions for close to fifty years. I was elected President and held that office for thirty years. The club was our shared delight!

When we are weak, our God is strong in us! Truly, I found that out as time passed on. There were more goodbyes to other family members, dear friends, and special church members. Life is only a short journey, even if you live more than a hundred years. There's no way that I could include the surplus of names, but I will add just a few more.

A month before Pete's ascension, Mary Ruby High, who had married a Banfield, met her maker on the 7th of March. A couple of years later, her sister, Ramona High, who married a Graham, "flew away" in June 2004, followed by Katie Jones Wilcher, Yi's daughter, on the 15th of November. Mary Ruby and Pete were born in 1925, Ramona in 1926, and Katie in 1927. Pete and my three nieces were all young ladies in their prime of life.

Along with our Denise departing from us in 2013, we said farewell to the wonderful father of Syvil and Allan, Jr., the month before—February 25th. Allan Summers, Sr., the love of Pearline's life, was a God-fearing, hard-working, strong example of a man. He fought a lengthy battle with the cancer culprit. Allan, Sr. totally enjoyed all the family functions, and he was present at hundreds of them, you could depend on him to be there!

Another beloved father in our extended family succumbed on the 20th of September 2013; Beverly and her brothers, Kenneth and Brian, felt the pain of losing their hero. Mary became a widow when Robert Earl (Royster) Coleman, after a brief illness, slipped away. When he was young, I remember him playing baseball. He, too, like me and Buster, loved the game, and he was a great ball player.

After Buster passed, I depended on Mack and Willie to help me with maintenance, other household issues, and emergency transportation. They were always there for me. Willie had celebrated his ninety-sixth birthday on March 9, 2016—a strong nonagenarian. He was sharp-minded, although he had a few visits to the hospital and rehabilitation center. Gradually, I could see him declining and weakening. As he got frailer, his son, Leroy, came to care for him.

He entered Duke hospital around the beginning of December. Beverly came from Georgia on many occasions to spend time with him. She reminded me that "because of Uncle Willie, I had a paper route in the second grade. He helped develop that entrepreneurial spirit in me." Willie Lee "Sug" Johnson went to be with the Lord peacefully, on Wednesday, the 21st, right before Christmas. He was laid to rest beside his Christine at Woodlawn the next week.

I do remember Willie having a paper route with an African American Newspaper. He worked diligently, having his skills in auto mechanics, business, newspapers, and singing. His smile was infectious, and his heart was big as the ocean. A memory etched in my mind is when we took our picture together for Mount Vernon's anniversary directory. That photograph was a great reflection of the mutual admiration and appreciation that we had for each other.

The same day that Wille slept away, God called Yi's son, Rev. Junious "Bro" Jones, on home. He was Papa's namesake, and he's the only offspring that I can remember that followed in Papa's footsteps as a minister/preacher of the Gospel. He pastored Haw River Baptist Church in Pittsboro, NC, for twenty years. His wife preceded him in death, and he left his daughter and son, Christi and Christopher. He had turned seventy-one on his November 8th birthday. I always remembered "Bro" as a gentleman, even as a young boy. He possessed the politest behavior and the best manners. His life was a shining light for our Lord and Savior. Heaven welcomed two mighty men homeward—from labor to rest.

In 2017, it was approaching sixty-nine years that me and Mack would have lived next door to each other. I never thought that he nor I would live at any other address different than North Alston Avenue. I may have stated these words in a prior chapter, but they are worth repeating—"everything must change." Mack was able to care for himself until one day, he stopped. He'd forget to eat and take care of his body. He had moments where he wasn't sure what he had or had not done,

He trusted Pearline and agreed for her to take care of him to a certain degree. Allan, Jr.'s wife, Rita, and Syvil helped Pearline by bringing him meals and doing whatever cleaning they could do. After a short while, it became necessary for Mack to have 24-hour care. It was hard for him to agree at first; he'd talk to me, and I'd listen. It was the best decision for him.

He was accepted at the Rose Manor Nursing home, the same one that Buddy was in. Syvil took me to see him a few times. He always knew who I was, and we had good fellowship together. The facility recognized his ninety-second birthday on the 20th of April. It appeared that he was getting stronger. The daily routine agreed with Mack. His time in the Army had given him discipline and structure; that's also what he received at Rose Manor. He seemed at peace.

Mack's earthly journey ended early on a Monday morning, the 24th of July. When I got the call, I cried. Mack was my last connection to the country—the road leading to Jones Chapel, our days at Rosenwald, and all the fun we had playing in our big yard. Floods of great memories swirled in my head. I laughed out loud when I pictured me pulling Mack down the dirt road, and he, along with his mattress, slid out onto the ground! I was still pulling the carriage when a neighbor screamed out, "You dropped the baby!" It didn't hurt him; at least he didn't cry! Mack, Lizzie and Burt's only child, my steadfast nephew and another family nonagenarian was placed beside his loving wife of fifty-four years at Glenview Memorial Park.

No, I didn't expect to live this long, and at the same time, it was an eye-opening reality check to look back at all those I named who have gone on before me and those not named that are planted in my heart. They all played a cherished and important role in my life. Plus, when I recall the health challenges that could have taken me out, my expectations of long life were hazy.

I am a CANCER SURVIVOR! Not many knew or know that part of my story. It wasn't a secret; it was just a matter of acknowledging and dealing with that unexpected cancer culprit! Thinking back over a decade, I had gone to church that Sunday and went to visit Mary, George's wife, on Monday. During our visit, I got a catch in my side and couldn't move. I could feel a little lump in my stomach—soft and the size of a small ball. I felt heavy on one side of my body.

On Tuesday, I literally had shingles that damaged the nerves in my breast. They were red and tender. Berma stayed with me all day and held my hand while I was in pain. Then on Wednesday, Denise had a guy come to change her tire; he smelt badly, and the stench made me vomit. Denise insisted that I go to the doctor. I had made up my mind to go on that Friday. Several tests were run, blood taken, and a diagnosis was made immediately. It was the last test that showed conclusively; I had colon cancer. The medical staff was on it. Dr. James Wilson, a cancer surgeon, arrived promptly and showed me the pictures of what had to be taken out—the cancer and part of my intestines.

The only day that the operation room was available for the next week or two was Saturday morning, the next day! I didn't have time to be afraid or wonder should I have gotten a second opinion. It was Dr. Wilson saying, "I can do it at 7:00 a.m." and asking, "Mrs. McLeod, Do I have your consent?" I consented and said, "Let's go." He operated. God was in the midst!

Dr. Wilson informed me that he would know by that Wednesday if I'd have to do chemotherapy treatments. On Wednesday morning, he came in with a partial smile to confirm that no chemotherapy was needed. I rejoiced and thanked the Lord! Dr. Wilson had me follow up with him once a year for five years. After five years, still cancer-free, I quit going to see him. He and his wife retired and moved to the mountains to live. Both of them were genuinely nice people. A great "God bless" to all cancer survivors!

Later that same year, I encountered another vomiting spell that led to the removal of my gallbladder. When the doctor showed it to me, it crumbled up in his hand. Indeed, there were many occasions that could have stopped me in my tracks, so why did I live, and Lizzie lost her battle? Why have I outlived so many church brothers and sisters, so many family members, a boatload of friends, neighbors, and peers? The answers, my friend, are "blowing in the wind."

What I mean by that is—only our Heavenly Father is qualified to respond to those questions. He knows! I don't, you don't, and we don't know, but he does. Cora Jones "Boot" McLeod didn't expect to live this long, yet she is so grateful that she has! Thus far, God has not finished with her yet!

Chapter 15
A Century of Living—Centenarian!

Two thousand eighteen was an astonishing year! There was so much excitement stirring about activities, birthday celebrations, gatherings, and road trips. My great-niece, Catherline's daughter, Beverly, spearheaded the upcoming agendas.

She had organized an incredible birthday dinner for her grandparents, Budja and Launa, for their seventy-ninth and seventy-seventh birthdays in 1988, which brought together so many of our family members and friends before they were absent from our circle. It didn't seem like thirty years had passed so swiftly.

Beverly came to Durham to visit me in January 2018. She and her husband, Willie, live in Georgia. Her Uncle Ronald Rhodes had passed, and his homegoing service was held in Ridgeway, South Carolina; she attended the service and drove on up to spend a few days with me.

On that visit, we chatted each day about some of everything: what did I like to do, what were some of my favorite childhood memories, what were my favorite colors, foods, and tv shows; how did me and Buster stay married so long, how many years had I been a member of Mount Vernon, and what did it mean to me to have lived almost one hundred years? She got me thinking. She really zipped opened my mind to happenings that I hadn't thought about for a long time. I was talking, and she was writing in a teal-green, thick notebook, all that I said.

As we talked about a hundredth birthday celebration, I shared that I loved breakfast! She exclaimed, "I love breakfast, too!" So right then and there, it was decided that my birthday event would be a breakfast celebration. I never imagined, in a hundred years, that one hundred people would show up to celebrate my birthday!

During that visit was the first time that we talked about a book recapping my life—a true, historical account of growing up in the country, moving to Durham, getting married, starting a business, and all of the triumphs and victories, the trials and tribulations faced up to present, an autobiography.

She seriously discussed the value of sharing my history, my journey, and my life with readers around the world. "Imagine all the lives that you will encourage, inspire, and touch with the Autobiography of Cora Jones "Boot" McLeod," she asked, with her arms open wide and her head tilted back looking like *Rocky* in his movies reaching the top of his zenith! At first, my mind couldn't extend that far. But as time had its way, I could see it, because she could see it!

The wheels were in motion, and the train was on track. Beverly "Eagle" Rogers, as she is called, was on a mission and a venture! She set an appointment to meet with Pastor Washington to get his/the church's suggestions and support. She set up times to speak with James, Jr. and the granddaughters, LaKishia, Karleshia, and Krystal, to get ideas and opinions, recommendations, and thoughts to start the ball rolling in March and celebrate right up to my August month when I would become a brand-new centenarian.

I am not certain if I had ever heard the word centenarian. If I had, the question still would have been, "What's a centenarian?" By definition, a centenarian is someone who has reached a hundred years of age. One of my best classes at Hillside High was the English class. I remember prefixes and suffixes and how they help define a word. Centenarian derives from a Latin word, *centen(i),* meaning "a hundred each," and the suffix -an denotes a person.

This great-niece of mine shared with me that there are deluxe names for all the age brackets. Just for good information, if you are reading my autobiography and you are age ten to nineteen, you are a denarian; and what if you are between twenty and twenty-nine, you are saluted as a vicenarian. Beverly's oldest grandson, Christopher, just joined in March 2021 all of the thirty to thirty-nine tricenarian readers, and if you are in your fine forties, you are a quadragenarian.

Let's continue: if you are in your focused fifties, you are a quinquagenarian; to the sexagenarian reader, you are in your sixties; having hit your seventies, you are called a septuagenarian; if you are in your roaring eighties, your group is octogenarians; and as my eldest niece, Budja's oldest daughter, celebrated her *Big 9-0* in December 2021, she, like others of you in your nineties, will be classed as a nonagenarian.

To my fellow centenarians who are traveling back with me in history and to all readers of all age brackets and deluxe name titles, thank you and thank you again for allowing me to share with you my journey. It has been a great one, and with the blessings of the Lord, it continues on!

For the five months leading to my special day, a planned activity was put on the agenda beginning in March. Our first engagement was an afternoon church program on the 4th of March, held by the Durham Station of the National Council of Negro Women (NCNW) at Peace Missionary Baptist Church on Hwy 55. It was entitled, Women's History Month Service—"Phenomenal Women."

NCNW is a well-respected organization that was founded by Dr. Mary McLeod Bethune, a political activist, a prominent educator, and a community visionary, in 1935. She was born the same year as Papa (1875), and Buster didn't claim to be any kin to her. She was the fifteenth of seventeen children, and her parents were former slaves. Large families were a norm!

Education changed the direction of her life. She was involved in different community roles and organizations before she founded the NCNW as a platform "with a more explicit civil rights agenda." Her vision was to have a unified force of black women's groups "fighting to improve racial conditions nationally and internationally." It has an outreach of close to four million women. Based in Washington, DC, the NCNW continues to fulfill its mission through advocacy and over two hundred community-based services and programs in Africa and the USA.

I enjoyed the church gathering. It was an excellent program recognizing a variety of women from different professions in the Durham community who had excelled in the scientific field.

Two of the hosts, Pastor Rachel Green and President Joyce Scarborough, made me feel very welcome.

A reception followed the program. Krystal, Kayla, Beverly, and her daughter, Melody, and a family friend, Smitty, had accompanied me, and we all delighted in the fellowship and the food. I was blessed to meet and get acquainted with a few of the ladies present: Mrs. Mamie Alston, Mrs. Catherine Ferrell, Mrs. Cora Cole-McFadden, Mrs. Lou Barnes, and her daughter, Beverly Evans, Ms. Cole, Ms. Hunter, Ms. Packenham, Ms. Turner and Mrs. Vivian C. Samuels. It was a great start to my five-month countdown!

April's activity was more of a ladies' day out. It was just me and Beverly enjoying the day together on the 5th of April. It began with a manicure and pedicure at Hollywood Nail Spa in Morrisville, NC. The staff and technicians were so surprised that I was ninety-nine and could get around without extra help required. That is one thing that I constantly thank the Lord for, the gift of mobility. What a pampering and relaxing outing at Hollywood!

Our next pitstop was at the Sheraton Imperial Hotel, Emperor Blvd. Beverly chose this location for the August grand finale. We stopped there for Ms. Anita Johnson, the Catering and Sales Manager, to meet me and me to meet her. "Meeting the person responsible for the success of your celebration gives her a face-to-face connection to know for whom she's working so hard," urged my organizer, Mrs. Rogers.

It must have worked; Ms. Johnson was super excited to meet me! She laughed and was beaming bright like a Christmas tree. She introduced me to numerous employees and administrative staff. We took pictures, and everyone wished me a happy upcoming birthday! At the Sheraton, I also met a young man, Willie Joyner, and thru conversation, we discovered that we were kinfolk on the Peppers' side of my family. Joyner is married to one of Beverly's best friends in Durham, Evangeline. If I've said it once, I've said it twice, it's a small world, and you never know who you will meet on any given day!

Onward we proceeded to the North Point Drive IHOP Restaurant to satisfy our hunger pains. More friendly faces greeted us, and when the workers found out that I was counting down to my one-hundredth birthday, they gathered around me, clapping, laughing, smiling, and wishing me a great celebration. I was served the biggest pancakes that my eyes had ever seen, nearly big as tires on a compact car. Yes, I love breakfast, and I enjoyed my meal, especially those whopper-super-sized pancakes!

The May countdown occasion was an emotional one for me. Our function was on May 11th, the graduation of my granddaughter, Krystal, from Durham's historic North Carolina Central University (NCCU) in the master's program; the same school that my Denise, her mother, had graduated from in 1979. My heart was drowning in gratitude and happiness that my Lord had allowed me to see this day.

When Karleshia and Krystal came to live with me as little girls, I prayed and asked the Lord to sustain my life long enough for me to see them grow up to be able to provide and take care of themselves. He answered my prayer. High school graduations were special, their first degreed graduations were double special, and this Master's graduation was extra, extra special!

As we looked at the success and destruction of the Hayti District, the story of NCCU is a continuous success narrative of Negro vision. In 1910, Dr. James E. Shepard founded what was called the National Religious Training School and Chautauqua for the Colored Race, Inc. in the Hayti District.

Dr. Shepard was a civil servant, a prominent pharmacist, and a wealthy businessman. As President of the college, he boldly declared its mission and purpose as "the development in young men and women of the character and sound academic training requisite for real service to the nation."

After the North Carolina state legislature changed the school's name to the North Carolina College for Negros, it officially became the first state-supported liberal arts college for Negro students in the nation. Other school name changes occurred, but in 1969 the college was added to the University of North Carolina system and became North Carolina Central University. Krystal's graduation was the one hundred thirty-first commencement exercise at NCCU.

I was a little worried about the crowds of people and where I could be seated to get a good position to see Krystal. With Willie and Beverly's help, they found the exact entrance to the auditorium on the first level where the students would have their procession, and because I used a borrowed wheelchair for convenience, I was in an excellent spot to see everything clearly.

The ceremony was timely and touching. Afterward, a separate presentation of degrees for the College of Behavioral and Social Sciences was held at a different venue on campus. I was honored to present Krystal with her Master of Science degree in Criminal Justice. My short speech was from my heart, and it brought tears to many eyes, including hers:

"You've always been an obedient child, and you've always been smart. I know now nothing can stop you from achieving your goals. Keep going, Honey, don't let nothing stop you. Grandmama never thought she would be here to present you this degree. Keep your head up and keep going (2018)."

Her father, Robert Daye, attended and celebrated this great achievement with his daughter, as well as her cousin, LaKishia, and her parents, James, Jr. and Barbara Jean. Kayla was proud of her mother. It was a happy, family affair. Dinner plans emerged at the Bonefish Grill on NC Hwy 751. The meal I ordered was fantastic, but much more food than I could eat in one sitting (smile). Our celebration for the graduate continued. It was a long and momentous day. We were all so proud of Krystal Lynn!

The month of June came rather fast, and Beverly was oscillating between countdown options. I had been invited by Lydia Jane to the McLeod Reunion in Lumberton, NC. Lydia Jane is Buster's niece, his sister Sis's daughter. It had been quite a time passed since I had enjoyed the company of my McLeod side of the family. I asked Beverly if we could make that our June occasion. "Most definitely, Aunt Boot, this is your countdown, and whatever you want to add or subtract, it's fine with us," she responded.

The Lumberton trip was added to our agenda for Saturday, the 9th of June. When I told James, Jr., he was as excited as I was because he hadn't seen most of the family in a long time, too. He looked forward to spending time with his father's descendants. The two hours' drive didn't seem long at all. Me, Krystal, and Kayla rode with Willie and Beverly in their faithful, black Dodge caravan. LaKishia drove herself and her parents from Charlotte, NC., which was about the same distance as from Durham.

You should have heard all the screams and shouts when I arrived, "There's Aunt Boot!" "Aunt Boot is here!" or "Look, Aunt Boot made it!" They all were super elated and couldn't believe that I was still alive. They were happy, too, to see James, Jr. and his wife and daughter. It was so many babies and children there, and I kept trying to find out who was whose mother and father or grandmother and grandfather. It was a task unaccomplished.

They had piles and piles of food—chicken, fish, hamburgers, hot dogs, ribs, seafood, and a ton of mouth-watering side dishes. The McLeod ladies could always cook, it was no surprise that their children's children could cook, as well, and everything was delicious and finger-licking good.

Lydia Jane, who was born a DeBerry, and was now a Robinson, looked terrific. Her daughters were beautiful and stylish. Her son, John Wayne, gave me a big bear hug. Buster's great-nephew, Terry DeBerry, seemed thrilled that we had spent this time together. He was Lorraine's son, Lydia Jane's oldest sister.

We told everyone about the approaching birthday celebration planned for August. Many said they were planning to attend, and they did! I asked Terry's brother, Ardell McArn, if he would sing one of my favorite songs at my birthday breakfast. He delightfully accepted. We hated to leave. It was a cherished, great time. Buster's family always made me feel close to them, like my real family. They *are* my real family!

To say that July 2018 was a power-packed month might be an understatement! This hot summer month's agenda included a family trip to Washington, DC, the recognition and formal resolution from Chairperson Wendy Jacobs of the Durham County Board of County Commissioners (DCBCC), and the Live C-Span recognition from North Carolina's U.S. House of Representative, G.K. Butterfield on the House floor.

The Washington, DC trip was promoted as the crescendo before the grand finale. Many of the immediate family members desired to attend, but couldn't alter their schedules, so we proceeded forward with the planned agenda. Unfortunately, the faithful, black Dodge caravan was totaled loss when a driver ran a stoplight and crashed into Beverly a week or so before our scheduled departing time. Thankfully, she wasn't hurt or injured. God had his hand upon her!

We've heard older family members say, "Be careful; you can get another vehicle, but we can't get another you!" True statement! She and Willie rented another Dodge caravan, off-white, and we were back on course. A dear sister-in-Christ from Mount Vernon had called me earlier in the month to check on me. I told her about the July venture, and she got excited about the trip. I invited her to come along, and that was a great decision. Sister Edith Umstead became my room partner and a joyful bonus to our journey!

Early morning, Monday the 16th of July, Willie and Beverly picked up me and Edith, and we headed up Interstate 85 N toward DC. They had their grandson, Melody's little guy, Adrien Lucas, with them, and he was the best behaved, politest little fellow that I had met in quite a while. Edith fell in love with his genuine, calm, and cool nature. He would turn seven two days after I reached one hundredth.

The weather was perfect, not too hot, moderately warm with a gentle breeze. The traffic was light, considering it was a workday Monday. Willie was a great driver. His driving wasn't frightening to senior citizens, at least not this one (smile). We did stop midway to DC at the Golden Corral on Providence Road in Richmond, VA, for lunch.

I had not been accustomed to so much love and recognition from strangers, but it seemed like turning one hundred brings out the best in others. The manager at the Golden Corral and all the available workers came to my table and cheered and clapped and sang to me, making me feel so blessed and grateful to God for allowing my golden days to roll on and on!

We arrived safely to Washington, DC, and registered at the Days Inn, Connecticut Ave., NW. They had a nice welcome banner, just for me. How special of them! James Jr., Barbara Jean, and LaKishia arrived shortly behind us. After getting settled in our rooms, we were hungry again.

We found a well-known restaurant called the Potbelly Sandwich Shop—Good Vibes, Great Sandwiches.® It was within walking distance and had been serving since 1977. Using, once again, a rented wheelchair for convenience, we strolled along Connecticut Avenue till we got to the shop. We all had salads and a variety of classic sandwiches. The atmosphere was pleasant, and we chitchatted till time for them to close.

On the way back to the Days Inn, you could hear the sounds of the Capital City—animals barking and cooing at each other; music flowing and tingling thru the air; people conversing and debating their opinions; and traffic bustling and honking in rhythm as the crisp air reminded us that night had fallen. Back at the inn, the pull of a long day had us prepare fast for a comfortable night's rest. I said my prayers and thanked my heavenly Father for my adult adventure in DC.

For our Tuesday agenda, we headed to the unparalleled National Museum of African American History & Culture (NMAAHC). We (me and Beverly) decided earlier in the year to enroll as charter members of the museum, so I was beyond excited to tour this remarkable gallery as a new member. We met Debbie Williams Buffalo, a junior high school friend of Beverly's, who was there with some of her church family from the St. John Baptist congregation from Durham, NC. She had reserved the tickets for both of our groups.

The greeters were exceptionally pleasant and helped our approval to enter go quite smoothly. Charmelita, my great-great niece, Beverly's oldest daughter, met us there, along with Linda Phillips, Beverly's BFF, since seventh grade. We became the magnificent ten team!

If you and your family have been to the museum, you can give witness to the elaborate magnitude and overwhelming vastness that it covers in African American History. If you and your family have not been to the museum, mere words are not enough to encourage you to do so! If I could be a billboard—bold and huge—flashing across the screen of the sky, this is one purpose for which I would not hesitate to flash brightly. Hoping it would get you and yours to plan a trip to this unbelievable venue.

For good information: The National Museum of African American History and Culture (NMAAHC), located at 1400 Constitution Avenue NW, Washington, DC., is the only national museum exclusively dedicated to the documentation of African American culture, history, and life. It opened to the public in September 2016 as a result of an Act of Congress in 2003. It is the nineteenth and newest museum of the famous Smithsonian Institution.

Yet, it's not just for African Americans; it is for all people. One of its four pillars is, "It helps all Americans see how their stories, their histories, and their cultures are shaped and informed by global influences." The NMAAHC is a public institution open to all, where everybody is welcome to collaborate, participate and learn more about African American history and culture. It had collected more than thirty-five thousand artifacts, and like me, nearly one hundred thousand persons had become members. The Founding Director, Lonnie G. Bunch III, stated, "there are few things as powerful and as important as a people, as a nation that is steeped in its history."

Being at the NAAHC was one of the most powerful experiences of my life. We spent the entire afternoon at the museum, which is not nearly enough time to cover three levels of chronological history. We took a break to dine in the exceptional cafeteria inside the gallery. The menu was quite appealing, from down-home cooking like fried chicken and collard greens to homemade desserts and ice cream. Hundreds of visitors had the same idea because the cafeteria was filled with people from all over the nation and various countries of the world.

From exhibitions detailing the elaborate commerce of slavery, including a full-sized slave ship crossing the ocean to the eras of segregation and Jim Crow, to displays of African American accomplishments in—inventions, journalism, military, movies, music, politics, science, sports, television, theater, and many more—all the way to the African American presence in the White House, I was spellbound by all of the compelling history captivated in one immense locale. Never before, a museum so impactful, intellectual, intriguing, and stimulating to my thinking. I wanted to cry and shout at the same time!

We talked about the sheer joy of being there as we departed from our tour. We could only imagine what it would be like in decades from now when little Adrien comes back in his twenties, thirties, or forties and brings his children and family. A family legacy would be carried on into the next generations.

We left the museum and drove to the Martin Luther King, Jr. Memorial, located at 1964 Independence Ave. SW, which is adjacent to the Franklin D. Roosevelt Memorial. I thought about my brother, Yi when we passed the FDR's Memorial. The MLK, Jr. Memorial shared a direct sightline between the Lincoln and Jefferson Memorials. What an accumulation of American history within a short span of real estate.

The MLK, Jr. Memorial was created in honor of the Civil Rights Act of 1964, in which Dr. King played an important role. He was one of the most active, influential, and prominent leaders of the Civil Rights Movement. His speeches fueled support for his non-violence platform and protests. He helped organize the 1963 March on Washington and is remembered for his monumental "I Have a Dream" speech given only minutes from where we were, at the Lincoln Memorial. It is a lasting tribute to Dr. King's legacy, and it was the first memorial in Washington, DC, for a Black/Negro man.

We found a great parking space in front of the memorial entrance. The walkway led to the centerpiece of the memorial park—a 30-foot statue of Dr. King's image carved into the Stone of Hope. That stone is emerging from two large boulders, called the Mountain of Despair. Cut deeply into the side of the stone are the words, "Out of the mountain of despair, a stone of hope."

Different quotes from Dr. King were etched into the wall surrounding the memorial. We read all the inscriptions and soaked in those priceless moments. This, too, was touching to me because it made me think of how far we have come as a race of people and all the many, many people who donated their lives, willing and unwilling so that we could have the liberties and rights proper for all Americans.

As we were calling it a day, James, Jr. reminded me that Buster's nephew lived in Washington, DC, Joe Louis Love. Joe was Buster's sister, Julia's son. Julia and her husband, John Love, married about four months before we did in December 1935. Joe Louis would come to stay with us often; he and James, Jr. were good cousin friends.

We called Joe Louis, got directions, and made our way to visit him. As always, we talked about the good old days back in Lumberton and Durham. His wife, Carrie, joined in the fun and laughter. Joe Louis's only sister, Rhumel, was sick and not doing as well at that time. Joe Louis was excited that his eighty-third birthday was approaching in October. He was thrilled that I would be turning one hundred in a few weeks.

He and his wife promised to send me a birthday card. It was a short and sweet time of fellowship, and I was so happy to see Joe Louis after many bygone years.

Sheer exhaustion led to another restful night after we packed and prepared to pull out the next day, Wednesday morning. I was grateful to the Day's Inn Manager, Peggy, and some of her great staff, including Anna, Christina, Louise, Nora, and Steven. They treated me and my family with such great hospitality. I hoped to come again!

LaKishia and her parents spent a little extra time vacationing. But we arrived safely back to Durham on Wednesday evening. I was ever so grateful to Willie, Beverly, (and Adrien) for a well-planned and well-successful trip to our nation's Capital. I was appreciative to Edith for her great companionship. When asked how she enjoyed the trip, she remarked, "I really had a great time! The museum tour was 'worth its weight in gold.' I am grateful to have been invited. So thankful."

On the next Monday, the 23rd of July, The Durham County Board of County Commissioners (DCBCC) held their Regular Session meeting at 7:00 p.m. The Clerk to the Board, Terri Lea Hugie, MPA, had sent an email stating the DCBCC would like to recognize my upcoming birthday with a ceremonial resolution.

Karleshia and Krystal and my great-grandchildren, Kassan, Khalil, Kaiden, and Kayla escorted me to this session. LaKishia and her parents watched online. Beverly came back from Georgia. Edith and her husband, Deacon Ron Umstead, were present. And we all arrived right on time. Chairperson Wendy Jacobs opened the Session and called it to order.

Many items were listed for the board to address. The first recognition was in honor of the late Mrs. Peggy Johnson Tapp, who was the co-owner and proprietor of The Chicken Hut, formally the Chicken Box. It is a locally-owned restaurant that has served the Durham community for over sixty years. She was honored for her untiring service. It was shared that the Chicken Hut gives away five hundred meals a day to help feed people in need. Her son, Claiborne Tapp III, and her nephew, Jeff Johnson, were present to accept the presentation in honor of Mrs. Tapp, "A legend in our community," stated Jacobs.

My resolution presentation immediately followed with Chairperson Jacobs acknowledging that it was" fitting that the second ceremonial item is in recognition of another great woman in our community with a resolution honoring her upcoming century birthday" (DCBCC 2018). Commissioner James Hill read the resolution with true passion. Each commissioner voiced special sentiments and well wishes. It was heart-warming to hear from Commissioners—Heidi Carter, Brenda Howerton, and Ellen Reckhow. Chairperson Jacobs closed with these words:

"Mrs. McLeod, it's really such an honor to be able to see you and have you here. It's really amazing to recognize your century birthday, and we all, I think, aspire to be like you, if we have the opportunity to live to be one hundred years old. Just to see you here with your family, grandchildren, and great-grands… We really appreciate you coming tonight."

They gave me an honor that I will remember for the rest of my life! (youtube.com/Durham County BOCC July 23, 1918)

The month wasn't over yet! Two days later, on Wednesday, the 25th of that incredible month, another special surprise arose. Thanks to my pastor, Rev. Jerome Washington, Congressman G.K. Butterfield, the United States Representative from NC, surprisingly spoke on the House Floor at the Morning Hour. The Morning Hour permitted members to speak on any topic for a designated time of five minutes. Can you imagine the topic that he spoke upon?

Yes, he spoke on the upcoming hundredth birthday celebrations. Now, it wasn't just about my birthday. He acknowledged three members of Mount Vernon Baptist, Durham, NC, who would reach their one-hundredth birthdays soon to come.

Indeed, I was blessed to be in the number, along with Mrs. Christine Johnson Umstead and Mrs. Annie Bell Gilmore Rogers. Mrs. Umstead would celebrate her centenarian birthday on the 16th of August, and Mrs. Rogers would celebrate her centenarian birthday on the 20th of October. We were the three most senior citizens at our church.

Congressman Butterfield shared nationwide about our backgrounds and our different, unique accomplishments individually and about our Christian faith collectively. Mrs. Rogers's family were founding members of our church. I shared with you about Papa and our family joining in 1934, and Mrs. Umstead joined the church in 1948. We were referenced as pillars of Mount Vernon Baptist Church, and we were thankful for our spiritual foundations. He concluded his floor time with these words,

"And so, I am grateful to these remarkable women for their love of humanity and contributions to their community. I ask my colleagues to join me in wishing these three great Americans our very best wishes as they each celebrate one hundred years of life. Thank you, Mr. Speaker."

July 2018 concluded as one of the busiest months that I can recall. Consequently, it was a magnificent and meaningful month. My heart was so filled with magical moments. I was looking forward to the joys of the August month!

The Grand Finale:
100th Birthday Breakfast Celebration August 2018

The 3rd of August arrived on a bright and sunny Friday morning. I couldn't sleep the night before my birthday breakfast celebration. As I told Kayla, the sheer reality of reaching this milestone age brought tears to my eyes. Earlier during the year, the Lord had called Dr. Billy Graham home, and he celebrated his centenarian birthday on the other side, in paradise. Yet, God was allowing me to celebrate my special day with family and friends. How was I so truly blessed?

We had been instructed to arrive at the Sheraton Imperial by 9:00 a.m. I got myself dressed and fancied up with my new pink blouse, my dress-white pants, and my white knitted shawl across my shoulders. I found my pinkish clip earbobs, my white pearl-stringed necklace, and my comfortable flat, white canvas shoes. Patiently, I waited as Krystal and Kayla finished getting ready, and we drove from North Durham to Emperor Blvd on the Southeastern part of the city. My heartbeat was skipping with excitement.

So many people were already present and waiting on the birthday lady! Birthday hosts and guides were in place to greet and seat everyone as we arrived in the combined Imperial Ballrooms.

My eyes were stunned to see the beautiful and impressive decorations: all the tables were draped with white linen table-cloths, place settings with pink, tent-shaped napkins, and frosted oil lamps on mirror-tiled centerpieces; twin six-feet columns of pink and white balloons with a huge numbered balloon on top of each—the number one hundred, one pink and one white; birthday banners all around the ballroom; professionally-created programs on all the tables; the handicapped-accessible, raised platform for the head table with oversized, rose-colored balloons as the backdrop on the wall; and a specialty designed portrait birthday cake. It was an astounding sight, extraordinarily picturesque!

I sat nearby the entrance, just inside the broad doorway, to meet and speak with everyone before the program began. My son, James, Jr., and his wife, Barbara Jean, greeted me with a loving hug. George "McLeod" Green, Buster's oldest son, and his son, George, Jr., came all the way from Rochester, NY, and we were so happy to see each other!

My great-great-nephew, Catherline's grandson, Jonathan "JD" Edwards, Sr., wife, Sierra, and their three children ("Mella," Andreia and Jonathan, II "Deuce") arrived from Saint Marys, GA. He was accompanied by his sister, great-great-niece Melody Lucas, one of the Birthday hosts, and her son, Adrien, who traveled with us to DC. They all made me so happy by coming! Several other guests arrived from many miles away. My great-niece, Donna Banfield, Mary Ruby's daughter (Cete's grand), traveled from Savannah, GA; Her sister, great-niece Sylvia Banfield-Clark with husband, Barry, made it down from Galloway, NJ, and The Fords journeyed from DC. My adopted great-niece, Linda Phillips, arrived from Maryland. My McLeod Family from Lumberton, NC, showed up in great numbers. Bobby (Joy) Ashe, my great-nephew, and Cousin Tilda Caudle came from Wake Forest, NC. My great-niece, Tanya Nurse, arrived from Raleigh, NC, as well as a special business partner of Beverly's, Vance Davenport, along with two of his business partners. A list of the guests are noted in the appendix.

Smiling faces, lots of hugs and kisses, cards, flowers, gifts, and pure joy exuded from every individual person. The atmosphere for an early Friday morning was electrifying! As I proceeded to the uplifted head table, my heart was humbled that so many people had come from far and near in celebration of this great milestone.

My firstborn granddaughter, LaKishia McLeod, served as the Mistress of Ceremony. Her outgoing personality made her an excellent choice. She followed the program as outlined. It began with the Welcome and Occasion by my great-great-niece, Charmelita Royster, from Saint Marys, GA. Her sons, Christopher and LaMichael, were present with her. Prayer was offered by Pastor Jerome Washington, followed by the serving of the hot breakfast buffet by table selection.

The delicious Carolina Sunrise Breakfast menu included a variety of fresh juices—apple, cranberry, grapefruit, and orange—and brewed Starbucks coffee and herbal teas. There was an assortment of breakfast breads, including bagels, danish, and muffins with added butter, cream cheese, and sorted jellies. The main entrees were crispy bacon, smoked link sausages, fluffy scrambled eggs, southern-style grits, and home-fried potatoes. I love breakfast! This one was mighty delicious, and there was plenty to eat, enough for second helpings. (smile)

While we enjoyed the scrumptious food, we enjoyed great, live gospel music by The World-Renowned Sensational Nightingales. Durham is quite famous for its gospel-grown talents. As mentioned, Gospel singer, Evangelist/Pastor Shirley Caesar hails from Durham; so does Gospel singer Pastor John P. Kee; and the lead guitarist of the Sensational Nightingales, Brother Joseph "JoJo" Wallace (seventy-two years with the group).

The Sensational Nightingales are a legendary gospel quartet group that has been singing since 1942. They are famous for their lyrics being "The Word in Song," meaning that the lyrics are from the Bible. In addition to Brother Wallace, the group consisted of Brother Horace "Shug" Thompson (fifty-seven years with the group) and Brother Larry Moore (twenty-four years with the group). They sang us happy!

After hearing great songs like "At the Meeting" and "Standing on the Promises of God," we were introduced to Rev. Mark Anthony Middleton from the Office of Durham's Mayor, Stephen Schewel. Rev. Middleton is a City Council Member and serves as Councilman of Ward Two. He read and presented the Proclamation from the mayor. He did an absolutely wonderful job. He brought the room to its feet when he declared:

"WHEREAS, the faithfulness of Mrs. McLeod is recognized and honored today by her Family, Pastor, Church Family, the NCNW, Friends, and Officials as she celebrates her 100th Birthday, and whereas, *A Century+ of Living: The Autobiography of Cora Jones 'Boot' McLeod* will be published, sharing the life and story of Mrs. McLeod; Now, therefore, I, Stephen M. Schewel, Mayor of the City of Durham, NC, do hereby proclaim August 3, 2018, to be **Mrs. Cora Jones "Boot" McLeod Day!** The whole day! And hereby, salute Mrs. Cora Jones "Boot" McLeod on this celebration of 100 years of life; and hereby urge all citizens to take special notice of this observation. WITNESS my hand and the corporate seal of the City of Durham, NC, this third day of August 2018."

The standing ovation lasted for several minutes, and I think I was blushing. I had never had a day dedicated in my honor!

The Councilman was a hard act to follow, but my great-niece, Tanya Nurse, followed in class and style. Tanya is the granddaughter of my sister, Cete, Ramona's daughter. She spoke of me as "the matriarch of the family and as a rock." She creatively used the old hymn, "Solid Rock," in comparison to our Christ as the solid rock on which we stand and me as the rock of the family on which the family stands.

The next speaker was one of my favorite mentees, Mrs. Shirley Lennon Abdullah. She spoke of coming to work at her first job at Tip Top Beauty Shop as a nineteen-year-old, fresh out of DeShazor's Beauty College. She shared that me and Gladys didn't have time for foolishness and treated her as our own daughter.

She choked up several times as she told how I was "a role model then in 1963 and still a role model today." She brought greetings from the NC State Beauticians & Cosmetologists Association, where she is now treasurer and where I served as

President of Chapter One for over thirty years. She also shared the story of how she knew she would be retired before twenty years. Everyone laughed with her and about her ideal, young-age plan.

My great-nephew, Ardell McArn, had come as he promised to sing my special song. He is the son of Buster's sister's daughter, Lorraine. He was next on the program, and what a fantastic job he did! The song that he sang is entitled "I Won't Complain" by Rev. Paul Jones. The first stanza is a major theme in my life:

> I've had some good days. I've had some hills to climb. I've had some weary days and some sleepless nights. But when I look around, and I think things over. All of my good days outweigh my bad days. I won't complain.

> "So, I'll just say thank you, Lord, I won't complain."

The program was nearing the end, but one more speaker had to take the podium. That speaker was none other than my former pastor for thirty-four years, Rev. Dr. Percy L. High. He and his wife, Sister Esther, were among the first to RSVP for this celebration.

Pastor High joked about my nickname of "Boot." He told us how his father, a stern man, didn't let them use nicknames growing up until he couldn't pronounce his sister's name, and his dad let him call her a name he could pronounce, *Wheezy!* He recalled that he told one of his relatives that he was called to pastor Mount Vernon Church in Durham, and the response was, "Oh, you Boot's pastor?" That's how he discovered my a.k.a (also known as) name. (smile)

Pastor High concluded by sharing that my birth name of Cora means someone who serves other people. He spoke of how I served others as a beautician in helping to make them look pretty and how I served others as an usher for over fifty years, helping people to feel welcome when they came to our church.

He, then, stated that a nickname must be earned and the special one that he would give to me is one that I've earned, and no one can take it from me; it was "C.C." Everyone, especially me, was waiting with anticipation of what possibly could it mean. "C.C. means," he paused, "Consistent Christian." He explained, before he took his seat, that it meant that I didn't change from Sunday to Sunday, that people knew where I stood for the Lord, and that if no one else said *amen* while the preacher was preaching, the pastor/preacher could count on one *amen* from Mother McLeod. He looked directly at me and said, "I don't know why you are so consistent, but I'm glad you are!" He closed with these words:

"What made her consistent as a Christian? I believe I've found the secret. Someone said that her life could be summed up in this pithy poem,
Others, Lord, Yes, others
Let this my motto be
Help me to live for others
That I may live like thee."

"Thank you, C.C.," from Pastor High.

LaKishia was doing a fine job moving the morning right along! Everyone appeared to be comfortably enjoying the agenda and the flow of the program; I certainly was!

LaKishia did acknowledge other letters and proclamations received in recognition of my special day. The list included messages from:

1. Governor Roy Cooper—NC Governor
2. Rep. Floyd McKissick, Jr.—NC Senate
3. Rep. Mary Ann Black—Member of the NC House of Representatives/ State Representative
4. Rep. G. K. Butterfield—NC Congressman
5. Cora Cole-McFadden—National Council of Negro Women (NCNW)
6. Rev. Rachel Green—National Association for the Advancement of
   Colored People (NAACP)

I was blessed and happy to have Government Officials—Former Durham Mayor William Bell, Durham County Commissioner Brenda Howerton, and Rep. Floyd McKissick, Jr.—present at my birthday breakfast celebration.

The finishing portion of the morning was a beautiful presentation of one hundred flowers by my grands and great-grands. What a glorious sight to see LaKishia, Karleshia, Krystal, Kassan, Khalil, Kayla, and Kaiden showering me with dozens and dozens and more dozens of pink carnations. What a heart-warming feeling! Everyone, then, joined in singing the "Happy Birthday to You" song.

As I made my way to the podium for Words of Appreciation, I felt joy, unspeakable joy, down in my soul. The standing ovation enhanced the inside joy. I began my remarks with a simple question:

"What can I say? Everything good has already been said. I'm so happy today. I have been blessed all my life! I serve a good God, and I know you know Him, too. Thank you all for coming. You have made this day for me! You know, God has been good to all of us. Let's give Him a hand of praise. I love you all!"

I asked everyone not to forget me and come see me some time. I reminded them that I had never had a day declared in my name and that I would enjoy it to the highest. Before I took my seat, I asked the gospel singers to help me sing MY song. It was an old-fashioned church chant:

"Lord, I thank you, thank you, thank you
Lord, I thank you, thank you, thank you
I just thank you all the days of my life.
Lord, I thank you, thank you, thank you
Lord, thank you, thank you, thank you
I just thank you all the days of my life."

The next verse goes on to say," When I was sick, Lord, you healed me," and I have already shared when I was sick and how the Lord healed me. So, this song was fitting for me to close out my blessed, one hundredth birthday breakfast celebration. I smiled and waved my hand to all the guests and reclaimed my seat.

The Closing Prayer was the final piece to this jubilant and unforgettable story. Pastor Clarence H. Burke was selected for this task. He is the esteemed pastor of Beacon Light Missionary Baptist Church here in Durham; and is also the cherished son-in-law to my beloved niece, Pearline. He married a very lovely and smart young lady, my great-niece, Syvil, who was responsible for the slicing and distributing of my birthday cake.

"To God be the Glory" was the opening salutation from Pastor Burke. He added that this was a great family affair! He requested that we hold hands with one another. Before praying, Pastor Burke took time to recognize Beverly for her dreaming of and organizing this outstanding celebration. Then he prayed:

"Father, we thank you. We thank you, Lord, for 100 years. Lord, an age that most of us cannot even imagine, Father, Thank you. Thank you for the 100 flowers, the balloons, we thank you for 100. Lord, thank you for the faith that she has had all these years that has carried her thru all these years. Thank you for all who have attended; it shows the love that they have for her, Father. We pray for her..."

Pastor Burke's prayer added the cherry on top of the best birthday celebration that I could not have ever imagined!

We took a ton of pictures with—all the family members, with my Mount Vernon Church Family, with the Governmental Officials, with the ladies from NCNW, with Family Heritage Guests, with members of the NCSBCA and the NAACP. The photographer, Jacqueline Perry, and the videographer, Charles Tucker, captured this amazing occasion in photos and videos, and for that, I am grateful. The awesome programs were created by Gwen McQueen of Jennings, FL; they are golden keepsakes of beauty and excellence!

Neither me nor the guests wanted to leave; it was like we all wanted the moments to stand still in time and last forever. After the wonderful breakfast celebration, many came by my home on North Alston Avenue and continued to celebrate and visit—it was my day for the whole day! (lol)

Two Sundays later, August 12th, Mount Vernon had a special recognition service in honor of the three church centenarians, Mrs. Annie Butler, Mrs. Cora McLeod, and Mrs. Christine Umstead. Our pictures were on the front of the church bulletin. We, the three honorees, sat at the front of the church on the first center pew.

The video was shown of NC Rep. G.K. Butterfield addressing the House Floor and dedicating his time to speak of Mount Vernon Missionary Baptist Church in Durham, NC, and its three centenarian members. Quite a few members had not seen the address and were super excited to hear their church and our names mentioned in a political setting. After the morning worship service, a parade of people came by, wished us happy, happy birthday, and put blessings in our hands. It was elegant, elite, and very graceful! Thank you, loving Pastor Jerome Washington and our Mount Vernon Church Family. We appreciated all the kindness and love.

CHAPTER 16
Ten Decades and Beyond

Back in the country, a senior gentleman used to come see Papa ever so often. When he got ready to leave, Papa would tell him to take it easy until they'd meet again. The gentleman replied in a vigorous way, "Rev. Jones, if I can make it thru January and February, I can sho' nuff see March!" What could he have meant? I offer my humble thought: if we can make it thru our wintery times, springtime is on its way! Perhaps, my meaning is different than what he meant; yet that's my personal interpretation.

I thank God that He brought me thru 2019, 2020 and 2021, and here we are in the year 2022. *I hardly know what to say.* Life has not been, as Langston Hughes wrote, "a crystal stair," but it has been the best life that I could have ever lived. God has shown Himself real in my life. Where would I be, had the Lord not been on my side?

After reaching the 100th Birthday milestone in 2018, a major decision had to be made in 2019. My address of 1309 North Alston Avenue, Durham, NC, had been my home for over seventy years. With my Buster, we had shared a good life together there. We raised our two children, James, Jr. and

Denise, in a loving and stable environment. My business was built onto that address, and I was able to provide beauty-care services for more than forty years at that same location. When our grandchildren and great-grandchildren came along, our home provided a haven for them when needed, always with unconditional love.

Prior roof work had been done by Cedric Rogers, Sr. of Rogers' Home Improvement; now, an inspection of the house determined that mold had formed in several places in the home. I had to decide the next best option. Could I afford to get it fixed if it could be restored? Should I entertain selling it, and if I did, where would we live? I had to think about Krystal, Kayla, and Panda—the cat, and their well-being. It was hard to hear from the Lord, hard to pray, hard to sleep, and hard to think about uprooting after so many decades. I spoke with James Jr., and he had a temporary solution.

When James Jr. and Barbara Jean went to live with their daughter, their home in Old Farm, a prestigious, well-established community, was left unoccupied. He suggested that we sell my house, move to his house, and stay until a new decision is made to get a different home. Offers to buy our house came in on a consistent basis. Budja's house was purchased swiftly after Launa passed. Mack's house had sold even faster after Mack left us. The offers weren't elaborate compared to houses selling for 200,000 and 300,000 dollars all around us.

For me, it was the irreplaceable mountain of memories, not the money, that had me anxious and hesitant about leaving. Krystal had concerns about the health effects on our bodies, especially on Kayla, from prolonged mold problems. I did pray, and I received peace in my heart to go forward with that plan. We closed on the house and had to be out by August's end.

Because of previous pest problems, we chose to get all new appliances, bedding, furniture, and household items. It was like starting over, but this time without a mortgage in my name, repairs that I'd be responsible for, and taxes that I had to pay. At age 101, I didn't need those extra burdens on my plate.

Speaking of age—I celebrated my 101st birthday at the Golden Corral Buffet Restaurant on Apex Hwy in Durham. Of course, it was a breakfast buffet gathering! I love breakfast, as I've mentioned more than once (smile). The food was super delicious. Everyone was full to the brim!

They showered me with a beautiful birthday cake, birthday cards, birthday citations, birthday letters, bouquets of flowers and roses by the dozens, giant "101" numbered balloons, hundreds of multi-colored balloons, and maximum love. Durham's Mayor, Stephen M. Schewel, sent another Proclamation declaring my birthday, August 3, 2019, as my special day! Each person that attended spoke words of inspiration to me and sprinkled loving birthday wishes upon me! As always, I enjoyed the fellowship with my loving family and friends.

I was still getting accustomed to the new community and environment, the different house layout, and the various adjusted routines. The hardest part was being further away from my church, Mount Vernon. When Krystal worked twelve hours all Saturday night, drove over an hour to and from work, and arrived home early in the morning, she needed her sleep. For her to get up and get me to Sunday School by 9:30 a.m. and come back and pick me up by 1:00 p.m., that was asking a lot, especially when we were ten more miles north in the opposite directions from the church. So, I missed a few Sunday services. But on the weekends, when Krystal was off, I was able to go worship in the House of the Lord.

Prior to moving, it was normal for me to cook my breakfast every morning. I was used to my stove and my kitchen. One major change for me was the stove at our new dwelling. It was wired electric instead of gas. I had used gas for cooking, the hot water heater, and the furnace for seventy-one years, and boy, is there a difference? Yes, to me, most definitely!

I remember when we moved to North Alston Avenue, the electric company was right down the street on Alston Avenue. I went to see about getting a gas air conditioner. The lady working there sent me to L.D. Swain & Son—a heating and air conditioning company. Every gas air conditioner and gas furnace, thereafter, I got from them until they discontinued making them. Then, my first electric air conditioner unit came from Sears, the same store that Mr. Julius Rosenwald was president! Life is a circle, isn't it?

Anyway, my dilemma with the stove was the knobs. On the gas stove, the knobs are in front of the stove; on the electric stove, they are in the rear of the stove. I'd have to reach over the burners to control the level of heat. As you get older, you get shorter, at least that's my case. I'm shorter than I used to be and about as tall as the stove; it was hard for me to reach all the way to the back of the stove to cook. Krystal, smartly, began cooking my meats and grits and storing them in the refrigerator, along with a fruit mixture, where I could reach them easily.

Let me give a shout-out to the organization Meals on Wheels Durham (MOWD) for their services of meals to senior citizens. Their mission and vision include "helping the convalescing, elderly, disabled, frail, and others who are not able to provide proper nutrition for themselves." Ruth had told me about Meals on Wheels after Denise got sick. I inquired and qualified. Volunteers used to deliver meals each day, Monday-Friday. After the pandemic started, things changed. They now deliver seven delicious, nourishing, well-prepared frozen meals each Monday, with bright smiles and kind words. Cat food is included for Panda, too! MOWD—people caring for people!

A wonderful occasion happened on the first Sunday in November 2019. The World-Renowned Sensational Nightingales celebrated their 73rd singing anniversary at Mt. Zion Christian Church on Fayetteville Street, Durham. Bro. Wallace, Bro. Thompson and Bro. Moore had invited me and my friend, Mother Catherine Ferrell, who had turned 107 years old in October, as their special guests. I invited my friends, Edith, and her husband, Deacon Ron. Willie and Beverly escorted me there. Mother Ferrell's daughter, Shirley, escorted her. We had front row seats, and it was the best anniversary concert ever! They honored and recognized me and Mother Ferrell and presented us with a dozen of roses. Apostle Donald Q. Fozard, the pastor of Mt. Zion, greeted us with so much excitement because he's looking to live for 110-years, and he was glad to see that we were almost there (smile)!

Our first Thanksgiving at our new abode was celebrated with James, Jr., Barbara Jean, and LaKishia coming to visit. Krystal had to work on the holiday, but like Denise, she enjoyed preparing for the festivities and creating a tasty, traditional Thanksgiving dinner. Karleshia and the boys, Kassan, Khalil, and Kaiden, joined us for the celebration. Kayla really liked her new school. But she was enjoying her school break and spending time with her family. I was getting to feel more comfortable at our new residence. I thanked God for my family and for making a way!

The Christmas holidays brought jubilation, peace of mind, and preparation for 2020. It promised to be a great new year. Krystal had planned her trip to Africa at the closing of the year. Willie and Beverly came to stay with me while she was gone. December 29th, the last Sunday in the year, we attended Sunday School and morning worship at Mount Vernon. The Male Chorus sang so wonderfully, and Rev. JaVaughn Troxler brought forth an inspirational message, "Get Your Feet Wet," to close out the 2019 year.

Most churches had a Watch Night Service on New Year's Eve, around 10:00 pm. It was suggested that we bring in the New Year at Beacon Light Missionary Baptist. I gladly agreed and was excited to hear Pastor Clarence Burke preach. Beverly, me, and Willie arrived on time, and we enjoyed the singing, preaching, and testimonies. Pastor Burke is a great teacher, too!

Refreshments were served as the New Year 2020 came in. I enjoyed seeing Syvil, the First Lady and my great-niece, who gave me a loving hug, my great-nephew, Allan Jr., who we call June, along with his dear wife, Rita. Clarence and Syvil's daughter, Mia, my great-great-niece, greeted me with her beautiful smile. She married a kind, young man, Michael, who was home with their newborn son, Desmond.

Clarence and Syvil's son, Cedric, my great-great-nephew, is also faithful at Beacon Light; he married his true love, Jennifer, and was out of town with her for the holidays. I missed Pearline from this great New Year's service. Everyone was so friendly and welcoming. There was so much fellowship, love, and joy! Perhaps it may be an extreme understatement to say, "no one expected what the year 2020 would bring!"

I was able to sleep later than usual on that Wednesday, January 1, 2020, as Willie prepared our hot breakfast. He also prepared to cook the traditional black-eyed peas and collard greens along with a big pot of homemade chili. He's rather famous for his cooking; folks from many cities and states have called to request his cabbage, chili, and collard greens. He could fix cabbage for me any day; his cabbage tastes better than mine!

I had a surprise visit that evening. Mike and his mother, Ruth, came by to wish me Happy New Year! We hadn't seen each other since my 100th birthday celebration; I was so happy that they thought enough of me to come and spend some time. We offered them something to eat. At first, they weren't hungry. After more catching up, laughing, and talking, they obliged me by sharing our delicious New Year's meal. They made my day and promised to come again!

Willie and Beverly left out early that Friday morning, heading to Raleigh. Willie's last aunt, his father's baby sister, Mrs. Lois Rogers Caudle, had passed the last Saturday in December 2019. Willie's people were from Wake County. We had known some Rogers, too, in the country. Along with her only son, Rev. Anthony Rogers (Sylvia), the extended family joined in the celebration of a life well-blessed. Like me, she had been preceded in death by her parents and all her sisters and brothers.

On the first Sunday of the New 2020 Year, we had communion service at Mount Vernon. The harmonic voices of the Inspirational Choir blessed my soul, as well as the message from Pastor Washington, "Don't Look Back." What a sermon to begin a New Year! After service, we headed to Golden Corral for lunch. They had a splendid array of mouth-watering dishes, but my favorite—they served crispy, whole catfish, all you can eat, and I dined like a queen!

Me and Beverly went out after breakfast on Monday morning to Gurley's Medical Supply on Guess Road to get a price on what I called "a walker that you can sit on." Gurley's name for it was a "walkabout lite four-wheel rollator." It had a little basket on it, and it could fold in one process. It was nice and was priced in the hundreds. We put it on hold to address later. We, then, decided to visit a few persons who were sick and shut in.

One sweet lady that we visited was Sister Carrie McNair, the widow of Mr. McNair, who got me to join the usher board. She was to celebrate her 99th birthday this 2020 year, and she looked so well and smiled so brightly when she saw me. We spent a short time with her, and I felt like Mama Olivia, doing missionary work.

We thought about visiting my only other living niece, Frances Jones Parker, Honey's daughter, who I hadn't seen in decades, probably not since Catherline's homegoing service. She and Cat were friends till the end! Beverly knew exactly where she lived because Landis, her nephew, had lived in the same complex. I wondered if I could make it to her front door;

there was a small incline, but I didn't have any problem. I was on my no-seater walker.

When I walked in, Frances screamed for joy and started weeping in sheer surprise! We embraced, hugged, and kissed, shedding non-stop tears. It was a reunion arranged by God. I patted and comforted her and told her, "It's alright, it's alright." My heart was overjoyed to connect with Frances. I loved her from a little girl. She was kindhearted, obedient, and smart.

Millie gave approval for Frances to marry as a young girl. She bore a daughter and five boys. "All are doing fine," she said proudly. I remembered Bill, Jr., and Francine. Last count, Frances had eighteen grandchildren, twenty-seven great-grands, and seven great-great-grands. I hope to meet them all one day soon. We could have talked for hours.

Before we left, we had prayer. I then, out of the corner of my eye, noticed a rollator like the one we saw at Gurley's. I shared with Frances that we had priced one of them at a store earlier. She replied that she had more than one and for me to take one for mine own. I was amazed how God blessed me with a "walker with a seat"—just like that! Thanks to my niece, Frances, and to my God, who supplies all our needs!

Things still seemed normal in the world, yet the second week in January, the CBS morning news reported a strange virus that was affecting people in China and was spreading to other parts of the World; the first case in the United States had been announced. I heard the initial physicians say that the risk to the public was low. From the White House, the same type of message came across that the virus was like a cold or flu and would go away on its own.

By March, The World Health Organization (WHO) declared a "global pandemic." It was projected by experts that nearly 70% of our world's population might be infected. I watched the news daily. The 2020 Olympics had been officially postponed in January. After the declaration by the WHO, businesses, churches, companies, dental offices, doctors' offices, hospitals, governments, law firms, nursing homes, schools, and universities started closing their doors, one right after the other.

It hit home for our family when, on the 12th of March, Willie and Beverly drove to Atlanta for the birth of their first great-granddaughter, arrived at the hospital shortly after noon, and was prohibited from entrance. The hospital enforced a no-visitation policy thirty minutes before they found a parking space. Despite the hospital closure, a healthy 6 pounds 11 ounces, 19.5 inches, Da'Zayiah Matthews was born to Christopher and Sanoia, becoming the baby sister to their older daughter, Kiara. I was excited to have a new great-great-great-great-niece!

Assisted living facilities, long-term care centers, nursing homes, and rest havens struggled desperately to care for their residents and keep them protected and safe from this new, deadly disease named COVID-19. Yet, acquaintances, church members, family, and friends succumbed to this out-of-control pandemic. I adopted Linda from Maryland a while back, as she's been Beverly's best friend since the seventh grade. I'd ask about her 98-year-old mother, Mrs. Sadie, each time we spoke.

Sadly, her mother was diagnosed with COVID-19 while in her quarantined, restricted residential facility. Five days later, on the 22nd of April, Linda and her brothers became motherless. I pondered in my mind, "What if I had been put away in a home or taken to a facility? Would I have been a statistic—one of the hundreds of thousands affected or lost to this virus?" With my hand over my heart, I wish that I could express my deepest gratitude to James, Jr., Barbara Jean, LaKishia, Krystal, Bai, Kayla, and my entire family for being there for me!

Daily, the COVID-19 numbers kept climbing, soaring, and tumbling over the last reported numbers. The term "social distancing" became a practiced method, plus handwashing, masking, and sanitizing to fight this monster of a virus. By May, the national news confirmed USA's 100,000 deaths from this unprecedented pandemic. Though I was reminded of the year that I was born and the 1918 Influenza Pandemic, I had no recollection of how bad it really was.

History, however, reported that roughly 500,000 million individuals, equal to one-third of the world's population, became infected with that specific virus. Hazily, I can recall Papa and other older adults making references to that year and the impact of the pandemic; maybe because 1918 was the same year that Papa dedicated Jones Chapel, and there was concern for the member's health.

My health experienced challenges this 2020 year. I was hospitalized at Duke for a few days in February, April, and May. Thankfully, there was no COVID-19 issue. First, my blood count was down, and my oxygen level was low. Next, the doctors found an infection in my spine. Lastly, I did something to the rotator cuff on my shoulder and couldn't raise my arm. Neither time was major; I was treated and sent home to get better. Each hospital admission had limited and restricted visitation. I could only imagine how hard it was for those in hospitals for weeks and months, all alone, fighting for their lives. I practiced staying safe at home and prayed for those in hospital confinements.

May became a painful month for America and the world—no matter one's class, culture, gender, politics, race, or religion. The death of a young man named George Floyd shifted our American binoculars from the pandemic to police brutality, from disease to disparity and injustice. I felt agony within my soul when I heard this young man crying out for his mother only moments before he passed, pressed down under the knees of a police officer. My thoughts went straightway to my own James, Jr., and what if I had lost him as a result of an unexpected encounter with a police officer? I shuddered at the unbearable thought!

Demonstrations, marches, protests, riots, and uprisings sprang out in cities across the nation and in foreign countries across the globe. Banners and signs of declaration—Black Lives Matter, Blue Lives Matter, George's Life Mattered, My Life Matters, and All Lives Matter—displayed amply on television channels, the internet, news networks, and in the streets. I saw where many police officers kneeled in solidarity with protestors in many cities. The reality of how far we haven't come as a nation is shocking to some; yet, all Americans have a right to equality, humanity, and justice!

Bereavement found another path into our lives in the middle of pandemic infections and purposeful protesting. Lennon Earl Royster, Jr., called Red, left us so unexpectedly a few days after his 33rd birthday, on June 9, 2020. He and his Aunt Beverly facetimed and talked lots of times on his birthday. "He was so elated and thrilled to be on a good road, having completed

OSHA trainings and excelling in his career with Metro Group, City of Long Island," she shared.

His body was transported from NY to Holloway Memorial Funeral Home. His mother, Doris, his sister and brothers, many other relatives and friends came together for a graveside service at Glenview Memorial Gardens. His brother, Landis, read the Old Testament scripture, and his brother-in-law, Jerrell, Shamika's husband, read the New Testament verses. His niece, Nakiyah, sang a beautiful song, "Missing You." Shamyra, a family friend, live-streamed his solemn service.

Pastor Clarence Burke delivered his eulogy. He was laid to rest beside his daddy, Lennon Earl Royster, Sr., and close to his grandmother, Catherline, as well as other relatives on his mother's side of the family. Many days, Lil' Earl would come by the old house and sit and talk. Whatever was on his mind, he confided with me, and I listened respectfully. His sudden departure shocked me deeply!

In July 2020, there was a resemblance of normalcy when Major League Baseball finally returned. It, too, like NBA and other professional sports closed in March. My love for the game has continued through the decades. I did change teams, mainly because the Braves kept losing (smile) after winning so much in earlier years. I chose the Washington Nationals as my team because they were a new team who came to Washington DC in 2005. They struggled at first but started to win division titles. I was a happy camper in 2019 when they made it to the World Series and defeated the Houston Astros in a seven-game comeback. It was their first championship! Buster and Denise would have really enjoyed watching that series.

Mid-July, I was getting excited about my 102nd upcoming birthday. Krystal had mentioned plans for a down-home fish-fry party. Out of nowhere, pipes burst in the kitchen, and water gushed and streamed everywhere throughout the house. We were relocated to a hotel suite across town. What was to be a few weeks' hotel stay multiplied into months away from home for me, Krystal, Kayla, and Panda. It was a major renovation.

The pandemic continued to strike hard, especially in the African American community and in lower economically stable families. Families were not group-gathering, so in lieu of the fish-fry party, Willie and Beverly came from Georgia with grandson Deuce and cooked my favorite meal at the hotel. Everyone already knows—it was breakfast-and what a scrumptious breakfast it was: bacon, eggs, grits, and toast—along with my everyday joy, my cup of Maxwell House coffee. Monday, August 3, 2020, God shined upon me to live 102 years. *I hardly know what to say!*

Because of social distancing, people began using different forms of technology to call and communicate. Beverly had set up a Zoom Birthday meeting, and it was marvelous. Many friends and relatives joined the Zoom call and wished me *Happy 102*! Imagine me, a Centenarian+, greeting and seeing people by way of Zoom and FaceTime! My friends, Edith and Cynthia from Mount Vernon, came by and brought me birthday gifts. It was a low-keyed celebration, but high in appreciation, humility and love!

To add to the unpredictive 2020 year, it was a forceful hurricane season on our side of the Atlantic Ocean with more hurricanes and tropical storms than ever recorded. Various meteorologists had forecasted from thirteen-twenty-five hurricanes; the last record-breaking number that I heard was thirty. Normally, the season extends from the first of June to the last day in November. I paid attention to these developments because NC tends to reap a backlash from many of these hurricanes and tropical storms.

This 2020 year also happened to be an election year. The debated topics included: climate change, coronavirus outbreak, economics, ethnic inequality, foreign policy, gun laws, health care, immigration, systemic racism, Supreme Court appointments, and violent crimes, to name just a few. The topics concerning me the most were harmony, love, and peace between one another. Sounds naïve; still, I have wanted those topics to be a reality since I was a young girl. Krystal took me for early voting before leaving for Africa.

The arguments among candidates fighting for their party's nomination were heavy and intense. Election day came fast, it seemed, and America voted on Tuesday, November 3, 2020. President Donald Trump and Vice President Mike Pence did not come out on top. The American people voted to elect former Vice-President Joseph Biden for President and Senator Kamala Harris as Vice President. History was made on behalf of aging, diversity, HBCUs, poll voting records, senior adults, and women. Denise would have been proud that the new Vice President-elect was a member of her AKA sorority.

The 2020 Thanksgiving and Christmas holidays were homebound and quiet-natured due to the overwhelming increases of COVID-19. I wasn't afraid but cautious as to who came and went into our house. At the end of December, WHO globally reported for the month over 4 million new COVID-19 cases and 72,000 new deaths. That brought the total global number to nearly 80 million reported cases and over 1.7 million deceased since the beginning of the pandemic. What unbelievable numbers to try to wrap your mind around as real? Tragically, they were true numbers. What we all could do and continue to do—is call on the name of the Lord and pray that he would heal our land.

My 2021 New Year came in peacefully. Beverly was in Durham writing on my book. I was grateful to God for keeping me alive to see another year. Tears of joy ran down my face as I thought about the goodness of God! Because of the coronavirus, most churches were still closed for in-service worship. Like Mount Vernon, lots of churches were online and virtual. Krystal set up on her computer for me to watch worship services.

I was appreciative of the virtual computer connection, but I really missed fellowshipping and seeing my Christian brothers and sisters, hearing the live choirs, and having a sermon preached from the pulpit by Pastor Washington. I longed for the church experience we had before the pandemic. Everything had changed; nothing remained the same. How different were things for you and your family as the New Year started?

Kayla had surgery on her tonsils on the 6th of January, the day after her mother, Krystal, hailed her 34th birthday. Grandsons Khalil (12) and Kassan (13) flipped birthdays in January. Kayla healed well and enjoyed her 10th birthday on the first Thursday of February. The next week, I found myself back at Duke hospital. After the doctor's examination and minimum testing, I was back home the same day—all was fine.

However, on January 6th, all was not fine in our nation's capital. The joint session of Congress had gathered at the Capitol to confirm the 2020 election results. I couldn't believe my eyes when news interruptions flooded the television displaying thousands of protestors violently attacking, disrupting, forcing entrance, looting, and vandalizing our nation's Capitol Building; assaulting and totally ignoring the police officers positioned out front and within the building.

People were harmed, injured, screaming, squeezed, and killed! I was horrified and shocked! Rioters held American flags, Confederate flags, and Trump flags; they had combat gear, tools, and weapons. The mob of protestors sought our Vice President and other lawmakers, who had been removed from the building, and had planned on hurting them. Did they think what they did was right?

Democracy prevailed; the lawmakers did not allow the insurrection, as it was reported, to derail them from formalizing the electoral votes and officially verifying the results of November's election. They preceded forward into the wee hours of the next morning and got it done.

On the 20th of January, the world, myself included, watched the inauguration of the 46th President and Vice President of the United States of America. A highlighted moment during the ceremony was the poem read and written by the youngest inaugural poet in U.S. history, Amanda Gorman, "The Hill We Climb." Watching her gave me, and the world, so much pride! It's what you want your grandchildren and great-grands to see to give them hope that they can achieve goals and greatness by being committed and focused!

Many great activities happened in the first part of this year. I joined a Zoom Birthday call on the 28th of February for my great-nephew, Bobby Ashe, Buddy's grandson. His family honored him for his 77th year of living. I met descendants that I had never known or seen. Wandolyn, his niece, told us about the call, and Beverly joined me right in. It was a happy event!

Krystal took me to get my vaccine. I was in one of the first groups allowed because of my age. It went well, and I had no pain or reaction to it. So, the first Wednesday in March, I planned a road trip to Raleigh to visit Janet Young, Uncle Joe's granddaughter, whom I hadn't seen in decades, and Tanya Nurse, Cete's granddaughter, who lived nearby.

Janet had gotten her doctorate degree and was working on a documentary about incest in the family. She knew first-hand the toll of the hidden secrets. She was always smart. The Lord blessed her to be a breast cancer survivor. I didn't get to see her brothers: Carl, who lives in Holly Springs, and Ronald, who lives in Garner, but Janet had a ton of pictures of the Hunter/Jeffers/Martin/ Peterson/Young side of our family. I truly enjoyed our visit together.

Tanya didn't live too far from Janet, but in Raleigh, traffic is epic every day, and not too far could still take extra time. She had sold her big house and was living in a charming townhouse with lots of beautiful flowers and a pond in the back. We chatted and laughed and took pictures. Tanya has a sweety spirit like Cete and always has that beautiful smile on her face. Our time was pleasant and special, quite enjoyable!

Throughout the writing of my history, I was introduced to various influential individuals. Educator, filmmaker, and writer

Claudia Stack, from Rocky Point, NC, produced a documentary on Rosenwald Schools, along with other Stack Stories of African American Culture. When we connected, she inspired me to write on and share my history with the world. She has plans to interview me as a new centenarian writer and possibly create a documentary on my life. I lift her up daily in prayer as her current challenge is her fight with cancer. Whisper a prayer for my friend, Claudia.

Another positive and powerful person that I made acquaintance with is Jamaal Scott of New Jersey. He is a young historian, orator, and poet. He recorded oral renditions about our Hayti District of Durham, NC; The Tulsa, Oklahoma Massacre; The Jewel of the Delta, Mound Bayou, MS; SC State College Shooting in Orangeburg, SC, and about many other famous happenings and people. He has committed to creating an oration about my story and 103 years of living. Jamaal is leaving a strong legacy to the world! www.historicag.com

One day in April, I had a facetime call with two amazing young girls, Blair and Grace Ross of Jacksonville, FL. Their parents, Brian and Lisa, are successful business owners. They brightened my day and encouraged me to finish my book so that they could learn about my journey. I saw their videos on Facebook—Blair (10) is a great soccer player, Grace (12) dances like a professional ballerina, and they told me about Adam, their brother, who I am 100 years older than he is. (lol) What a great influence and inspiration from this younger generation. Thank you, dear girls!

Lastly, Dr. Charles D. Johnson influenced me considerably. He is the Assistant Professor of History and Director of Public

History at NCCU. Our friend, Beverly Evans, referred me to him. He contacted us and set up an oral interview for Sunday, May 2nd, at 3:00 p.m. It was an airy, sunny spring afternoon, a perfect time to share my life story. He asked lots of questions about me, Papa, Mama Olivia, my siblings, the farm, and moving to Durham. Dr. Johnson's interview sparked even further my belief that others will read, enjoy and gain historical insights from my life story. He let me know that the interview will be stored in the archives of North Carolina Central University.

Granddaughters, LaKishia and Karleshia, had celebrated their birthdays in March and April, respectively. LaKishia reached the milestone of forty-one, and Karleshia was close to her, turning thirty-seven. We were getting excited about Kaiden's birthday in August when he would be double-digits, ten years old. His birthday comes the day before mine, and I felt sheer joy approaching our birthdays!

However, a newly found Delta variant of the coronavirus was detected in the US during May in Texas; by 1 July 2021, news channels reported that Delta had been detected in all fifty states and Washington, DC. Delta was labeled as more aggressive, double times contagious, and highly infectious, even threatening those who had been vaccinated. Many people in America were feeling like things were getting amended and back to some form of "normal." Businesses, churches, restaurants, and schools had either reopened or planned to reopen. My church, Mount Vernon, reopened in July with an outdoor service; then, the first Sunday in August, we gathered in the sanctuary with new guidelines and safety measures.

Worship service in our newly renovated sanctuary was joyous and uplifting! Me and Beverly arrived early and got a seat close upfront such that I could hear well. The opening song, "I'm So Glad Jesus Lifted Me," had us clapping, rocking, and singing spiritedly. Pastor shared his appreciation to all who helped in any capacity to complete the church project. His message was entitled, "An Encouraging Word." We participated in Holy communion and left the building as directed by the ushers—no hugging and kissing.

After church, I prepared for an exciting event—my 103rd Birthday Parade! The usher board from Mount Vernon had joined with my family to invite church members, friends, neighbors, and other special guests. Gospel radio host, Carolyn Satterfield, announced it on her radio program. Our yard was decorated so fancy in my favorite color of pink with a white accent. The chairs were covered in white coverings wrapped with pink sashes. Hundreds of pink and white balloons were scattered around the yard, on the mailbox and the banisters. Happy Birthday banners and signs displayed boldly between the trees and on the pink, shaded canopy where I would sit. Willie's daughter, Millicent, made special 103rd birthday shirts for me and Beverly. I wore a golden birthday crown upon my head; I felt like a queen for a day!

The Reverend and the DJ presented live, great-sounding gospel music for my birthday parade. If you've never heard them, they have an Inspirational Gospel Show each Sunday morning, 8:00 a.m. on OAK 93.5. God uses DJ Maurice and Rev. Tanya Coleman Johnson for his glory and certainly used them to make me overjoyed by playing all my favorite songs! Come to find out, Tanya and Beverly are first cousins. Her father was Rev. William "Bill" Coleman, Robert Earl's youngest brother, who came and prayed with me on many occasions.

Cecil and Willie organized the parade processional, which began promptly at 4:00 p.m. Brian, a family friend, live-streamed and videoed the parade celebration. His friends joined in and helped pass out the birthday bags and received flowers and gifts. Cars, cars, cars, and more cars kept on driving by; the occupants tooted, sang, shouted, and waved! The air was full of cheer, excitement, grins, laughter, love, music, and praise.

Family came from Charlotte, Lumberton, Raleigh, and Wake Forest. Friends that I hadn't seen in decades came to wish me a happy 103rd birthday. What was planned as an hour parade turned into several great hours of celebration, chatting, eating, fellowshipping, fun, memories, and reminiscing. I didn't want to go into the house. The sun set, and those who were still present, sat and watched the horizon change shifts. At the closing of the day, James, Jr., Barbara Jean, LaKishia, Kayla, Beverly, and Willie watched me blow out my candles and eat cake and ice cream.

I wasn't tired at all, even though I woke up early that morning, and it was about to turn into a new day. I looked a James, Jr. and thought about how he has been with me most all my life. He's been an earthly anchor for me—my firstborn. I looked at Barbara Jean and thought about how she has loved and been with James, Jr. most all of her and his life and how she's been his anchor; together, they stand as one.

Kayla reminds me so much of her grandmother, Denise. I looked at her and could see her strong abilities. I pray for her life's anchor. I pray for all my grands and great-grands, that the

Lord will touch their hearts, and become personal and real in their lives. My eyes, then, focused on Willie and Beverly, and my heart overflowed with gratitude. What they have meant to me has become irreplaceable. Like an anchor, they have been consistent, dependable, and steadfast in my life; they, too, are each other's anchor.

When I looked at LaKishia, my thoughts flew back to the tomato garden that I had on the hill in the backyard of North Alston Avenue. She was so excited to pick tomatoes with me. I taught her how to choose the right ones. We took them into the house and placed them on the windowsill in the kitchen until they ripened. She'd check them every day while I worked in the beauty salon. When they were ready and ripe, I'd combine cucumbers, tomatoes, and vinegar into a salad. She's like those tomatoes. She has grown in her parents' garden. She was specially picked to be there for them in this stage of life. Her anchor is her faith, and it will hold her strong on her journey.

Life is like a garden. God plants us in the soil to grow. Our soil is our family. Within our family, we are cared for, nurtured, pruned, and ripened. We get off the windowsill to start our own garden—planting and nurturing and pruning until our offspring are ripened and ready to produce future generations of offspring.

I thank God for the Jones's Garden in which I was planted. All that I've grown to be, I owe it to my soil. Each day, the Master Gardener chooses to pluck one of his creations from this earth. When He does, our gardening days are fulfilled. I'm ready when he calls for me. Until then, I'm a centenarian and beyond, and whatever my life holds for the future, I must give all the glory, honor, and praise to Him! He's my life-long Anchor!

With Gratitude and Love,
Cora Jones "Boot" McLeod

About the Author

Dr. Beverly "Eagle" Rogers, a Durham, NC native, knew in her heart that the story of her great-aunt, Mrs. Cora Jones 'Boot' McLeod, had to be shared with the world. "She is a brilliant woman with the gift of life, longevity, and overwhelming love and has seen a century-plus of changes, growth, and history. With her sharp and witty nature, Aunt Boot recalls vivid details of her childhood, the country community in Wake County, NC, where she grew up, her large Jones family, and settling in the 'Bull City.'"

Dr. Rogers is a proud graduate of Durham's Hillside High School- Class of 1973. She is a loyal alumna of The University of North Carolina-Chapel Hill- Class of 1977. Her Master's Degree was obtained from Brenau University, Gainesville, GA- Class of 1996. At the University of Phoenix, she completed studies in 2004 for the Doctorate of Management, ABD and received her Doctorate of Ministry (DM) in 2006 from South Georgia's Refreshing Bible College.

Since 2000, Dr. Rogers has served the Southeastern USA communities thru the Globe Life: Family Heritage Division by providing supplemental healthcare plans for businesses, churches, families, individuals. and organizations. She truly loves serving people!

Married to her high-school sweetheart, Allen "Willie," together they are proud parents of six offspring, with eight grandchildren, and one great-granddaughter.

REFERENCES

1. FDR on His Houseboat: The Larooco Log 1924-1926, Karen Chase 2016
2. *Rosenwald: The Remarkable Story of a Jewish Partnership with African American Communities—The Harvey B. Gantt Center for African-American Arts + Culture.* Ganttcenter.org. Retrieved July 7, 2017
3. *History of the Rosenwald School Program.* National Trust for Historic Preservation. Retrieved December 14, 2013
4. Rosenwald School. En.wikipedia.org
5. Booker T. Washington. En.wikipedia.org
6. The North Carolina Institution. American Annals of the Deaf and Dumb/Vol. 13, No. 4, November 1868
7. www.governormorehead.net
8. www.governormorehead.net
9. Herbert Hoover, The 31st President of the United States. www.whitehouse.gov
10. "The Star-Spangled Banner" becomes official U.S. national anthem. www.history.com (March 3, 1931)
11. Longley, Robert. *Hoovervilles: Homeless Camps of the Great Depression.* ThoughtCo. Dec. 6, 2021, thoughtco.com
12. FDR creates the Works Progress Administration (WPA). www.history.com (May 6, 1935)
13. Billy Graham: Preparing for Death—The Billy Graham Evangelistic Association of Canada. www.billygraham.ca

14. Carter, Jr., Robert. The American Tobacco Company. https://ncpedia.org. 2006

15. Carter, Jr., Robert. The American Tobacco Company. https://ncpedia.org. 2006

16. Duke Health History. www.corporate.dukehealth.org

17. Women in Duke Medicine. www.digitaldukemed.mc.duke.edu

18. Jones, Beverly; Egelhoff, Claudia. *Working in Tobacco: An Oral History of Durham's Tobacco Factory Workers*. www.archive.org (1987)

19. North Carolina's Tobacco History & Culture. www.CarolinaK12.org

20. History—Hampton University. www.hamptonu.edu

21. Johnson, Nelson. The Northside: African Americans and the Creation of Atlantic City. (2010) www.nelsonjohnson-author.com

22. Magnus, Amanda; Stasio, Frank. The History of Hayti, The Anchor of Durham's African-American Neighborhood. (March 2019). www.wunc.org

23. Background Information on the Hayti District. www.ibiblio.org/hayti/background.html

24. Town of Butner, N.C. www.butnernc.org

25. Van Riper, Tom. *America's Most Affluent Neighborhoods*. (2012) www.forbes.com

26. April 27, 1956: Boxing Champ Rocky Marciano Retires. www.history101.com

27. Roosevelt's Little White House at Warm Springs. www.nps.gov

28. Remembering James Baldwin and Urban Renewal. (2020) www.itslibrary.berkeley.edu

29. Truman Announced a Fair Deal, January 5, 1949. www.americaslibrary.gov

30. Dismantling Hayti—Bull City 150. www.bullcity150.org

31. Definition of "Uncle Tom." www.merriam.com
32. "What prompted land loss for black farmers? An obscure property law." (2017) www.thefern.org
33. Motion Picture *42*. Directed by Brian Helgeland, performances by Chadwick Boseman and Harrison Ford. Warner Bros. Pictures. (2013)
34. Lake Rogers Park—A Creedmoor Family Recreation Site. www.cityofcreedmoor.org
35. Jordan Lake State Recreation Area. www.jordan.lake@ ncparks.gov
36. Lake Michie. www.dprplaymore.org
37. Durham High School. www.enacademic.com
38. www.legacy.com/funeral-homes/north-carolina/durham/
39. School Desegregation. www.ncpedia.org
40. The Parnassians Club. Ancestry.com. U.S. School Yearbooks, 1900-1999.
    (database on-line). Durham High School, Durham, NC
41. Alpha Kappa Alpha Sorority, Incorporated. www.aka1908. com
42. Y2K /National Geographic Society. www.nationalgeographic.org
43. Our History-National Council of Negro Women. www. ncnw.org
44. NCNW. www.blackpast.org
45. North Carolina Central University. www.nccu.edu
46. NCCU. www.nccu.edu
47. NMAAHC. www.smithsonianmag.com
48. NMAAHC. www.nmaahc.si.edu
49. "Out of a mountain of despair, a stone of hope"/MLK Memorial brings famous speech to life. www.10tv.com/ article/news

50. DCBCC. www.youtube.com/Durham County BOCC July 23, 2018
51. DCBCC. July 23, 2018
52. Morning Hour. www.c-span.org. U.S. House Meets for Morning Hour U.S. House of Representative/July 23-2018
53. Sensational Nightingales. www.en.wikipedia.org
54. Meals on Wheels, Durham. www.mowdurham.org
55. US passes 100,000 coronavirus deaths as states relax lockdown measures. www.theguardian.com
56. 1918 Pandemic (Influenza Flu). www.cdc.gov
57. Weekly epidemiological update—29 December 2020. www.who.int
58. How Dangerous Is the Delta Variant? July 2021. www.asm.org

Family Tree Pastor Junious and Olivia Young Jones				
Name	Age	Born	Passed	Spouse(s)
Junious Jones	59	6/15/1875	11/3/1934	Olivia Young
Olivia Jones	83	12/25/1879	6/7/1963	Junious Jones
LeRoy Jones	88	5/22/1896	12/6/1984	Luzelia Hartsfield Queen Perry
William Arthur Jones	94	4/15/1897	4/05/1992	Lonie May Lyon
Nathaniel Jones	40	6/15/1901	5/1/1942	Millie Moore
Lizzie Alma Jones	80	5/30/1903	11/30/1983	Lonnie Burt Dunn
Aldonia Jones	91	12/05/1905	7/27/1997	Otha Lucas Lumas Young, Jr
Annie Dora Jones	54	4/22/1906	9/21/1960	John High Adolphus Davis
Lennon Jones	79	2/12/1909	1/22/1989	Launa Thompson
Otis Jones	21	4/21/1910	8/15/1931	Never Married
Clelly Jones	82	4/15/1913	12/31/1995	Robert Wall William A. Gailes
Hattie Mozelle Jones	83	8/12/1917	1/23/2001	Never Married
Cora Jones	103	8/3/1918	Alive	James McLeod, Sr.
Christine Jones	80	1/6/1921	6/30/2001	Willie Johnson

Attendees 100th Birthday Celebration for Cora Jones "Boot" McLeod August 3, 2018- Sheraton Imperial Hotel	
James & Shirley Abdullah	Karleshia Daye Jones/ Kassan, Khalil, Kaiden
Mammie Alston	Barbara Jones
Bobby & Joy Ashe	Peggy McLeod Kirkpatrick
Donna Banfield	Eric Lennon
Barry & Sylvia Banfield-Clark	Janis Love
Michael Batts	Melody Edwards Lucas/ Adrien Lucas
Former Mayor William Bell	Larry & Barbara Massenburg/ Holly
Ava Best	Christopher Matthews
Rev. Clarence & Syvil Burke	Ardell McArn
Tilda Caudle	Bertha McCrae
Gail Clay	James & Barbara McLeod
Gigi Clemons	LaKishia McLeod
Richard Cole	Senator Floyd McKissick
Rosalyn Cole	Wandolyn Merritt
Vance Davenport	Councilman Mark A. Middleton
Bennie Daye	Alecia Tapp Mitchell
Donald & Jennifer Daye	Tanya Nurse
Gloria Daye	Linda E. Phillips
Terry DeBerry	John Wayne Robinson
Jonathan & Sierra Edwards/ Karm'Ella, Andreia, Deuce	Lydia Jane Robinson/ Beulah Robinson
Michael Evans	Allen & Beverly Rogers
Smitty Evans	Mother Annie Bell Rogers
Alma Ford	Charlene Rogers-Taylor
Hazel Ford	Deacon Ronald Rogers
Mother Catherine Ferrell	Reatha Ann Rogers

Camille Gallagher	Reathie Rogers
Cheryl Gee	Charmelita Royster
Krystal Daye Giles/ Kayla	LaMichael Royster
Janet Gooch	Ruth Sanders
George Green, Sr.	Pearline Summers
George Green, Jr.	Lizzette Tapp
Rev. Rachel Green	Deborah Walker Taylor
Alma Hamilton	Edna Thompson
Rev. Percy & Esther High	Deacon Ron & Edith Umstead
Gassennie Hodge	Phillip & Sabrina Vereen
Deacon Thad & Lois Hodge	Pastor Jerome Washington
Commissioner B. Howerton	Michalle White
Liddie Howard	Cynthia Williams
Jean Johnson	Deacon Jairus & Velma Wilson
Barbara Jones	Geraldine Young

HOUSE OF REPRESENTATIVES
of the
NORTH CAROLINA GENERAL ASSEMBLY

SENDS CONGRATULATIONS TO

Cora Jones "Boot" McLeod

Durham, NC

in recognition of her
100ᵀᴴ BIRTHDAY

This 23ʳᵈ day of July, in the year two thousand and eighteen

MaryAnn E. Black
North Carolina House of Representatives
29ᵗʰ House District
Durham County

National Council of Negro Women
Durham Section

August 3, 2018

Mrs. Cora Jones McLeod
P. O. Box 318
Durham, North Carolina 27702

Dear Sister McLeod:

What a joy and blessing it is to bring words of congratulations on behalf of the Durham Section, National Council of Negro Women as you celebrate your 100th birthday.

Just think of all the lives you've touch during your lifetime and will continue to touch as God blesses you in years to come. We are so blessed that God created you and placed you among our people in Durham where you are so appreciated and loved.

So many changes have occurred since you were born. Thanks be to God that you have been able to depend on a force in your life that has not and will not ever change. I'm reminded of one of my favorite hymns, "Great Is Thy Faithfulness"."Great is Thy faithfulness, O God my Father, There is no shadow of turning with Thee. Thou changest not, Thy compassions, they fail not, As thou has been Thou forever wilt be."

As we celebrate your life, we celebrate and thank God for blessing you to see this special day.

Sincerely yours,

Cora Cole-McFadden, President

OTHERS, LORD, YES, OTHERS

Lord, help me live from day to day
In such a self-forgetful way
That even when I kneel to pray
My prayer shall be for others.

OTHERS, LORD, YES O`THERS,
LET THIS MY MOTTO BE,
HELP ME TO LIVE FOR OTHERS
THAT I MAY LIVE LIKE THEE.

Help me in all the work I do
To ever be sincere and true
And know that all I'd do for You
Must needs be done for others.

Let self be crucified and slain
And buried deep: and all in vain
May efforts be to rise again,
Unless to live for others.

And when my work on earth is done,
And my new work in Heav'n's begun,
May I forget the crown I've won,
While thinking still of others.

Charles D. Meigs

Attendees 101st Birthday Celebration of Cora Jones "Boot" McLeod August 3, 2019- Golden Corral Buffet Restaurant	
Shirley Abdullah	Rev. James McCoy
Ava Best	Mrs. James McCoy
Ursela Cocerham	Cora Jones "Boot" McLeod *
Herman Davenport	Tanya Nurse
Krystal Daye Giles	Allen Rogers
Kayla Giles	Beverly Rogers
Jimmy Harris	Reatha Ann Rogers
Karleshia Jones	Sam Rogers
Kassan Jones	Charmelita Royster
Khalil Jones	Deacon Ron Umstead
Kaiden Jones	Deaconess Edith Umstead
Willie Joyner	Stephanie Watson
Peggy Kirkpatrick	Deacon Jairus Wilson
Adrien Lucas	Deaconess Velma Wilson

State of North Carolina
Roy Cooper
Governor

Birthday Commemoration

The State of North Carolina and
Governor Roy Cooper are pleased to honor

Cora Jones "Boot" McLeod

on the occasion of her 101st birthday.

_____
Governor

August 3, 2019
Date

CONGRESSMAN G. K. BUTTERFIELD
UNITED STATES HOUSE OF REPRESENTATIVES
FIRST DISTRICT OF NORTH CAROLINA

A TRIBUTE TO

Cora Jones "Boot" McLeod

At this blessed and special milestone in your life, I am honored to extend my best wishes to you on the occasion of your 103rd birthday. I pray that God will continue to bless you with health and happiness for many years to come. On behalf of the United States House of Representatives and the people of North Carolina I wish to you a wonderful celebration with family and friends.

G. K. Butterfield
Member of Congress

STATE OF NORTH CAROLINA
OFFICE OF THE GOVERNOR

ROY COOPER
GOVERNOR

August 13, 2021

Mrs. Cora Jones 'Boot' McLeod
5500 Whippoorwill Street
Durham, North Carolina 27704

Dear Mrs. McLeod:

On behalf of the State of North Carolina, it is a pleasure to congratulate you on the recent celebration of your 103rd birthday. The strong men and women of your generation invested decades of aspiration, diligence and devotion in making a better state and country, and we are deeply grateful.

My wife Kristin and I hope your birthday was full of joy, love and time with those you cherish. May you enjoy fond memories from the past and look forward to more of them in the future.

With warm regards, I am

Very truly yours,

Roy Cooper

RAC/oo

20301 MAIL SERVICE CENTER • RALEIGH, NC 27699-0301 • TELEPHONE: 919-814-2000
WWW.GOVERNOR.NC.GOV

July 23, 2021

Ms. Cora Jones "Boot" McLeod
PO Box 318
Durham, NC 27702

Dear Ms. McLeod,

It is my privilege and honor to congratulate you on your upcoming 103rd birthday, there are few of us that reach this historic milestone, however, you have done so with dignity, honor, but, most importantly, a life of unselfish service and commitment to your family and to your community. I commend you on your many distinguished accomplishments, and I thank you for touching and positively impacting the lives of so many in our community.

I look forward to joining you and congratulating you on your 104th birthday next year!

With Love, Respect, and Appreciation,

Floyd B. McKissick, Jr.
Member, North Carolina Utilities Commission

CITY MANAGER

CITY OF DURHAM

August 3, 2021

Ms. Cora Jones "Boot" McLeod
5500 Whipporwill Drive
Durham, North Carolina 27704

Dear Ms. McLeod:

On behalf of the City of Durham, I am so honored to write this letter to celebrate you on the occasion of your 103rd BIRTHDAY!!!

I don't think I have ever written such a special letter before and I am proud and humbled that you are the recipient.

You have been a wonderful asset to the Durham community for a very long time. Your faithful service to God, your family and community has been recognized and is worthy of all the accolades you receive.

Thank you so much for the kindness, respect and contributions you have shown to Durham. You are so appreciated! Your 103 years is a blessing and we are grateful to stand in witness of your beautiful life and spirit. Continue to shine!

Sincerely,

Wanda S. Page

Wanda S. Page
City Manager

101 City Hall Plaza, Second Floor, Durham NC 27701 | 919.560.4222 | DurhamNC.gov | Follow Us @CityofDurhamNC

೧ Proclamation ౭౧

WHEREAS, longevity of life is a blessing for an individual and for the community which benefits from the knowledge, experience, and legacy this individual brings to all; and

WHEREAS, the City of Durham recognizes with respect and admiration the contributions of senior citizens in our community; and

WHEREAS, Mrs. Cora Jones 'Boot' McLeod was born in Wake County, NC on August 3, 1918 to Reverend Junious Jones and Olivia Young Jones, and was the knee-baby girl of twelve children. She relocated to Durham in 1932 and has spent most of her life in this city, attending Durham City Schools and DeShazor's Beauty College, where she graduated as a licensed cosmetologist in 1943. After working a few years for someone else, she joined with the late Gladys Best and Dorothy Steele to establish Tip Top Beauty Shop in the famous Hayti community and worked industriously to teach new beauticians the business of cosmetology and customer service; and

WHEREAS, urban renewal affected the businesses of the Hayti community to the extent of closure. The late Mr. James McLeod, Sr. provided his wife with her own home beauty shop, affectionately known as McLeod's Beauty Nook where she offered her professional haircare services for over fifty more years; and

WHEREAS, Mrs. McLeod, along with her family, joined Mount Vernon Baptist Church in Durham in 1933 under the leadership of Pastor W.C. Williamson and has been a member for 88 years. She joined the Mount Vernon Usher board in 1950, served as secretary for over 50 years, and attends church regularly each Sunday. She has served under Pastors Bass, Thomas, Thompson, Browne, and High, and is now under the leadership of Pastor Jerome J. Washington; and

WHEREAS, the faithfulness of Mrs. McLeod is recognized and honored today by her family, pastor, church family, the NCNW, Inc., and friends as she celebrates her 103rd birthday.

NOW, THEREFORE, I, Stephen M. Schewel, Mayor of the City of Durham, North Carolina, do hereby proclaim August 3, 2021 as

"MRS. CORA JONES 'BOOT' MCLEOD DAY"

in Durham, and do hereby salute Mrs. Cora Jones 'Boot' McLeod on this celebration of 103 years of life.

Witness my hand and the corporate seal of the City of Durham, this the 2nd day of August 2021.

Stephen M. Schewel

Stephen M. Schewel
Mayor

9 781685 562502